# SAS: Sea King Down

# SAS: Sea King Down

## MARK 'SPLASH' ASTON
## AND STUART TOOTAL

MICHAEL  JOSEPH

MICHAEL JOSEPH

UK | USA | Canada | Ireland | Australia
India | New Zealand | South Africa

Michael Joseph is part of the Penguin Random House group of companies
whose addresses can be found at global.penguinrandomhouse.com

Penguin
Random House
UK

First published 2021
001

Copyright © Mark Aston and Stuart Tootal, 2021

The moral right of the authors has been asserted

Inset picture credits: p.2, top, © Imperial War Museum (FKD 53); p.5, bottom, © PA Images; p.6, top,
USS *Slater* / Destroyer Escort Historical Museum, Albany, New York; p.6, bottom, 'NA'; p.7, middle,
HMS *Glamorgan*; p.9, top, © Imperial War Museum (FKD 393); p.10, top, credit not known,
via Santiago Rivas; p.10, bottom, © Imperial War Museum (FKD 192); p.11, top, Carl Rhodes;
pp.14–15, bottom, John Moore; p.16, bottom right, Antony Bysouth.

Every effort has been made to trace copyright holders and to obtain their permission for
the use of copyright material. The publisher apologizes for any errors or omissions
and would be grateful to be notified of any corrections that should be
incorporated in future editions of this book.

Set in 13.75/16.25 pt Garamond MT Std
Typeset by Jouve (UK), Milton Keynes
Printed and bound in Great Britain by Clays Ltd, Elcograf S.p.A.

The authorized representative in the EEA is Penguin Random House Ireland,
Morrison Chambers, 32 Nassau Street, Dublin D02 YH68

A CIP catalogue record for this book is available from the British Library

HARDBACK ISBN: 978–0–241–40098–2
TRADE PAPERBACK ISBN: 978–0–241–40099–9

www.greenpenguin.co.uk

For those warriors that did not make it home.

*We are but warriors for the working day; our gayness and guilt all besmirched.*

*Henry V*, Act 4, Scene 3, by William Shakespeare

# Contents

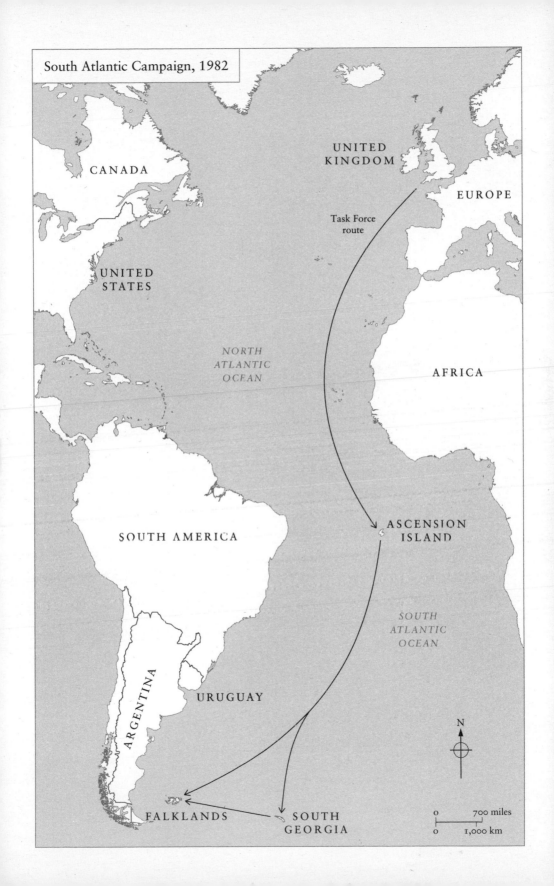

South Atlantic Campaign, 1982

CANADA

UNITED KINGDOM

EUROPE

Task Force route

UNITED STATES

NORTH ATLANTIC OCEAN

AFRICA

SOUTH AMERICA

ASCENSION ISLAND

SOUTH ATLANTIC OCEAN

ARGENTINA

URUGUAY

N

FALKLANDS

SOUTH GEORGIA

0        700 miles
0        1,000 km

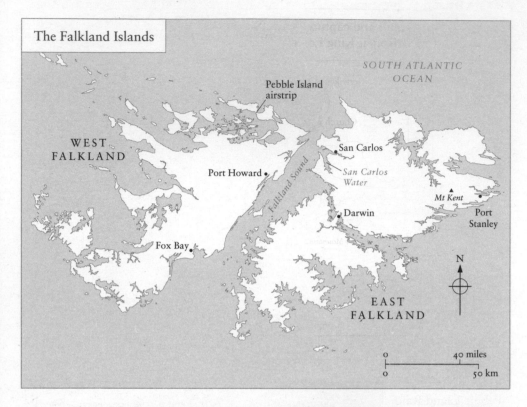

## The Falkland Islands

SOUTH ATLANTIC
OCEAN

Pebble Island
airstrip

WEST
FALKLAND

San Carlos

Port Howard

San Carlos
Water

Falkland Sound

Mt Kent

Port
Stanley

Darwin

Fox Bay

N

EAST
FALKLAND

0           40 miles
0           50 km

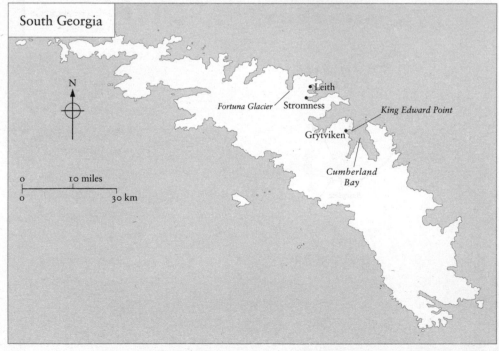

## South Georgia

N

Leith

Fortuna Glacier

Stromness

King Edward Point

Grytviken

Cumberland
Bay

0        10 miles
0        30 km

Assault and capture of the Argentine garrison at King Edward Point

Grytviken
Church
Santa Fe
King Edward Point
King Edward Cove
HMS *Antrim*
Brown Mountain
Sea lions
Helicopter insertion point
N
0   0.5 miles
0   1 km

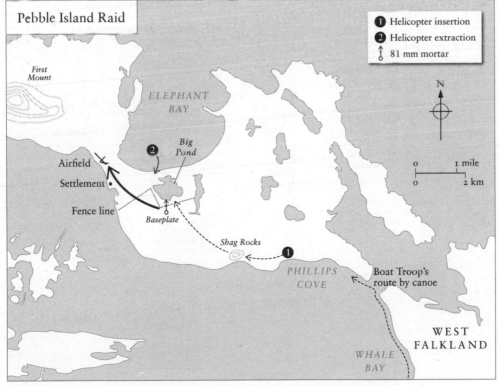

Pebble Island Raid

1 Helicopter insertion
2 Helicopter extraction
81 mm mortar

First Mount
ELEPHANT BAY
Big Pond
Airfield
Settlement
Fence line
Baseplate
Shag Rocks
PHILLIPS COVE
Boat Troop's route by canoe
WEST FALKLAND
WHALE BAY
N
0   1 mile
0   2 km

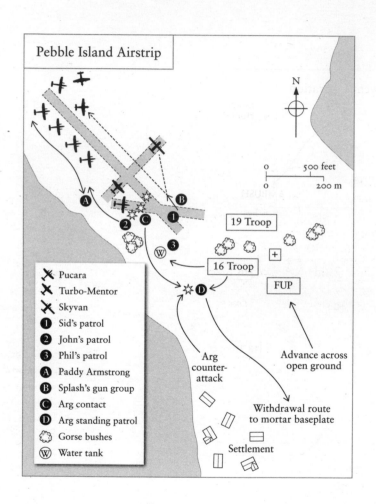

Pebble Island Airstrip

N

| 0 | 500 feet |
| 0 | 200 m |

19 Troop

16 Troop

FUP

Arg
counter-
attack

Advance across
open ground

Withdrawal route
to mortar baseplate

Settlement

✗ Pucara
✗ Turbo-Mentor
✗ Skyvan
① Sid's patrol
② John's patrol
③ Phil's patrol
Ⓐ Paddy Armstrong
Ⓑ Splash's gun group
Ⓒ Arg contact
Ⓓ Arg standing patrol
Gorse bushes
Ⓦ Water tank

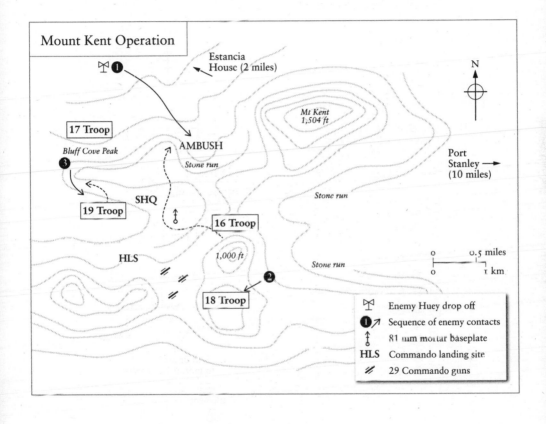

Mount Kent Operation

Estancia
House (2 miles)

N

17 Troop

Mt Kent
1,504 ft

Bluff Cove Peak

AMBUSH

Port
Stanley →
(10 miles)

Stone run

19 Troop

SHQ

Stone run

16 Troop

HLS

1,000 ft

Stone run

o          0.5 miles
o          1 km

18 Troop

Enemy Huey drop off

Sequence of enemy contacts

81 mm mortar baseplate

HLS    Commando landing site

29 Commando guns

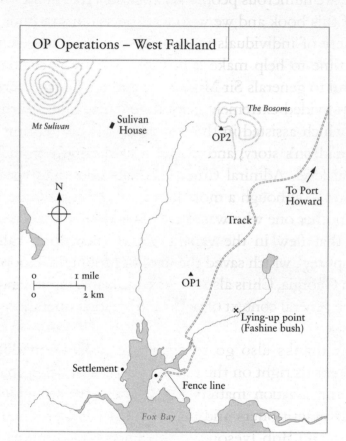

OP Operations – West Falkland

Mt Sulivan

Sulivan
House

The Bosoms

OP2

N

To Port
Howard

Track

0      1 mile

0      2 km

OP1

✕ Lying-up point
(Fashine bush)

Settlement •

Fence line

Fox Bay

# Acknowledgements

There are numerous people who played a role in the writing of this book and we wish to express our gratitude to a variety of individuals who were so willing to give up their time to help make it possible. We are particularly grateful to generals Sir Mike Rose and Sir Cedric Delves who provided extremely helpful guidance and information, which assisted in the compiling of this account of D Squadron's story, and placed it at the more granular tactical level. Admiral Chris Parry also deserves special mention – although a more junior officer at the time, he was another one who was there. As a member of the aircrew that flew in the valiant Wessex helicopter called 'Humphrey', which saved the lives of Mountain Troop in South Georgia, Chris also imparted valuable input regarding the general context of naval and aviation operations at the time.

Our thanks also go to a host of other individuals who kept us right on the relevant details of other maritime and aviation matters. As former serving subject-matter practitioners and experts: Mike Evans, Charlie Wilson and Bob Iveson provided a mass of important information regarding Sea King helicopter operations, amphibious ships and Harrier jet sorties respectively. Martin Reed and Suzie West must also be thanked for the help they provided from their experiences of being part of the remarkable crew on board the SS *Canberra* during the conflict. Likewise, as a naval officer on HMS *Endurance* at the time, Andrew Lockett provided a wealth of information regarding Operation Paraquet, which was supplemented by the explorer Neil Laughton who has retraced Shackleton's steps and supplied much helpful data regarding the nature and characteristics of the Fortuna Glacier. We also owe a debt of gratitude to Dave Morris, who as the senior aircraft curator at the Fleet Air Arm Museum in Yeovilton, devoted a huge amount of his time in providing useful points of research and allowing us to access several exhibits that flew in the conflict and were part of this story.

Danny West and Roger Edwards, who were part of D Squadron during the conflict also deserve our thanks. Additionally, we want to express our gratitude to Roger and his wife Norma, for the hospitality and kindness they showed to us when we visited the Falkland Islands as part of writing this book. Other members of the Squadron who contributed their thoughts and views are also worthy of mention. Although, out of respect for their wishes they will remain anonymous, but they know who they are. The one exception is Bilbo, who kept a diary of his time down south and was generous enough to make parts of it available to us. Our appreciation extends to individual family members of some of those who lost their lives, as well as the women in our lives, Mandy and Sasha, not least for the many hours that we were absent from them when engrossed in conversation and travelling together as we conducted our research.

As ever, acting as our agent, Phil Patterson was always

there providing unbounded enthusiasm and encouragement for the project, while lending his exceptional eye
for detail and guidance from the impressive breadth of
his own knowledge. Finally, we would like to thank Row-
land White and his team at Penguin for having faith in us
and bringing this story alive in published form.

# Prologue

I felt my breathing heavy in my lungs and throat, my leg muscles aching with the effort of it as I pushed higher up towards the stony outcrop of Shag Rocks. It was harder back then, when we had been burdened by weapons and the heavy kit that we carried as we laboured through the dark, our feet stumbling over rocks and among the clumps of grass and heathery scrub. Now I was loaded with the weight of advancing years and the effects of a long flight across thousands of miles of the South Atlantic.

The incessant wind blew hard in my face from across the empty sea in the west, just as it did before, although it was night-time then and a different season. The sun warmed the back of my neck, and I felt the first trickle of sweat as I crested the rocky bluff that stood proud from the rest of the coastline. The sea was a brilliant aqua blue below me down to my left, the sunlight sparkling off the gentle swell of the waves, no longer whipped by the fury of the storm we had faced that night. I caught my breath as I reached the top and, looking inland, I saw it.

The settlement lay a few miles off in the distance of the lower ground, its buildings discernible as a cluster of small white dots nestling among the dark smudges of gorse bushes, with the slight dash of an orange windsock just visible as it flapped in the breeze on its eastern edge. Beyond it lay the target. As I gazed across the open ground in front of me, taking in the marshy ponds and the mountains in the background, the detail of it all came flooding back to me as if it was yesterday.

Keyed with frozen fingers, the Morse code message sent over high-frequency radio to the D Squadron, 22 SAS operations room on board HMS *Hermes* was short and precise.

*'Eleven, repeat eleven aircraft. Believed to be real. Squadron attack tonight.'*

# I

It all started with the knock on the door of my pad in Hereford on 4 April 1982. It was a Sunday evening; the signature tune from *Dallas* blared out from the TV set in the living room as I made my way into the small hallway of our married quarter to answer the unexpected caller.

Phil Currass, the troop sergeant of Mountain Troop, stood on the doorstep. 'All right, Phil, what's up?' Phil and his family lived a few doors down on the pad's patch of tight-packed two-up, two-down houses, but something in his manner told me it wasn't a social call.

'Sorry to bother you on a Sunday, mate. A Scale A has been called for the Squadron, and everyone needs to be in camp for a briefing at 1000 hours tomorrow morning.'

'What's up?' I repeated.

'I dunno,' he replied, 'but it's got to be something big, as the boys from G Squadron have been called in too.'

Thirty-four years old, the quietly spoken, sandy-haired Midlander was a former medic from the Army's medical corps. Phil was also a decorated Special Forces veteran and, as the 'troop staffie' of Mountain Troop, he ran the small sub-unit of sixteen men with something of a bedside manner, which oozed confidence and a soothing balm of authority. But it didn't mean that he knew what the brief was about; his job was to make sure that we were there for it.

The absence of any more information didn't concern

me overly. I had been in 22 SAS for just over two years, and the Regiment was always on permanent standby to provide a response to any brewing crisis. It usually came to nothing. We were used to being stood up at short notice only to be stood down again just as quickly. However, Liz took a very different view.

'What did Phil want?' she asked with a trace of acid suspicion in her voice, as I shut the door and walked back into the living room.

I told her about the briefing.

'And, of course, you will be going in?'

I resisted the temptation to say, 'Of course I am fucking going in. I'm in the fucking SAS.' I knew it wouldn't help the situation.

Sensing my indignation, she shot me a murderous look, pushing herself back hard into the sofa and throwing her arms tightly across her body.

*Oh shit. Here we go again*, I thought.

Liz turned up the volume on the TV to signal the beginning of the silent treatment. JR Ewing was getting a slice from Sue Ellen Ewing on the box, and I felt for the poor bugger.

Had we been watching the news that night, however, we might have had an inkling that events taking place thousands of miles away were about to impact on us.

Ask any soldier about loyalty, and they will speak of their regiment in an ascending order of priority starting with its smallest constituent part. In my case fidelity began with the sixteen-odd men of Mountain Troop. It then ran to D Squadron, formed of us and three other troops, before ending with the Regiment and its four

4

other similarly formed sabre squadrons. This was my military family. But my civilian wife, Liz, had a distinctly different take on things.

Liz was a nurse, and we had met while I was on a medical attachment with the A and E department of a large London hospital. We had married just before the end of December in 1981. She had hardly seen me since. In the first week of January, the Troop deployed with the rest of D Squadron on a two-month exercise in Kenya, which was followed almost immediately by two weeks of troop training in the Bavarian Alps. I had just got back from Germany and had been given a week's leave, so it was perhaps not unsurprising that me going into work the next day promoted some harsh words of disappointment, hurt and then silence.

I could hardly blame her. Liz was discovering that the reality of married life was somewhat different from what she had expected. Home and family are a secondary commitment in the Regiment, and it takes a special kind of woman to maintain a lasting relationship with an SAS soldier.

The next morning, I left a tense atmosphere at home behind and made the short walk into the camp. The barracks had been the home to the Regiment since 1960, after the SAS had been re-formed as a regular unit in response to the Malayan Emergency. The camp had recently been rebuilt, as a new redbrick construct of two-storey buildings to accommodate our Special Forces role, and renamed as Stirling Lines. It included an aquatic centre, complete with a helicopter mock-up for fast roping into the pool and an artificial beach to practise seaborne covert insertion techniques using collapsible Klepper canoes and inflatable Gemini boats. The barracks also boasted a brand-new close-quarter battle range building. Known as the 'Killing House', it was fitted out with rubber-coated bullet-absorbing walls and was designed for the purpose of hostage-rescue training.

I went into camp through the back gate and made my way past the new single blokes' accommodation to the briefing room, located in the main Regimental headquarters building in the centre of Stirling Lines. Known as the 'Blue Room', it was laid out like a small theatre, with a short 2 foot stage at one end and enough seating to cater for 200-plus people. It was busy.

A mild buzz of anticipation filled the air as I walked in. Most of D Squadron were already there, and the blokes from G Squadron were also filtering in. I spotted Binsy and Bilbo standing by a large stainless-steel urn of coffee and went over to join them.

'All right, my lover?' Binsy said in a West Country burr. 'What's occurring?'

'All right, Binsy. All right, Bilbo?' I replied, acknowledging the shorter of the two fellow members of the Troop. 'I haven't got a clue, Binsy. Phil didn't know either when he came round last night, but he said it must be big.'

'It must be: the director and the CO are both here.'

I followed Binsy's gaze as he nodded over the top of his coffee cup in the direction of the two officers who were in deep conversation at the edge of the stage. The younger of the two men was the CO. He gestured to the more senior man he was talking to, then looked to his right and said something to the RSM. The regimental sergeant major cleared his throat and then raised his voice to tell us to take our seats. The three of us made for a line of chairs placed towards the back of the room and sat down together. The noise of hastily replaced coffee cups and scraping chairs subsided as the room was called to order.

As a brigadier and the senior SAS-badged officer in the Army, the director went first. Brigadier Peter de la Billière was a former commanding officer of 22 SAS, and we might have been distracted by the fact that he had his green elbow-patched army pullover on back to front, had it not been for what he told us.

'Gentlemen, during the early hours of 2nd April, Argentine Special Forces and Marines invaded the Falkland Islands, overwhelmed its small Royal Marine garrison after a short, stiff firefight and are now claiming the islands and their dependent island of South Georgia as their own.'

There was a hushed silence. The director let the enormity of what he had said sink in. Then a murmur of disbelieving voices broke out among the audience.

Binsy nudged my arm. 'What the hell is Argentina doing invading an island somewhere up in Scotland and capturing Bootnecks?'

Binsy was no great student of geography, but the rest of us were little better informed when it came to knowing where the Falklands were.

The RSM called for quiet, and the brigadier went on to elaborate, with the aid of a small atlas-type map stuck up on the wall of the stage, that the Falkland Islands were in fact located at the southern end of the South Atlantic 400 miles off the east coast of Argentina. He told us that a naval task force was being assembled to make ready to take back the islands and, as far as he was concerned, we were going to be part of it. On the trip back from Bavaria I had read an article on the Falklands. It mentioned sabre-rattling by a military junta in Buenos Aires as much as it did about arctic wildlife and colonies of penguins. At the time I thought little of it; but as I sat there in the Blue Room, the penny suddenly dropped.

'Bastards,' Binsy hissed under his breath next to me.

It was a sentiment shared by everyone in the room. Our blood was up. The sense of indignation and national slight was immediately strong, but the prospect of imminent action was even stronger.

The director went on to describe how we would be employed to conduct direct-action tasks and covert information-gathering operations against Argentine targets, which met with a murmur of approval. Gathering covert intelligence, by spending long hours dug into concealed observation posts established deep inside hostile territory, and raiding critical strategic targets behind enemy lines were our bread and butter.

But there was a sting in the tail. Firstly, the brigadier told us that the UN had already condemned Argentina's action and that frantic diplomatic efforts were being led by the US to avoid a conflict occurring between two of its allies. He made it clear that there was every chance of a political resolution to the crisis being found. Secondly, it was apparent from what the brigadier said that the Regiment had not been officially warned off to join the Task Force. This was confirmed by the CO, when he stood up to speak after the brigadier had finished.

With hair beginning to show the first traces of grey at the temples, Lieutenant Colonel Michael Rose was an energetic and highly competent operator who had originally been commissioned into the Coldstream Guards. He had been in command of 22 SAS for over two years and had a reputation as a 'go-getter', which made him popular with the troops. Since he had found out about the Argentine invasion in advance of the brief on the preceding Friday, Rose had spent the weekend rushing between Hereford and 3 Commando Brigade's headquarters in Plymouth, lobbying hard for our inclusion on the ORBAT (order of battle) of any force being sent to the South Atlantic. He told us that the brigade of three commando units was being reinforced by at least one Para battalion, and his intention was that D and G Squadrons should join them.

The CO didn't indicate whether he had been successful in his lobbying efforts but, regardless of official orders, he was true to his charismatic form and told us, 'Pack your kit and be ready to drive to RAF Brize Norton, where an aircraft is being organized to fly you from the UK to Ascension Island.'

The briefing broke up with a resumption of animated conversation and more scraping of chairs, and NCOs began calling out over the noise. D Squadron's own sergeant major stood out among them.

Lawrence Gallagher was an engineer who had come from 9 PARA, a unit that prided itself on always trying to be tougher than the Parachute Regiment soldiers they supported. He looked the part. Gallagher was a big man and possessed square-set features. With a displaced nose and thick black droopy moustache, his face suggested that he had seen his fair share of bar-room action in enhancing the reputation of the outfit he hailed from. As our sergeant major, he enjoyed a huge measure of respect, although it had nothing to do with his background or physical stature. Instead it stemmed from a steady disposition and good-natured generosity of spirit that made him popular both with officers and the rank and file, whom he considered it was his duty to serve in equal measure. Gallagher gathered us round.

'Right, guys. You heard what the boss said. Get yourselves down to the stores and help Graham and Wally sort out the Squadron stores ready for the move to Brize. I am organizing a bus to take us there later this afternoon. Timings to follow, but the married blokes among you should be able to get a couple of hours at home before ETD.'

I didn't relish the prospect of telling Liz that we would be heading off that afternoon one little bit.

'Any questions?' Gallagher asked. There were none.

'Right then, let's get cracking.'

I headed down to the Squadron stores with Bilbo and Binsy. James Grey fell in with us. We were all part of the same troop, but to the casual observer we made for an incongruous group. Binsy was as tall as Bilbo was short; like me they were both non-coms from regular Army units. With a thick head of dark hair that was beginning to recede at the front, Binsy was an easy-going bloke who originally joined the Army as a Green Jacket. As his nickname suggested, he needed glasses. That he wore an illegal set of contact lenses was a poorly kept secret from the Regimental hierarchy in a unit that demanded that all its soldiers had 20/20 perfect vision. Short-sighted or not, he was an excellent shot. Binsy working up a close-quarter battle range or handling a sniper's rifle was something to behold. When not training with the unit, he spent all his spare time rough shooting and was a natural when it came to living in the field and knocking things over with a rifle or shotgun.

In comparison, Bilbo was squat, powerfully built and as broad as Binsy was tall. At 5 feet 4 inches, the former commando engineer looked like a Hobbit. He also hated heights – an interesting quality in a member of Mountain Troop.

James, not 'J' and certainly not 'Jim', had no nickname and was my best mate. Fresh-faced with mousy brown hair, James had joined the Regiment straight from university, serving first in the Territorial SAS before attempting and passing Selection to join 22 SAS. The fact that he had a degree was not the only thing that made him something of an oddity. He also hadn't served in the regular Army. Consequently, the Regiment made him complete the gruelling six-month recruit training course for the Parachute Regiment before they would finally accept him, despite the fact that he had already passed Selection.

The other thing that stood out about James was that he could have been an officer; he spoke like one, initially dressed like one, and his father had been one. But he was content with his chosen path, and the thought of having to do another training course in the form of spending a year at Sandhurst if he applied for a commission filled him with horror. It would also have meant that he would have had to spend several years serving as a junior officer in a conventional Army unit before he could apply to reattempt Selection to join the Regiment.

'It doesn't make sense,' he said. 'Britain doesn't go to war with countries like Argentina, when the real threat comes from the Soviets. It's just not something that we do.'

'You might be right, professor,' remarked Binsy with a grin. 'But I doubt we will get beyond Brize. Although, not without first being pissed about with lots of hurry up and wait, then getting on the bus and getting off the bus, before being finally stood down again.'

'Yeah,' Bilbo chipped in. 'We are not even on the ORBAT of units warned off to go.'

'Do you think B Squadron's do at Prince's Gate will make a difference?' I countered, airing a thought that was stirring on all our minds.

Captured on TV screens across the country, the Regiment's daring rescue of the hostages taken during the Iranian Embassy siege two years previously had propelled the SAS into the full glare of an awe-inspired British public.

Bilbo beamed back at me with a mischievous glint in his eye. 'Yeah, it just might. But did you see the brigadier's jumper? He had it on the wrong way around. Bloody Ruperts, who would believe it? He comes all the way down here to brief us from London that we might be going on operations and can't even put his jumper on properly.'

We burst out laughing, a strong sense of the ridiculous cutting through the more weighty strategic affairs of state and the prospect of war, however remote, as we arrived at the stores and started packing the Squadron's kit for God knows what.

## 2

The Regiment's role in ending the siege at the Iranian Embassy was as dramatic as it was short. On 5 May 1980 counterterrorist teams from B Squadron stormed the Embassy, killing five terrorists and rescuing twenty-four hostages. The images of armed and hooded SAS men, dressed in a black kit of overalls and respirators abseiling down the white stucco-fronted building in Prince's Gate in South Kensington and effecting entry with explosives and stub grenades, propelled the Regiment into the public consciousness.

Occurring over a bank holiday weekend, the seventeen minutes of action took place in the full glare of TV press coverage and was beamed into the living rooms of millions of people. Overnight the SAS gained celebrity status, became a household name and gained a near-mythical status as a daring breed of super soldiers capable of anything. As in all things, legend and reality are often divergent, and none of us subscribed to being part of some superhuman martial strain, but we hoped that the cachet the Regiment had accrued might secure us the ticket we needed to join the Task Force.

Prior to the transmission of those spectacular TV images, few people in the UK had any real idea about the existence of the SAS and its capabilities. As a Special

Forces unit, it was an anonymity that many would have preferred to keep.

The SAS had been set up as an irregular outfit during the North African campaign of the Second World War, and the behind-the-lines attacks on German airfields by the likes of David Stirling and Paddy Mayne had become the stuff of legend. But the Regiment's initial operations were clandestine, a heritage that was fiercely preserved, and most of the post-war activities of the SAS were shrouded in secrecy.

It was also an obscurity that had pertained in the wider Army. After the siege, all that changed, and the Regiment became overwhelmed by the numbers wishing to join its ranks. There is no direct entry into the SAS: its soldiers are drawn from the members of the armed forces already serving in the Army, as well as the Navy and RAF. Having attained the requisite military experience, any candidate must then pass a gruelling selection process before being badged as a full-blown member of the Regiment.

My own route to the SAS started when I joined the Army as a fifteen-year-old in 1964. By the early 1960s, service in the armed forces was no longer a norm. National Service had ended. It had been an unwelcome intrusion into the lives of a generation wanting to embrace the increasing liberalism of the age, and an almost anti-military culture developed among young men. But that hippy culture of long hair on blokes and smoking pot was not really my thing. I also saw little value in completing a more formal education, which was only likely to lead to my getting a job making radio parts in a factory in Chelmsford, where I grew up. Compared to that of a 'squaddie', the pay might have been better, but even as a teenager I was aware that it would lead to a dead-end life. Money could not buy what the life of a soldier offered.

I had also been in the Army Cadet Force, which provided a sense of the adventure and the prospect of manly purpose that I knew I could pursue as an adult if I joined the Army's regular ranks. My father had come to Essex when he married, but he grew up in the Forest of Dean, in a family with a strong service affinity stemming from a clutch of uncles who had served in the local county regiment. As a consequence, joining the 1st Battalion of the Gloucestershire Regiment seemed an obvious choice when I completed my training as a junior boy-soldier in September 1966.

What wasn't so obvious was the nickname I was given on joining the battalion.

'What's your name?' the guard sergeant asked me when I reported for duty in the guardroom.

'Private Mark Aston, sergeant,' I replied.

'No you ain't,' a grizzled old corporal interjected from the side of the guardroom.

'Yeah,' the sergeant retorted, 'you needs a nickname. I know – from now on you will be called Splash.'

No explanation was given, but from that moment on I was 'Splash'.

I had enjoyed basic training and took the initial bullshit of endlessly cleaning kit, polishing barrack-room floors, show parades and interminable drill every Saturday morning in my stride. We also learned about infantry weapon systems and basic tactics. When not living in the field or on rifle ranges, we also went adventure training and furthered our education. These were activities that piqued my interest and provided me with a good foundation of soldiering. Within a year of reporting to the Glosters, I had completed a promotion cadre, and by the time I was twenty, I was serving in the intelligence section as a full corporal in Berlin.

In 1969, we deployed to Northern Ireland to protect the Catholic population from the sectarian violence that had engulfed the province. However, we were soon lifting terrorist suspects within the Republican community and being shot at and bombed by the IRA. Military engagement in the 'Troubles' of the 1970s and 1980s drove a predictable routine for Army units, which the Battalion followed, as it bounced between serving in Germany as part of the British Army of the Rhine and deploying on repeated four-month emergency tours to Ulster. However, it was during a subsequent stint of service back with the Battalion in the UK that I first met the SAS over a few beers in the sergeants' mess of our barracks in 1977.

Having commanded a section of eight infantry soldiers, before becoming a platoon sergeant to thirty men and then eventually commanding a platoon, I had risen to the rank of colour sergeant and was expected to take my turn in running the stores in one of the Battalion's rifle companies. It was a necessary step to progressing my career. But filing endless equipment registers, ammunition returns and accounting for soiled mattresses and making sure the hundred-odd souls of the company were properly fed was a far cry from the soldiering I had relished as a rifle platoon infantryman. I was twenty-nine, bored rigid with what the Army calls 'G4 matters' and knew that the frontline aspects of soldiering, which I had loved, were over. If it came my way, further promotion would just mean more G4 and administrative management on a larger scale. I was at a career crossroads and needed to do something different. The men with longer hair, beyond-regulation-length sideburns and wearing flared jeans and bomber jackets who frequented our mess looked like they might be able to provide the answer.

Although they had nothing to do with the Battalion, the SAS NCOs lived and took their meals in the mess while they were training on the nearby ranges. The fact that they were instantly different wasn't just down to their civilian attire and the fact that they never seemed to wear uniform. There was a distinct air about them of professional self-confidence and a focused operational mindset regardless of rank or position which seemed to be the very epitome of what they were about.

All the SAS blokes that came into the mess had spent time with the Regiment fighting in Dhofar in support of the Sultan of Oman on what the Army called 'Operation Storm'. Over a few beers they talked about ambushing rebel tribesmen and attacking their camps high up in the Jebel peaks and across gravel desert plains. It sounded like real soldiering, and I wanted some of it. But to get there I would first have to gain my own regiment's formal permission to apply to attend the SAS Selection course, the passing of which was the gateway to joining the Regiment.

No infantry commanding officer wants to lose good

people to a volunteer Special Forces unit. The CO of the Glosters said to me when I walked into his office to gain his permission to attempt Selection, 'Colour Sergeant Aston, in a few years you will be the RSM of the Battalion if you stay with us.'

'I know what I might be giving up, sir,' I replied. 'But I have thought hard about this, and it's something that I need to do.'

The colonel sighed. 'OK. If you are sure, I will sign the paperwork, but I think you are throwing away a promising career.'

I thanked him, saluted and marched out of his office before he could change his mind. The thought crossed my mind: *Perhaps he let me go because he thought there was a good chance that I wouldn't make it through Selection.*

The Regiment may have enjoyed an obscurity it later lost after the siege at Prince's Gate, but anyone who knew anything about the SAS also knew that passing Selection and getting into the Regiment was not easy. There was every chance that I would return to the Battalion in a few months' time having failed to make the grade. I was determined that wasn't going to happen.

As the New Year of 1978 dawned, I shook off my hangover and began a punishing six-month regime of physical self-preparation to get ready for the course that would start at the beginning of August. I started running with a heavy bergen rucksack on my back. I would go out in the morning and do several miles, go out again at lunchtime, swim in the afternoon and then go for a run in the evening. By July I was as ready as I was going to be, and I made my way to Hereford and reported to Stirling Lines.

SAS Selection is billed as the toughest course in the British Army. It runs twice a year, once in the winter and once in the summer. It is broken down into five distinct phases, and its major constituent parts take place in the rugged hills of the Black Mountains and the Brecon Beacons, as well as the inhospitable primary jungles of either Brunei or Belize.

The first phase lasts four weeks and is called 'Endurance', or what is colloquially referred to as the 'hills phase', which is designed to test a candidate's aptitude for physical and mental toughness. The first part of 'Endurance' lasts three weeks and is spent building up an applicant's fitness to march and navigate over long distances with a rifle and pack, using a 1:50,000 scale map and a Silva compass. Each day, weights and distances are increased, and navigation becomes more demanding. 'Endurance' culminates in 'Test Week', where every aspiring SAS soldier marches against the clock and needs to maintain a punishing pace if he is to complete an allocated route within a set time, which is kept from them. Consequently, all they do know is that they must march hard and fast to pass. Failure to do so results in a candidate being 'returned to their unit' or RTU'd. By the time we reached Test Week we were already exhausted.

Of the 150 individuals who had started our course, over seventy had already dropped out of their own accord. By the time we finished the final Test Week endurance march of 40 miles, carrying a 55 lb bergen plus rifle, another fifty-plus had been told they had not made the grade and were RTU'd. With just under thirty others left on the course, we began continuation training and spent the next two weeks learning about standard operating procedures used by the Regiment, which included tactics, patrolling, weapon handling, signalling and an element of medical training. Much of what we covered was already familiar, but the focus of the training was to bring non-infantry candidates up to speed on the basic skills they would require.

During this period, the officers on the course were taken away to undergo 'Officers' Week', which was the Regiment's own version of hell for anyone attempting to join with a commission, who were referred to disparagingly as 'Ruperts'. Each Rupert was tasked to plan a Special Forces-type mission, which included conducting covert reconnaissance of local hypothetical targets such as power stations and military installations. They were deliberately deprived of sleep and beasted by their instructors to keep them under physical and mental pressure, before facing the ultimate test of presenting their plan to a large audience of SAS men of all ranks drawn from across the Regiment.

Having sat in the audience myself, to describe it as 'critical' and 'hostile' is something of an understatement. Each presenting officer candidate could expect to have his plan torn apart publicly by men who were junior in rank to him. It made today's *Dragons' Den* look like a baby shower. But those officers who could overcome their fatigue, maintain their cool, accept criticism and show that logical thinking and reasoned decision-making lay behind their plans were likely to pass. Those who demonstrated the converse would fail, and the process highlighted that soldiers had some say in who would lead them.

With the trauma of Officers' Week behind them, the successful Ruperts rejoined the rest of the course to undergo six weeks' training in the jungle, where we practised patrolling and navigating through the dense primary vegetation and the sticky humid heat of Belize. We laid ambushes and conducted live firing jungle camp attacks. We were permanently wet and exhausted, and the jungle tested our field discipline and our ability to work as a team in a demanding environment. Not everyone measured up to the exacting standards, and another four candidates were RTU'd.

Those who remained returned to the UK to complete the penultimate three-week phase of 'Combat Survival'. The year had progressed, and we were tipped out into the countryside of a freezing English winter wearing nothing more than old Second World War battledress. We were rarely fed, and were expected to live off the land, as we attempted to evade capture by a hunter force, while using rough sketch maps to make a series of meetings with friendly agents. Ultimately, an agent would deliberately betray us. Once captured we were bound, hooded and went into twenty-four hours of interrogation, where we were expected to reveal nothing more than our name, rank, number and date of birth, known as the 'Big Four'.

As Special Forces personnel operating behind enemy lines, we viewed the risk of capture as an occupational hazard, and resistance to interrogation was a vital element of our training. If we were caught by enemy forces, what we revealed under questioning could threaten our comrades still at large and the success of a mission. It was essential to be prepared to know what to expect – to deal with the shock of capture and hold out under the utmost pressure. Hunger, stress positions, heavy handling, cunning, psychological inducement and sleep deprivation were all used to wear us down and get us to divulge more information and to test our resistance to interrogation.

I kept telling myself that it was only an exercise and all I needed to do was to hold out. But I was exhausted and desperate for sleep after two weeks of living rough out in the freezing open. Each time I was screamed at when I failed to answer a question or kicked back into an agonizing stress position, I could feel my resolve slipping as I doggedly stuck to revealing nothing but the 'Big Four'. The seemingly endless session of interrogations, interspersed by hours spent in contorted, muscle-agonizing postures, confined in hooded darkness and regularly doused with cold water, felt like an eternity.

I had lost all sense of time and was at my lowest ebb when I was dragged into yet another session for questioning. I was forced into a chair, and my hood was pulled off. I winced painfully against the sudden harsh glare of light from a single bulb burning brightly above me. Facing me across a rough wooden table sat my tormentors. *Here we go again*, I thought. *Mutt and fucking Jeff playing the good cop, bad cop routine.*

It was a classic tactical questioning (TQ) technique, straight out of a movie, but used for good reason.

'Colour Sergeant Aston. We know who you are,' started Jeff, the 'good cop'. 'You've done very well, but why don't you do yourself a favour and tell us what we want to know? Then this can all be over,' he said in a soothing voice, beguiling in its enticement.

I was tempted. Then Mutt cut in, slamming his fist down on the table and screaming in my face, close enough that I was flecked by his spittle.

'Fucking tell us about your mission, you bastard! Who was in your patrol and where are the code books!'

*Fuck you*, I thought, but instead just mumbled: 'Aston, Colour Sergeant, 45778992 . . .'

And the fist slammed down hard on the table.

And so it went on. For how long I have no idea, but the continuous sweet and sour combo was gradually weakening my resolve. At one point, I was stripped naked, and a woman came in and mocked my manhood, which I admit was probably not at its best, but the humiliation and sense of vulnerability stung.

*This is just an exercise. Hold on. Hold on*, I kept telling myself until eventually I was told to get back into my clothes, the hood came on, and I was dragged out in the darkness and pushed into another back-breaking stress position, before an icy-cold bucket of water was thrown over me, and they switched back on the blaring white noise, which seared the brain, further confounded the senses and added to the sense of disorientation and desperation. I fought against it in my head.

*This is just an exercise. Hold on. Hold on*, I repeated over and over to myself.

When the interrogation element of the Combat Survival phase finally ended, another clutch of individuals was removed from the course. Any man can be made to crack under interrogation, especially if torture is used, and it is only a matter of time. But in Special Forces operations, time is critical, and the longer you resist giving up information, the more time you buy for your uncaptured comrades to have a chance of completing the mission, making good their own evasion from capture and giving your headquarters a better chance to adjust to the implications of some of their people being in the hands of the enemy. Hence, if you cracked in a twenty-four-hour exercise, there could be no place for you in the SAS.

It is a basic requirement that all SAS soldiers are parachute trained, so the twenty-five of us who survived the interrogation went on to complete the fifth and final phase of Selection, in the form of passing the basic military parachuting course at the Number 1 Parachute School at RAF Brize Norton. We made eight static line parachute descents, including one from a balloon and a night jump. Each jump involved building up to jumping with kit and with more people, to simulate a whole unit going out of a C-130 Hercules transport plane into a combat situation. Even at the hands of the gentler RAF parachute jump instructors, I was glad to get the course done. Any refusal to jump would have resulted in an instant RTU, although no one did on our course; they had been through too much to fail due to a momentary inability to master their fear and jump out of an aircraft. However, as far as I was concerned, parachuting was a necessary evil and not something that I enjoyed.

More importantly, earning the right to wear my jumps wings meant that I had passed Selection and had become a 'badged' member of the Regiment, and I had earned the right to wear their sand-coloured beret, with its winged dagger cap badge. It also meant that D Squadron and Stirling Lines would become my new home – at least for the moment. While Selection entitled initial entry to the Regiment, it was no guarantee that you would stay in it. All of those who passed the course would be joining on a probationary twelve-month basis. The slightest indiscretion or failure to live up to the exacting standards expected of us, and we would be out.

I was told that I would be joining Mountain Troop, with two others who had also made it through Selection out of the total of fifteen candidates who had passed the course. One of those posted to Mountain Troop with me was Roy Fonseca. Roy was a Royal Signals soldier who came from the Seychelles. As this was a former British colony, he had joined the Army under a scheme that offered a limited number of places among its ranks to individuals from Commonwealth countries. I hadn't seen much of him during Selection, as he was in a different batch of candidates. But Roy had a disposition that was as sunny as the country he came from.

With a head of tight-wired frizzy hair and big white teeth, he was always smiling, regardless of how difficult the circumstances could get, which became immediately apparent during the resistance to interrogation training. When 'end ex' was called and his hood came off, he refused to believe the DS when they told him that the training was over. Fearing an elaborate ruse, he just kept repeating the 'Big Four' back to the instructors, and it took them an age to convince him that the resistance to interrogation phase really had finished. The more frustrated they got, the surer Roy was that it was a trick, until he eventually relented, broke out into a broad grin and acquiesced to getting on the transport back to Hereford with the rest of us.

Despite the diversity of our backgrounds, Roy and I were both entering a different world to the one that we were used to, where there was little time for the more orthodox military traditions of drill, dress regulations and ceremonial bullshit. Both of us had started Selection as NCOs in our parent units, but while we would maintain the pay of our former rank for the next twelve months, in terms of the SAS hierarchy we would revert to the rank of private. Effectively we were 'Toms' again – derived from Tommy Atkins, the term described the most junior of soldiers in the military hierarchy. Regardless of status, and the fact that we no longer had any, everyone in the Regiment is on first-name terms, except for the officers, who were addressed as 'boss' rather than 'sir'. But a rigid rank structure didn't mean that a relaxed carefree attitude prevailed. A fierce discipline of professionalism and personal conduct pervaded the Regiment, which was evident in the intensity of training.

If we went to the ranges to practise and enhance our weapon skills, we would often work late into the night, endlessly going over repetitive drills until they were honed to perfection. Then we would start all over again the next day doing exactly the same thing. We were also joining an environment where there was a seemingly initial contradictory requirement. On the one hand we had, in part, been selected because of our ability to think as individuals who could demonstrate self-reliance and independence of thought. On the other, we were expected to do as we were told, keep our mouths shut and not venture an opinion unless asked to express one or until deemed to have proven ourselves as being worthy of the right to do so. No one cared where you came from and no one expected you to talk about it. Keeping my head down and working hard to establish myself as a trusted member of the team was the obvious imperative of fitting in and being accepted.

While the more basic soldierly skills of an SAS trooper quickly became an ingrained part of our DNA through the incessant application of hard training, we also had to learn the specialist skills associated with the troop we had been assigned to. The SAS is organized into a regimental headquarters squadron and its four principal sabre squadrons, each designated by the prefix letters of A, B, G and D. Each sub-unit is commanded by a major and in turn is divided down into a squadron headquarters troop and four specialist theatre entry troop-level sub-units, which gives rise to their functional titles: Air, Boat, Mobility and Mountain. In D Squadron, these were respectively numbered as 16, 17, 18 and 19 Troops.

Regardless of specialization, each troop was divided into four groups of four-man patrols, which were each commanded by one of the three senior NCOs and the captain in the troop, who was also the troop commander. While the other three troops would focus on their environmental specialisms of parachuting, using boats and canoes and specialist mobility vehicles, Mountain Troop was trained in climbing and rope work to facilitate the rest of the Squadron being able to operate in any area where mountains might be encountered. It meant that we spent much of our time in places like Snowdonia and the

Alps learning to become proficient as rock leaders and snow and ice climbers. However, previous experience or personal preference had little to do with which troop you were posted to.

When Bilbo joined D Squadron, having passed a later Selection to my course, he was desperate not to be posted to Air Troop, due to his acute fear of heights: the thought of having to specialize in freefall parachuting terrified him. On reporting for duty in the Squadron office, he couldn't quite catch what the OC told him regarding which troop he would be joining. Meeting the Squadron sergeant major in the corridor, he asked for clarity, praying that he wasn't being posted to 16 Troop, hoping for either Mobility or Boat Troop.

'No,' Lawrence Gallagher replied, 'you are going to Mountain Troop.'

Bilbo spent the next year being hauled up mountains and dragged across precipitous ridges by seasoned mountaineers in the Troop, like John Arthy. Also known as Lofty (he was well over 6 feet tall), John was a newly promoted sergeant in the Troop and a former Guardsman, who referred to everything good as 'gleaming', as all woodentops seem to do. He was also a brilliant climber who had summited Everest. They made for an incongruous climbing partnership, as the veteran enthusiast mountain man shepherded the acrophobic Bilbo up severe grade climbs at the end of the rope. On reaching the top of a pitch, Bilbo would arrive shaking and thanking his lucky stars that he had made it through another death-defying experience, while Lofty would just sit back and say, 'That was fucking gleaming.'

As well as mastering the specialist environmental skills of the troop we had joined, we were also expected to develop individual specialisms, such as signalling, learning a foreign language or becoming a patrol medic. I qualified as a patrol signaller in high-frequency Morse code, which involved learning to key out coded messages, receive them and decipher them at a rate of sixty characters a minute. Given the nature of having to conduct extended-range operations anywhere in the world, when there was no internet and satellite communications were in their infancy, it was an essential qualification to have. But applying hand-coded formulas and mathematical cyphers made it a tedious and mind-numbing course to pass.

We started by learning the Morse code alphabet, with each letter being distinguished by dots, called 'dits', pronounced as 'di', and by dashes, called 'dahs', or by a combination of dits and dahs. Every letter had its own distinctive beat. The letter 'H' was a series of four dits and sounded like a galloping horse in a hurry when tapped out on a Morse code telegraph key as 'di, di, di, di', with the letter 'M' having a more heavy-footed sound of two dashes or 'dah, dah'. It was like learning an entirely new language, and we had to commit the sound of each letter to memory and learn that rhythm was the key to good sending: dits had to be uniform and short, dahs had to be precise and long and the spacing between characters exactly right if the message we sent was to have any meaning.

Over three long, torturous months, our coding gradually became second nature. As regime and rhythm blended, we also developed our own unique signature in the transmissions we sent, to the extent that an experienced

Morse signaller could begin to recognize a specific oper-ator's keystroke style in a manner not dissimilar to recognizing an individual's handwriting. By the time I finished the course, I could write, think and speak in Morse like some deranged robot, and a good signaller at the other end of the net would know whether it was me transmitting to them or another member of the course. It also meant that, as part of an SAS patrol, I could com-municate in any terrain and over any distance back to a headquarters location, either to relay information about an enemy target or, more importantly, to call for help if we got into trouble.

The patrol medics' course was an entirely different affair. After two months of theoretical training with the Royal Army Medical Corps, we were sent on a four-week attach-ment to the A and E department of a major hospital. I went with a bloke from the SBS to St Helier in Carshal-ton, a large Art Deco facility built in the late 1920s as an overspill hospital for the expanding suburbs of London. We assisted the doctors and casualty nurses with every type of injury resulting in the main from road traffic acci-dents and nasty domestic mishaps. It was a hands-on experience, albeit under close supervision.

The first thing I was asked to do was to amputate the damaged toe of a little girl who came into the ward one evening, which was sobering. But it brought home the importance of being able to conduct trauma medicine when we might find ourselves operating in an environment a long way from normal medical support, where the ability to diagnose a bleed, find and clip an artery, stem a rup-tured vein or conduct a basic amputation would make the critical difference to whether someone hit by bullets or shrapnel could be kept alive until they could be evacuated to a proper hospital facility.

Although it was harrowing on occasion, I loved it. What really bothered me was the large number of drug addicts and drunks that we had to deal with, especially when they became abusive and violent towards the nurses. Late one Saturday night, a pissed bloke made the mistake of kicking off with one of the female medical staff, unaware that there were two hairy-arsed Special Forces blokes at the other end of the ward. We didn't wait to be asked to intervene.

The bloke at the end of the ward was a big unit, off his face and clearly fancied himself. 'Mate, you need to calm down and behave,' I said.

'Yeah? And what are you going to do about it, nursey?' the drunk replied in a voice full of sarcasm and menace. No doubt the blue ward scrubs we were wearing served to diminish any sense of threat we might pose.

'I have told you once . . .' I started, when the bloke suddenly came swinging at us with his fist flailing wildly through the air.

My SBS companion and I were sober, superior in numbers and in no mood to compromise. So it ended almost as soon as it started.

I am not sure if the drunk had a genuine injury when he arrived at the hospital, but he certainly left with one. I suspect the story grew in the telling, but it made us popular with the medical staff. It certainly enhanced our status in their eyes and probably played its part in the relationship that began to blossom with Liz.

By the time the sojourn at St Helier ended, a year had passed. The good news was that I had been accepted by the Squadron and would be staying. The bad news was that I would lose the pay I drew as a colour sergeant, and my salary would drop to that of a corporal, two ranks lower. There was no Special Forces pay in those days, and the additional 'Para pay' of about a quid a day, which we received for being jumps qualified, did little to compensate. Financially, I was impoverished, but in every other way I was opulent.

Although I had effectively dropped to the bottom rung of the Army's rank hierarchy, I was responsible for no one other than myself, Mountain Troop and the Squadron. Not having to chase private soldiers in the Battalion for guard duty or when they went AWOL, and not having to complete another administrative return for a sodden Army mattress, was liberating. But more importantly, I had joined an exclusive club beyond the preserve of most men, which led to a professional fulfilment absent in serving with a conventional Army unit. And I had met the girl of my dreams.

I was blissfully happy. The one gap in it all was that we hadn't deployed on operations. What I didn't realize when I applied for Selection was that Operation Storm was all but over. With the aid of British support, the Sultan of Oman had largely defeated the rebel forces by 1978, and the UK had been able to withdraw direct military assistance to his government, which included the SAS.

One prospect of some action lay with assuming the lead for the Regiment's counterterrorist role. The anti-terrorist capability had been set up in response to the killing

33

of eleven Israeli athletes by the Palestinian Black September terrorist group at the Munich Olympics in 1972. The need for the capability was also reinforced by the growing threat of Irish Republican terrorism to the UK mainland. In 1974, it proved its worth, when a four-man terrorist cell took two hostages and holed up in a flat in Balcombe Street in London. After a six-day stand-off with the police, the terrorists immediately surrendered when it was announced by the BBC that the SAS had been called in to deal with them.

Each of the four sabre squadrons rotated through the role on a six-monthly basis. In the autumn of 1979, D Squadron began preparing to take over the task from G Squadron. We were issued with blackhooded overalls, 9 mm Browning pistols and Heckler & Koch MP5 sub-machine guns. We also had Remington pump-action shotguns to blow off the locks and hinges of doors, and stun-grenades, known as 'flashbangs', which could be thrown into a room to stun and disorientate a terrorist, without causing any lasting harm to any of the hostages we would be attempting to rescue. The role also came with the provision of fast, powerful cars and access to helicopters to get us to a potential terrorist incident at speed.

A month of intense activity ensued. We trained incessantly in the 'Killing House' in Stirling Lines and became expert in every method of building entry, using fast ropes, explosives charges and the shotguns. We practised with flashbangs and CS gas and used live ammunition. The bullets were designed to stop dead in a target to avoid the threat of ricochet and follow-through, which would present a threat to any innocents, as the focus was all about killing terrorists and saving hostages. To get the drills right, civilian 'friendly' targets representing hostages were always mixed up among those representing the bad guys.

Each of the troops were at it night and day as we hardened our endeavours into ingrained drills and precision, which allowed us to make split-second judgement calls about selecting and engaging the right target in every circumstance and under every type of pressure. When deemed ready four weeks later, we went on standby and waited for the call. At any one time, two troops would be at thirty minutes' notice to move in Stirling Lines. The other two troops were held at three hours' notice, which meant that they had to carry bleepers and had to remain on call in close proximity to Hereford 24/7. Troops swapped between the readiness criteria to provide some respite, but for the next six months we were a coiled spring. The call did come, in the form of the Iranian Embassy siege. But it was too late for us. We had just handed over the counterterrorist role to B Squadron the month before, and they got the job.

Given the events that unfolded at Prince's Gate, it was a profound disappointment to every man in D Squadron. What we didn't realize at the time was the level of interest in the Regiment the siege had generated with the politicians. The counterterrorist capability had been set up by Edward Heath, but it caught the imagination of another Conservative prime minister, and was the start of what became an increasingly close relationship with Margaret Thatcher.

Mike Rose had just taken over command in Hereford at

the time. Rose oozed charm and had a demonstrable intellect and presence to go with it. It was a disposition that appealed to Thatcher, an appeal considerably enhanced by what the SAS had achieved in 1981, which she described as a 'brilliant operation'. She had been in power for just over two years and was battling against the pressures of soaring unemployment, economic recession, high inflation and the fallout from the riots in Brixton and Toxteth, which were the UK's worst civil disturbances since the Great Depression of the 1930s. Thatcher's government was not popular, and the successful and dramatic conclusion of the siege provided her with a welcome boost.

From that moment, the prime minister had taken a keen interest in the Regiment, which included paying a visit to Stirling Lines, where she readily volunteered to act as a hostage in a live firing demonstration in the 'Killing House', much against the wishes of her personal advisor. Bursting into the darkened target room with flashbangs, the assault team neatly double-tapped the terrorist cardboard cut-outs with a couple of rounds apiece, which had been positioned on either side of the prime minister. When the lights came on, she was sitting calmly between the smoking targets, but her minder was spread-eagled on the floor. She looked at the masked armed men in black overalls in front of her, then down at the floor at her prostrate aide, before sighing and saying, 'Get up, George, you are embarrassing me.'

A rather meek civil servant replied, 'Yes, prime minister,' as he sheepishly got to his feet.

It was a mark of the 'Iron Lady', the strength of the relationship she had developed with the Regiment. It also represented a favourable point of leverage, which was enhanced by the fact that the director had been in post at the time of the siege and also sat on the Cabinet Office's crisis committee known as COBR.* Consequently, we would have been surprised and disappointed if Rose and the brigadier were not utilizing the Regiment's reputation and affiliation with senior politicians like the prime minister to ensure that our capabilities would be included in any force being assembled to sail south to the Falklands. While such high-level matters may have been on our minds, their resolution was beyond our pay grade. Our focus was to get ready to leave Hereford, and we would have to wait and see whether the events of two years previously would play to our favour.

* COBR stands for 'Cabinet Office Briefing Room' in the Cabinet Office buildings, which is where COBR (now known as COBRA) was convened.

# 3

Those of us who were married kept ready-packed bergens in the 'pads' room in the single blokes' accommodation, which we picked up on the way to the Squadron stores, where they would be centralized for onward loading to Brize Norton. We then spent the rest of the morning helping pack the tons of Squadron kit, including rations, parachutes and a mountain of heavy signals equipment, which we took with us on every sub-unit-level exercise. Our weapons systems were also drawn from the armoury and bundled together in canvas sleeves, so that they could be dispatched with us on an aircraft.

It was a well-oiled process, and, regardless of our rank or status, we all lent a hand under the direction of the Squadron quartermaster sergeant, Graham Collins. He was originally a Fusilier and another Londoner: the capital was one of his parent regiment's recruiting grounds. Graham had passed Selection years previously but was doing the type of stores job that had provoked me to leave the Glosters. The difference was he was doing it in the Regiment and had a stack of combat experience from Operation Storm.

His able storeman assistant was equally content with his lot, although Wally Walpole wasn't badged and still wore his parent unit cap badge on his sand-coloured beret. Wally had an open, honest face and he was as unassuming as he was unambitious. He had applied to join the SAS as a lance corporal in a support role, which meant that he didn't have to do Selection. His duties were purely administrative, and he would not be expected to deploy on direct combat operations, although he would be coming with us if we managed to go south with the Task Force, to help Graham provision our logistic functions. Although Wally wasn't badged, he was acccptcd wholeheartedly as being one of the Squadron and valued for the important role he played. He was also accepted because he was a good bloke, looked after us and grafted hard. His job didn't have great promotion prospects, but he loved it, just wanted to be with the Squadron and was as excited about what might be afoot as we were.

By lunchtime the kit was packed, and we had all seen the news bulletins on the TV of large Argentine armoured vehicles tracking up and down the streets of Port Stanley in the Falklands, festooned with Argie soldiers giving the 'V' for victory sign. We also saw the images of the Royal Marine garrison lying prone on the ground, with their arms over their heads, as thcir gun-toting captors stood over them, with their faces smeared in camouflage cream.

'Poor buggers,' said Binsy, as we made a brew back in the 'pads' room. 'Doesn't look like the Booties stood a chance.'

'The sooner we get down there and sort those neckie bastards out, the better,' Bilbo replied, referring to the black-capped Arg Special Forces soldiers, who were being filmed leading away each of the Marines.

'Yeah,' said James, 'we need to get stuck in amongst them. But I just can't see how we can get down there in time. The Falklands are thousands of miles away, and the politicians will be desperate to avoid it coming to blows.'

'Let's just hope we get moving, then,' I replied, with half my mind on the footage we were watching on the box and the other half on the reception I was likely to face when I went home to collect the rest of my gear and tell Liz that we were heading off to Brize later that afternoon.

Liz was the one person who remained completely unenthused by it all. She was still in high dudgeon when I finished at the stores and went back to our quarters later that afternoon. It was not helped when she found out that I had only returned to pack some last few personal items, as the buses taking us to Brize Norton would be leaving from camp later that afternoon. I went into our bedroom and threw a few things into a large Para grip-bag before heading back downstairs to endure a difficult farewell.

To be fair to Liz, she had been slow to realize the significance of what was happening and that we might have to fight to get the Falklands back. The precious leave that we had planned to spend together may have been broken by events 8,000 miles away, but it was the loss of precious and much-needed time together that was uppermost in her mind.

She was nursing a cup of coffee in the kitchen. 'I have spoken to Mum,' she said in a low, miserable voice. 'She said that you might be off to war.' Her mother was a paragon of good sense.

'Yes, love, we might be,' I replied, as gently as I could, and followed this with an attempt at some level of assurance: 'But it could all come to nothing.'

Liz softened a little and looked at me with her dark,

hazel eyes, momentarily dulling the edge of awkwardness between us. I felt a sense of longing and guilt but was torn by the need to get going.

'Well, love, I better get a move on. The bus leaves in half an hour.'

'Yes, I suppose you have to.' The edge of hurt and disappointment creeping back into her voice.

I picked up my grip from the kitchen floor and gave her a brief kiss on the lips.

'Right, love, that's me, then.'

'Look after yourself,' she said.

'I will and I love you,' I replied.

There was a pause, and then she said, 'I love you too.'

I turned and walked into the hall, opened the door and pushed it shut behind me.

Caught between a troubled wife and my enthusiasm for what might lie ahead, it was a relief to leave the domestic awkwardness behind.

An hour later, I boarded a blue-grey coach.

I found a seat by a window, and Bilbo sat down next to me.

'How was leaving home, mate?' I asked.

'In truth, pretty shit,' Bilbo replied. 'It's my boy's fourth birthday next week, and it killed me to have to tell him that I wasn't going to be there for it. How was Liz? Pissed off?'

'Yep. Well unimpressed,' I said. 'Chances are we'll be back here in a day or two, though. You might make your boy's birthday, and I will be getting an earful from Liz.'

'At least we are on the bus. If this does kick off, Roy will be pissed,' said Bilbo.

Roy was on a Mountain Guides course in the German Alps. Lots of the blokes who were away from the Regiment had tried to get back to Hereford as soon as they heard about the crisis. Some had made it, and some had not, which included Roy.

The trees were not yet in full leaf when we pulled out of Stirling Lines and turned on to the old Ross Road and headed for Oxfordshire and RAF Brize Norton. As we left Hereford behind us, I noticed that the hawthorn in the hedgerows was spotted with white, the sun was still high in a clear blue sky, and I was filled with a sense of prospect and purpose.

My optimism was nearly dashed by the RAF movement handlers when we arrived at Brize. A VC-10 passenger jet was waiting on the tarmac to take designated personnel warned off for potential operations in the South Atlantic to a staging post, which was in the process of being set up on Ascension Island. The problem was that D Squadron wasn't on the manifest. A lively discussion between the aircrew and our command element, known as the 'head shed', ensued. While they negotiated our passage, the rest of us took seats in what passed for an arrivals and departure area to await the outcome.

Through the large windows of the terminal building we watched another VC-10 disgorging a body of Royal Marines. They trooped down the steps of the jet and began to file into the area near where we were sitting.

'Look at that lot,' Binsy said as the Marines trudged into the terminal.

'They must be the Bootnecks we saw on the TV,' said James.

He was right. The Marines were members of Naval Party 8901, who had been captured on the Falklands and South Georgia and had been returned by Argentina via Uruguay.

'Poor bastards, they look done in, but it sounds like they put up a pretty good fight and gave the Argies a bloody nose,' offered Binsy.

'Sounds like it,' I said.

'Fucking good job, Royal,' Bilbo said, as the Marines began to gather at one side of the terminal.

They were indeed a subdued and sombre-looking bunch. But they had put up a brief, stiff resistance against over-whelming odds. On the Falklands, the main force of 'Royals' had killed and wounded a number of the Argentine invaders and had taken out an armoured amphibious vehicle. On South Georgia, a smaller detachment of Marines, under a lieutenant called Keith Mills, had shot down a Puma troop-carrying helicopter and nearly sunk an Argentine warship with an anti-tank weapon, which we thought was pretty good going.

It didn't take long before we were told to grab our kit and get ready to board the aircraft. The head shed had won their argument with the RAF. We suspected that influence in high places and a veiled threat to use it had prevailed over bureaucracy.

We walked on board the VC-10 as our accompanying freight of stores, equipment, weapons and ammunition were loaded into the aircraft's hold. Each of us was given a white cardboard box containing some thin, flat-looking sandwiches filled with dubious-looking fish paste, and a can of cola and a packet of crisps, which both bore brand names no one had ever heard of. The nondescript packed lunch was an indication we'd been accepted by the RAF system and that our journey south was about to begin.

The VC-10 was soon taxiing out on to the runway. The engines built up power in readiness for take-off. We felt the brakes come off, and the aircraft accelerated down the runway before climbing into the sky as the sun began to dip to the horizon in the west.

Behind us we left a country indignant with a collective sense of national humiliation and outrage and a public demanding action, something Margaret Thatcher seemed determined to deliver. As we gained altitude, military bases, supply depots and ports across the country were marshalling ships and more men and equipment to follow on behind us.

Though the outcome was still in doubt, unlike some of the more discretionary conflicts the UK had engaged in since the turn of this century, the cause for war appeared straightforward. British sovereignty had been breached by an armed aggressor and had been condemned by international opinion. All of us shared the sentiment. But at the same time, the clear-cut righteousness of the cause hardly mattered. It was the prospect of being tested in combat that focused our minds most, and every member of D Squadron wanted to face that test.

# 4

If we had been given more information about the Falkland Islands, initial consideration might have suggested that they were not much of a place worth fighting and dying for. Lying 400 miles to the east of the South American Atlantic seaboard and 850 miles from Antarctica, the archipelago with its two primary islands of West and East Falkland is remote and desolate. Measuring just over 4,500 square miles, it is a treeless, windswept land of sodden peat moors, craggy stone-run gullies and whale-backed, rock-spiked hills. Most of its population (no more than 2,000 people in 1982) lived in the islands' capital of wooden and tin-roofed buildings at Port Stanley on East Falkland, which was little more than the size of a well-founded village. Linked together by only the most rudimentary of tracks, the remainder of its communities were scattered across numerous isolated farming settlements, which managed the half million sheep that provided the Falklands with its main economic output.

While the average Argentine probably didn't know much more about the realities of the Falklands than we did, every kid at school was taught that what they called the Islas Malvinas belonged to Argentina and had been stolen by the British in 1833.

The historical twists and turns regarding the sovereignty of the Islands were not uppermost in our minds as

45

we departed from the UK. What was clear was that the brutal and unpopular military dictatorship of General Leopoldo Galtieri's junta had invaded the Islands to forestall massive unrest in his own country. Crowds in Buenos Aires, which only a few days before had seethed in protest against repression, high unemployment and hyperinflation running at over 100 per cent, suddenly erupted in wild celebration of the regime's actions. It was also apparent that the UK's decision to phase out the Royal Navy's aircraft carriers and assault ships, while also dramatically reducing its fleet of destroyers and frigates in a planned round of swingeing defence cuts, had been taken by Galtieri as a sign that the UK had little interest in defending the Falklands. What the general did not take into account was the presence of Margaret Thatcher in 10 Downing Street.

But regardless of the balls Maggie had shown, her government had been caught napping. It was only Britain's possession of another small chunk of Atlantic real estate that would make any kind of military response possible.

Nine hours after we took off from Brize Norton, the wheels of our VC-10 thumped down hard on the 10,000 feet of single tarmac runway at Wideawake Airfield on the small British overseas territory of Ascension Island. Little more than 8 miles across at its widest point, Ascension rises out of the middle of the rolling surf of the Atlantic a few degrees below the Equator, as an isolated plug of black jagged volcanic rock. Positioned 4,500 miles from the UK and just under 4,000 miles from the Falklands, the island was about to become a vital staging post for the Task Force.

Critical though it was, Ascension was an eccentric place. Used as a British naval base during the Second World War, it had been leased to NASA as a space tracking station and alternative landing site for the Space Shuttle. The island also boasted a BBC World Service relay station, but apart from its American-built airfield and an array of radar dishes and antennae, it appeared as a barren wasteland of hardened lava rock and cinder ash. It was devoid of vegetation, except on the single high peak at its centre called Green Mountain, which at 2,800 feet above sea level was sufficiently high enough to attract rainfall to hydrate the scrub-thorn bush and Norfolk pines that grew on its upper slopes.

The purpose of flying to Ascension had been to hook up with a ship, which we had been told would provide us with onward passage to the South Atlantic. The arrangement seemed somewhat vague, and any reception party that might have been organized to meet us was conspicuous by its absence as we stepped off the plane into blazing sunshine and 30 degrees of tropical heat. The command element of the Squadron disappeared in the direction of a large hangar to inquire about finding our mystery vessel, while the rest of us kicked our heels on the shimmering tarmac and thought about finding some shade, which appeared to be equally absent.

With nowhere else to go, we sought shelter from the glare of the sun under one of the VC-10's wings and took in our surroundings, the sea-blown breeze drifting across the bay next to the airstrip doing little to reduce the stifling temperature.

'Fuck me. This is a bare arse-end of the world place.

I bet they don't get many visitors here,' said Binsy as he wiped his brow and we took in our surrounds, which consisted of nothing more than a few hangars with an air of loneliness and infrequent use about them.

'Yep, and no ships,' I replied, looking out towards the sea, which was empty to its horizon.

'No doubt they are still loading troops and kit back in the UK,' offered James. 'We must be the first troops to arrive.'

'So it's more hurry up and wait in this godforsaken place,' Binsy replied. But he was wrong on both counts.

In the days ahead, Wideawake would become one of the busiest airports in the world, as an increasing stream of cargo planes, air-refuelling tankers and passenger air-craft arrived, bringing personnel, material and equipment to sustain the seaborne element of the Task Force. The apron space at the side of the runway would begin to pile up with what would grow into small mountains of pal-leted ammunition and stores waiting to be collected by naval helicopters and ferried out to ships as they dropped anchor to be replenished and provisioned for the onward journey south.

A few minutes later, Lawrence re-emerged from the hangar with the OC and 2IC. He came over towards us, and we were about to get moving.

'Right, guys. Our ship is still at sea. But the matelot the boss has just spoken to –' Lawrence gestured back towards the hangar at a Royal Naval officer who had been dispatched to Ascension to help run the show – 'says that it should be here in a couple of days. Everything on the islands seems to be owned by Cable and Wireless, Pan Am or NASA, who also seem to run the place. There's no accommodation, but the Yanks are keen to help.'

We liked the sound of that. Whenever we were short of stuff, the Americans were always ready to chip in and help us Brits out.

'It won't be the Ritz,' Lawrence continued, 'but Cable and Wireless own an old schoolhouse further up the mountain, which we can doss down in, and the Americans are laying on some vehicles to take us up there.'

As if on cue, a couple of large US Army six-wheeled 2½ ton trucks drew up next to the aircraft. And with the knowledge of at least having somewhere to stay while we waited for our elusive ship to arrive, we loaded our kit and clambered aboard them.

Nowhere is very far away on Ascension Island, and after a few minutes' drive along traffic-free tarmac roads, which wound their way up through the rocky barren terrain, we arrived at the schoolhouse. It was located halfway up the northern slopes of Green Mountain near a small workers' village of white low-rise prefabricated buildings called Two Boats. A single-storey whitewashed building, devoid of any frames in its windows, it provided ample accommodation for our simple needs. 19 Troop was allocated a metal-framed bike shed, which would serve as our quarters for the next four days. Each of the Troop's patrols took an area of the rusty shelter to doss down together in their individual groupings of six men. Although not usually part of the same patrol, Binsy, Bilbo and I grabbed a piece of concrete floor space, along with Alex Brown, Chris Seakins and Sid Davidson, who made up the other three members of my patrol.

As a sergeant, Sid Davidson was the senior member of the patrol and its commander. Sid was a lean-built ex-Para and, like the rest of the senior NCOs in the Troop, he was a veteran of Operation Storm. Added to that, he had made a freefall combat jump into Oman in the mid-1970s, when parachuting into action had already become an historical anomaly that most airborne soldiers could only dream of. That Sid had done it for real lent him the aura of a fearsome warrior, but he was also a family man, with a passion for his two Shelties, and as gentle as he was kind. Back in Hereford, Sid would bring the two Shetland sheepdogs on long tabs, and when they got tired he would pick them up and carry them in his bergen for the rest of the route march.

Chris and Alex were also both ex-Paras – evidence that former members of the Parachute Regiment made up 60 per cent of the SAS. Not all of them passed Selection first time. Alex Brown had been on the same course as me but didn't make it through 'Endurance'. So he re-applied, went through it all again and got through Selection at the second attempt. A softly spoken Jock from Dundee, he was as bright as a button and an accomplished artist, which meant he always got the job of producing tactical sketch maps when the real things were in short supply. Alex was also a qualified *saucier*, one of the most respected positions in the French *Brigade de cuisine* hierarchy and the preserve of posh five-star hotels and smart restaurants. He was a heavy smoker and always had a rollie stuck between his lips – a habit that didn't sit overly well with the fact that he was the Troop demolition expert. He would happily select lumps of plastic explosive and roll them into shape as he puffed away on a fag.

Like Alex, Chris Seakins came from 1 PARA. Chris had joined the Paras as a boy-soldier and was one of the youngest members of the Troop. Lean and sinewy, he was as fit as a butcher's dog and could leave any man standing when it came to a Troop or Squadron run. Most days we would run part way up the slopes of Green Mountain; Chris did it religiously every day and was the only one who always went to the top and back again.

Though 22 SAS was now their first unit loyalty, their airborne roots remained a fierce part of their DNA. As Bilbo, Binsy and I were the only non-Paras in our little group, even though we had passed Selection they regarded us as 'crap-hats', a derogatory term Paras applied to everyone else in the Army who didn't wear the coveted maroon beret of the Parachute Regiment.

It also reflected the fact that, like all soldiers, we engaged in ceaseless banter, constantly taking the piss out of each other and stitching one another up. Surreptitiously slipping a deadweight, such as a rock, into someone's already overweight bergen during a training tab and then falling about in hysterics when they unpacked at the end of the march and discovered it, never got old. The ex-Paras found it even funnier if you got pissed off about it.

'If you can't take a fucking joke,' they would tell anyone who fell for it, 'you shouldn't have fucking joined up.'

Banter and how we engaged with one another was also conducted in the vernacular of the soldier, which was liberally sprinkled with jargon and Anglo-Saxon expletives. Almost every item, place, type of person and common adjective or activity possessed its own distinct terminology. Food was known as 'scoff', rubbish was 'gash', a cigarette was a 'bine', after Woodbines, a shelter was called a 'basha', where you slept in your 'gonk' or 'doss' (sleeping) bag, and the ubiquitous industrial-strength masking tape we used for just about everything was known as 'black nasty'. Pornography was 'grot' or 'Frankie Vaughan', and a spare or illicitly procured item of anything useful was known as a 'buckshee'. Being in the field was being out in the 'ulu', and the sea was called the 'ogin'.

If an item or event, such as the scoff or the 'Met', which was the weather, was bad it was described as being 'minging'. If something was good it was 'the dog's bollocks', or 'gleaming' if you were a Guardsman. They were also known as 'woodentops'. To do something quickly, such as your washing, which was referred to as 'dohbi', was getting a 'jildi on'. Truth or good information was known as 'pukka gen'. If something was no good it was 'duff', 'US' or, if it referred to a situation, was called a 'cluster fuck'. And the one thing you never wanted to do was to 'jack' on your mates.

As a team we were close, we ate, slept, dug in and patrolled together. We also drank together. On Ascension meals came in the form of ten-man compo rations of processed tinned food cooked up and served centrally by Graham and Wally. It was a bland, monotonous culinary affair, but Graham had also managed to procure some cans of buckshee beer to wash down the normal evening meal of anaemic, skin-pale sausages or corned beef, powdered mashed potato and baked beans. We couldn't have been happier.

The nature and size of a Special Forces sub-unit meant

that small-group loyalty snaked out from across each of the four individual patrol teams and extended to coil round 19 Troop as a whole. In comparison to an infantry platoon of thirty-plus soldiers, we numbered only sixteen to seventeen men at best. Smaller numbers helped increase the bond of fraternity, as did Selection and the attitudes imbued from passing it, which bred an easy familiarity based on professional respect and shared endeavour.

In conventional Army units, a traditional distance is maintained between the officers, senior NCOs and soldiers. In the Regiment the divide in rank structure was increasingly less marked, to the point of almost non-existence, except for living quarters arrangements when back in camp. While officers were still expected to make the decisions and rely on the senior NCOs to implement them, both commissioned and senior ranks in the Regiment were expected to do so within the confines of consulting with the men that they led. Harnessing the intellectual horsepower and professional opinions of the collective bred an equality found in few other places in the Army. It also presented a significant challenge of expectation for the newest member of 19 Troop.

John Hamilton joined as our new troop commander at the beginning of the year, having passed Selection in December 1981. He was a year or two younger than me and, as a captain in the Green Howards, he had survived the mental and physical agony of Officers' Week. Like everyone else, he had successfully passed all the other phases of the course. Unlike non-commissioned candidates, as an officer John had kept his rank on joining the Regiment. But just like the rest of us he would need to demonstrate that he could fit in and be accepted.

The difference was that as an officer he was also expected to lead; albeit with the informal consent of the men he was charged with leading. A young officer's lot is not an easy ride in the SAS. Serving as a troop commander is often considered as completing an apprenticeship to prove whether you are good enough to come back and serve as a squadron commander. The outcome is determined by the senior hierarchy of the Regiment, but without the backing of his men, an aspiring troop commander is unlikely to be invited back to the SAS for a second tour of duty in a higher rank.

In any small unit led by a single officer brand new to command, leadership success is often dependent on the rapport formed with the senior NCO of the troop. It is especially true in the SAS, where ultimate power rests with the troop staff sergeant, or 'staffie'. It is a relationship dynamic that also impacts on the well-being of the rest of the troop. Fortunately, for our new boss and us, John and Phil Currass got on well from the start. It was a mark of the professionalism of both men. Phil was willing to nurture and guide John while also allowing him to exercise command, albeit with his input and that of the 19 Troop shop floor. In turn, John was receptive to Phil's tutelage and the ideas put forward by the blokes. We had enjoyed a succession of good officers in D Squadron, and it was a positive legacy that helped John.

I summited Mountain Kenya with him at the beginning

of the year when he joined the Troop, and John and I also climbed together in Bavaria. Mutual dependence in a testing environment of ice and altitude provided a good barometer of his character, as a man who was determined and plucky, but also possessed a willingness to listen to the men he commanded and take our views into account.

Like the rest of the captains commanding the other three troops, John reported up to the major commanding D Squadron. Cedric Delves was also an infantry officer. Originally from the Devon and Dorsets, Cedric had served in the Regiment as a troop commander in Oman. He had been in command of the Squadron for just over a year. With a shock of reddish fair hair, he was a determined and experienced officer who possessed an easy style of command. But Cedric was also a man of few words.

As his second in command, Danny West was a perfect foil to Cedric's more introverted nature. An extrovert and talkative Scot, his Glaswegian accent had been softened by years spent away from his native city. Danny had come up through the ranks in the SAS and had been commissioned as a captain; Cedric brought him back into the fold of the Squadron from the Regiment's training wing to act as his number two when D Squadron was warned off to respond to the Falklands crisis. While Cedric and Danny were the only two officers in the head shed, they were backed by the Squadron sergeant major, Lawrence Gallagher.

The likes of Cedric, Danny, Lawrence, John Hamilton and Phil would be the men that I would go to war with, fight alongside and be led into battle by. But the prospect of combat still seemed a long way off. The Squadron still had no specific mission, and I was not even sure that we actually had official sanction to join the Task Force. News that there was a ship somewhere out in the ocean with our name on it sounded like a positive development. Until it arrived, though, we were largely left to our own devices.

# 5

The time on Ascension provided a welcome opportunity for the Squadron to catch its collective breath following our hasty departure from the UK. Even in the absence of detailed orders, a good soldier is never lacking in things to do. There was personal kit to check over, weapons to unbundle and zero and the chance to sunbathe. But first there were 15 tons of Squadron stores to sort through.

An SAS squadron is designed to be capable of conducting operations independently from the Regiment, which meant that it takes all the kit and equipment it needs with it. As the Squadron's quartermaster and storeman, Graham and Wally did most of the work, but shifting a large operational load of ammunition, outboard motors, inflatable boats and collapsible canoes took bodies, and we all mucked in. I half cursed Boat Troop under my breath, as they seemed to own most of the kit. Our own kit for Mountain Troop consisted mainly of ropes and climbing gear for scaling ice falls, rock faces and traversing snow crevasses. It was considerably lighter in comparison, but it had been left behind in Hereford, as we had been told that there were no mountains or deep snow-filled gullies in the Falklands.

Each troop was responsible for unbundling its own weapons and checking their serviceability. We were equipped along similar lines to an infantry company, although the difference was the mix and number of armaments, plus the fact that some of us also carried the American AR15 Armalite assault rifle, often referred to as an M16 and made famous by the Vietnam War. Other individuals carried the standard Army-issued L1A1 self-loading rifle, or SLR.

The main difference between the two weapons was the variation in the ammunition they fired. While they both came with a twenty-round magazine, the Armalite fired smaller 5.56 mm calibre ammunition and was also capable of fully automatic fire. The SLR chambered 7.62 mm rounds and could only be fired in semi-automatic mode, which meant that while the rifle recocked itself, only one round could be fired each time the trigger was pulled. Views on which was the better weapon were evenly split across the Squadron, and debates about individual preference were common. We discussed the relative merits of the two rifles over a beer one night in the bike shed. Bilbo was a fan of the AR15.

'Give me the Armalite any day. It's smaller, easier to handle, you can carry more ammunition and put more rounds down with it.'

'You're wrong, mate,' I countered. Although I also carried an AR15, I favoured the wooden-stocked SLR over the plastic-moulded American weapon. 'It may spit out less fire, but it's got more power and will knock over an elephant.'

'Yeah,' Binsy weighed in, 'the SLR has got 300 metres of extra range. It may be bigger and heavier, but it has got more punch. When a bloke gets hit with a 7.62 mm, he's going down and staying down.'

I wasn't done yet: 'Besides, our Armalites are old and knackered. The Regiment bought them off the Yanks during Borneo in the 1960s, and the barrels are all shot out.'

'Can't hit a barn door much over a couple of hundred metres,' added Binsy, 'and they also jam.'

Bilbo conceded that he had a point there. The ejected rounds had a tendency to become trapped in the Armalite's bolt mechanism, which meant that we had to carry a steel welder's rod taped with black nasty to the side of the weapon in the event of having to clear jammed empty cases.

The mainstay of our firepower came in the form of the Army's general-purpose machine gun, known as a GPMG, or 'Jimpy' for short. Each of the Troop's four patrols carried one. It fired the same 7.62 mm bullet as the SLR but was fed by a belt of linked ammunition. Weighing 26 lbs and equipped with a bipod, the GPMG was crewed by the firer and a number two, who was responsible for ensuring that the machine-gun belts were fed properly into the weapon. Chris got to carry the Jimpy in our patrol, as he was the junior and newest bloke, or what we referred to as the 'Joe Bag' or 'crow' of the team.

Depending on how it was set up, it could fire between 650 and 1,000 rounds a minute, which made it the modern-day equivalent of the Vickers machine gun in the First World War. But unlike the Vickers, it was not water cooled, and its fire had to be limited to twenty- to twenty-five-round 'killing' bursts to reduce the rate at which its barrel overheated. Spare 'quick-change' barrels were carried for that eventuality, and a worked-up team could swap out the barrels in a matter of seconds. The

GPMG made a heavy chattering thump when it fired, which was good for the spirit, as long as you were not on the receiving end of it.

At squadron level, support weapons systems, usually the preserve of specialist infantry platoons, were employed in much fewer numbers. They could only be crewed by robbing blokes from the troops to man them, but they provided the Squadron with much greater range and clout. The MILAN anti-tank missile system fired a wire-guided rocket out to 2,000 metres and, while designed to destroy armoured targets, it could also be used to take out bunkers and dug-in enemy, but it came with the price tag of weight and was a two-man burden to carry.

The one 81 mm mortar owned by the Squadron was even heavier. Consisting of a 50-inch-long barrel, bipod, sight and spring-buffered baseplate, it weighed in at around 80 lbs. The mortar bombs it fired were also heavy, but with a range out to just under six klicks they provided us with our own mini artillery capability.

Regardless of the personal weapon we carried, or the support weapon we had been trained to crew when required, every man wore a set of webbing. This consisted of a webbed belt and shoulder brace straps, with attached pouches for ammunition and water. Known as 'belt kit' or 'belt order', its pouches could also contain sundry items, such as grenades, a survival kit, medical kit and a day's spare rations; the idea being that you could live off your belt order for twenty-four hours or more if you needed to.

Belt kit was fashioned largely to personal preference, but it needed to fit like a glove, as once in the field it would be worn almost permanently. Like many of the blokes, I replaced the unwieldly buckle of my belt kit with a cargo quick-release strap. The standard-issue clip had a habit of sticking, especially when the canvas web belt became wet and was almost impossible to undo with freezing fingers, which made it a real pain in the arse. But it was more than just about convenience.

The cargo strap was an important modification if you needed to drop your belt order in a hurry if you found yourself operating in a confined space like a tunnel or when entering a building through a window. It also meant that you could release it with one hand, while keeping the other on your weapon. In short, you never knew when you might have to whip it off suddenly, and if you were fiddling around with both hands struggling to get it off when you needed to ditch it in an instant, it might just end up costing you your life.

The individual survival kit was a small tobacco tin containing, among other things, a button compass, waterproof matches and fishing hooks; it was designed for use in escape and evasion situations when you needed to live off the land. All other personal items carried into the field were packed into a bergen rucksack, which generally contained a doss bag (also known as a 'green maggot' due to its down-filled segments), jungle waterproof poncho, extra ammunition, rations and spare batteries for our radios. The bergens also contained our Army-issue waterproofs, which we called 'crisp packets'. They rustled like the devil when you moved about in them, and they were virtually useless when it came to keeping you dry. The magic of Gore-Tex had been discovered, but not by the British Army. Anyone who enjoyed the luxury of a civilian Gore-Tex bivy bag also enjoyed the means to buy one. As a cash-strapped full screw, I did not.

There were no hard and fast rules regarding uniforms. Most preferred wearing 'jungley' camouflage trousers, because they were light and dried quickly, although they incurred the disdain of the rest of the Army's hierarchy if they were worn out of the theatre they were designed for.

Interestingly, such prejudices didn't appear to apply to boots. Like the rest of the Army, we also suffered the general issue of DMS ('direct-moulded-sole') boots. Issued for the European front, where the emphasis of movement was by armoured vehicle rather than by foot, they were as short on the ankle as they were on the investment that went into their design and manufacture. DMS boots let water in, but rarely let it out again, so once your feet were wet, they stayed wet. I had a pair of higher-ankle Northern Ireland boots, made for the regular Army tours of the streets of Derry and Belfast. They were better than DMS boots, but not by much. Some of the blokes had civvy climbing- or walking-style boots, but again they were beyond my pay packet.

All of us wore windproof disruptive-camouflage smocks. Issued to the SAS and units deployed to arctic environments, they were loose-fitting zipped jackets adorned with a drawcord hood and large pockets on the hips and chest. Underneath them we tended to wear T-shirts and a Norwegian fleece-type pullover for warmth. Additional warmth came in the form of a black woolly hat and later from synthetic fleece-lined arctic caps with folding ear flaps. In those pre-risk-obsessed days, we hardly bothered with helmets unless we were parachuting, and when not cold most of us cut about bare-headed. Body armour had also not become the obsession it is in today's modern Army. It was only worn by the conventional troops serving in Ulster and was not something that we bothered with. However, given the tropical heat of Ascension, there wasn't requirement to wear very much at all, and with our personal kit squared away, we turned our attention to zeroing our weapons at a nearby beach the next day.

We regularly zeroed our Armalites and SLRs in Hereford, but in bundling and transporting the weapons over 3,000 miles, there was every chance that their alignment had been knocked off. We found a small, sandy cove and set up some plywood Figure 11 targets at one end of it and set about punching holes through them. The beach was deserted, and we fired out to sea, shattering the tranquil backwater peace of the island with short, well-aimed bursts of semi-automatic fire and the control orders of the range conducting officer. The fire orders were occasionally punctuated by frantic yells of 'Check fire! Check fire!' from the lookout we had posted on an outcrop of rocks every time a local boat looked like it was about to enter the nominal danger area of where the overshoot of our bullets was falling out to sea.

Zeroing was a standard basic practice, but Binsy was in his element. Not content to just fire the necessary grouping of five rounds to check his sights were on, he set about engaging as many targets as possible from different fire positions and ranges. He was an expert sharpshooter, probably the best in the Squadron, and a joy to watch as he moved, dropped to one knee and double-tapped neat holes through the centre of numerous targets, before moving and repeating the process.

I was a reasonable shot, but like some of the blokes in the other troops, I had been trained to operate the single 81 mm mortar tube the Squadron possessed. Its extended range and lethal blast effect precluded firing any live ammunition on Ascension. Instead we conducted dry training by going through the motions of responding to radio calls for fire, setting the sights to the required elevation and bearing of a given target and simulating the firing drills of dropping the mortar bombs down the barrel of the weapon.

An 81 mm mortar has a crew of three. While I had the necessary qualifications to control the firing of a complete platoon of nine mortars that would be found in an infantry battalion, I took on the role of the number three and most junior crew member. This involved preparing the mortar ammunition and slipping it down the barrel when told to fire. The sights were set by the number two, in accordance with instructions given by the number one and most senior member of the crew. This role fell to Nige Smith from 16 or Freefall Troop.

At 5 feet 4 inches and quietly spoken with a soft West Country accent, Nige was a most unlikely-looking SAS man. But he was as tough as they come and an absolute mortar devotee and expert. I had assisted him during the mortar training we conducted in Kenya at the start of the year. In the wide-open savannah scrubland, we fired hundreds of mortar rounds, with an impressive accuracy that only a mortar connoisseur of Nige's calibre could produce.

He was also a stickler for procedure, and we did everything by the drill book.

'Take post,' Nige shouted to initiate the start of the proceedings.

'Fire mission! Elevation 0965! Bearing 2200. Three rounds fire for effect!'

Adjusting the sighting system on the mortar, the number two shouted the words back at him finishing with:

'Set!'

Nige then bellowed, 'Fire!'

I went through the play-acting of preparing non-existent bombs for firing and then dropping the imaginary rounds down the barrel three times to rain make-believe mortar destruction on a make-believe enemy, before the number two screamed out, 'Rounds complete!'

We went at it for hours, and Nige berated us for even the most minor lapse in our drills. But make-believe or not, it was important to get it right. The mortar was probably the only instant source of heavy fire that we could count on as guaranteed if we got into a big contact with an enemy. If it was serious, there was a good chance that our lightly armed patrols would need every destructive ounce of explosive power the 81 mm mortar could deliver.

With our weapons tested, kit repacked and stores checked, there was little to do but wait, work on our tans and listen to the radio. With some intricate tuning of the large Army 320 HF radio sets, we could pick up the BBC World Service. The news from London was dominated by the crisis in the South Atlantic and the diplomatic efforts to avoid war. Through the hissing and crackling static of high-frequency radio waves the newsreader announced that the former US general and American secretary of state Al Haig had begun shuttling between Washington, London and Buenos Aires in an attempt to broker a negotiated settlement.

There was talk of setting up an interim administration for the islands and internationally backed discussions on their future sovereignty, in return for a withdrawal of Argentine forces. There was some positive commentary on the prognosis of success. I did no more than shake Maggie Thatcher's hand when she came to Hereford, but the impression she made and her courage in the 'Killing House' suggested that she wasn't someone who did compromise.

The announcement of Lord Carrington's resignation as foreign secretary provoked our ire.

'The man should have stayed and seen it through,' scoffed James.

'Aye, right,' said Binsy. 'Bloody politicians, they can just throw in the towel when they want to.'

'It's those leftie MPs that really piss me off, like Tony Benn,' I said. 'Spouting on about imperialism, avoiding war at all costs and that we are all going to get killed if we don't.'

'Wankers,' Bilbo muttered over one of Graham's buckshee beers.

When not listening to the radio, escapism also came in the form of Thomas Hardy's *Far from the Madding Crowd*. Hardy's novel may have seemed an odd choice for an SAS trooper, but it had sat unread on my bookshelf at home, and I had been meaning to tackle it for a while.

But I didn't get to spend much time in nineteenth-century Wessex before Binsy suggested an early-evening stroll down to the beach.

It was close to sunset when we found the baby turtles. The heat of the day was still in the air, and a steady tropical breeze blew in from the sea, when we noticed small, faltering shifts of movement in the sand, as a mass of baby green turtles began their slow, dangerous journey towards the surf, having hatched from their eggs further up on the beach.

Overhead, a noisy, swooping flock of terns was doing its best to stop them. We watched in fascination as the gulls dived down shrieking in excitement and plucked up the unfortunate infant reptiles with their beaks. Amidst the carnage of nature's screaming chaos and death, the surviving turtles ploughed on in with agonizing slowness, as if knowing that it was a matter of sheer numbers and chance as to whether they made it to the safety of the sea or not.

'Let's try and even the odds in their favour,' Binsy said, as he began beating away the angry birds.

We picked up the tiny, helpless creatures one at a time and delivered them into the relative safety of the incoming waves.

Binsy gave each one a send-off with, 'There you go, little fella', as the tiny reptiles dipped under the surface of the water and disappeared out of sight.

We became lost in our task of bucking the trend of Darwinism. And it was only when the last baby turtle had slipped into the water from my fingers that I saw them. A mass of maritime vessels of all shapes and sizes laid out at anchor in the bay in front of us. We had seen a few ships arrive over the previous days, but now there seemed to be a whole fleet of them.

'Fuck me, Binsy. Will you look at that? The whole bloody Navy has turned up.' If I had been a Guardsman, I might have followed up with the word 'gleaming'.

The growing number of ships arriving to anchor off the island, combined with the intensifying frequency of air traffic landing at Wideawake, was testimony to the national intent to resort to force of arms if diplomacy failed. And, as it turned out, it also meant that we were about to have our last compo supper at the schoolhouse.

# 6

We joined our vessel the next day, 9 April. At over 23,500 tonnes, RFA *Fort Austin* was one of the largest of the Royal Fleet Auxiliary's ships. Painted battleship-grey and fitted to transport troops, the ship was principally designed to carry ammunition, food and water to replenish the Royal Navy's warships at sea. As part of that purpose, *Fort Austin* was equipped with two Wessex Mk V troop helicopters, which clattered through the early-morning haze to pick us up from Wideawake Airfield and began shuttling us on board along with all our kit and equipment. Large stacks of outsized wicker hampers, crates and boxes soon built up on the two flight decks located on the stern of the ship, which then had to be manhandled through seemingly endless passageways to stowage areas on the lower decks. It was a time-consuming task, and by the time we had finished, the ship had weighed anchor and was heading out to sea.

Looking like a cross between an ocean liner and a cargo vessel, *Fort Austin* was a roomy ship, built with a degree of troop comfort in mind. It was hot and stuffy below decks, but we were accommodated in spacious three-bunk tiered cabins, with access to showers and a bar. The food in the main galley was excellent, without a compo sausage or a can of corned beef in sight. There was an assortment of other military personnel on board, including some members of the SBS, but we saw little of them even when we went for runs around the large cargo holds and flight decks. However, the sight of hardened bodies, glistening with sweat, as we thudded round the superstructure wearing only boots and shorts, caused a stir in other quarters.

Binsy noted some crew members ogling us from one of the upper decks during one session of PT and ribbed Bilbo about it.

'Hey, mate, I think that one on the right has eyes only for you. Obviously likes short blokes like you, my lover.'

'Fuck off, Binsy, I don't fancy yours much.'

The audience we had attracted on the rails above us picked up on the banter and started calling out with the odd 'Cooey!' and 'Ooh, I do like him!', which were followed by excited giggling and our own good-humoured laughter in response.

In the days when homosexuality was still illegal in the UK, the merchant navy became one of the few refuges where members of the gay community could openly display their sexuality without fear of harassment or prosecution. Consequently, a significant number of gay men joined up and went to sea as stewards. We were ordered to cover up, although one member of the Squadron called Al, who possessed a particularly ripped torso and aquiline features, had left an indelible mark on one member of the crew and continued to attract attention. At one stage during the voyage, Al was approached in the heads by one of the stewards wearing blue hot pants with pink love hearts stitched across the bottom. Looking down at him across the urinals, he said, 'Oooh, Al, you

piss like a gangster; would you like me to be your moll?'
The encounter did not end romantically.

The attentive nature of the stewards reflected a general
willingness of the whole crew to go out of their way to
accommodate us. At one point the captain slowed the
ship to facilitate some specific troop training activities.
17 Troop broke out their Geminis from the Squadron
stores and launched the boats to test their engines in the
water around the sides of the ship. 16 Troop appropriated
one of the RFA's helicopters and used civilian rigs they
had brought with them to make a few freefall parachute
descents into the water.

The weather was glorious, and the sea was a crystal-
clear blue calm of idyllic flatness. But given our distinct
specializations, there was little Mountain or Mobility
Troops could do, so the blokes of 18 and 19 Troops gathered on the side rails to watch the antics of the boys in
Freefall and Boat Troops. We weren't the only spectators
and were soon captivated by a large humpback whale,
accompanied by its calf, as it broke the surface and nuz-
zled the hull of the ship with its knobbly head. The
brightly coloured chutes of 16 Troop popped open in the
cloudless skies above us, and then the blokes under their
canopies began splashing down near one of *Fort Austin*'s
boats, which had been sent out to gather them up.

The whale picked up the sound of bodies hitting the
water and, with a slow flick of its pectoral fins, turned
from the ship with its calf in tow and swam out to investigate the alien noise. Some of 16 Troop were still several
hundred feet up in the air when they spotted the dark
submerged shapes, as they headed towards their mates

and where they were about to splash down. It resulted in some agitated shouting. I think the word 'shark' might have featured, and it provoked an ecstasy of excited scrambling as folk in the water and about to land made frantic efforts to get into the boat as fast as possible, much to the amusement of the more grounded elements of the Squadron watching from the rails of the ship. The antics and excitement of the day over, the boats and men of D Squadron were recovered back on board intact. The screws of *Fort Austin*'s engines began to turn again, and we resumed a steady 20 knots as we continued our journey south, no doubt leaving a bemused humpback whale and her calf in our wake.

We were halfway to the Antarctic Circle, but the potential conflict that we were heading towards might have been another world away. We were yet to receive any details of a mission. The weather was balmy, and so far, apart from testing a few weapons and running around the ship with our tops now on, we had also undertaken a spot of sport parachuting, messed about with small boats and engaged in whale watching. We had a ship with a bar and were waited on by adoring stewards in their rig of crisp white shirts and shorts. From the news media we received on board, there was also increasing talk that a diplomatic solution to the crisis was in the offing and the chances of having to fight appeared to be receding. All of which seemed to suggest that our rather enjoyable excursion might all be for nothing. However, our world was about to change in dramatic fashion.

After four days spent aboard *Fort Austin*, D Squadron cross-decked to a small flotilla of naval ships led by HMS

*Antrim*. It was 13 April. If I had the inclination or ability to read a maritime chart, the coordinates would have told me that we were now 23 degrees south of the Equator, but it was as if we had travelled to another planet. As our small group of ships left RFA *Fort Austin* in its wake, our days of easy sailing were over.

# 7

The warm sunshine, gentle breeze and kind seas of the Tropics vanished behind us. Ever-strengthening winds, a heavy rolling swell and white-capped waves greeted our approach to the sea of the South Atlantic known as the Roaring Forties. The temperature began to drop, and the clear blue skies were replaced by a smothering grey vista. In joining a warship preparing for operations we were also entering an environment which was as alien to us as the unforgiving weather that surrounded it. There was also a distinct sense that a specific mission was about to come our way.

With a displacement of nearly 7,000 tonnes and over 500 feet in length, HMS *Antrim* was one of the Navy's older County Class destroyers. Armed with a twin forward-mounted 4.5 inch gun turret and an array of anti-ship and anti-aircraft missiles, she was a formidable fighting vessel. Crewed by some 450 sailors and designed with war in mind, she had little space to quarter the best part of half a squadron of Special Forces soldiers. What accommodation there was came in the form of hot bunking with the junior NCO naval ratings on their mess deck. When a bunk space became free, you got in it; when the previous occupant came back from a four-hour watch, they woke you up, you got out of it and set about finding another vacant bed space, if there was one.

The sleeping arrangements were as unfamiliar to us as was the language and system of communication used to run the ship. 'Matelots' or 'Jacks' were naval ratings, toilets were known as 'heads', a mug of tea or coffee was a 'wet', not a 'brew', 'all hands' meant everybody, and if you were told to go 'amidships', you were expected to know exactly where that was and that it was not 'aft'. The ship's propellers were called 'screws', and food was 'scran', not the Army's equivalent of 'scoff'. Everything was 'pussers' (derived from 'purser's'), which meant it belonged to the Navy, and direction to the crew was passed over a tannoy in a series of terse messages referred to as 'pipes'. They were the equivalent of old Army bugle calls, which had been replaced by a more modern tannoy intercom system. Each broadcast started with an announcement of 'Dye hear there. Dye hear there.' And would then be followed by something like: 'Top part of the ship muster on the flag deck at 1800.'

'What in Christ's name does that mean?' I asked.

'Haven't got a scoobies,' came the reply from Binsy. 'Might as well be speaking in Martian.'

The alien environment was not helped by the fact we had to get used to operating on 'Zulu' time, which meant, despite the four-hour local time difference, all watches and timings were set to GMT. It meant that every element of the Task Force was using the same time as that being used back in the UK by the headquarters in Northwood and Hereford. As a result, we got up at 0200 in the morning and would eat lunch around 0800 hours. I suspect that the rest of the Squadron dispersed throughout the flotilla were as confused as we were, but there was clarity just around the corner.

On the first night aboard the destroyer, John Hamilton got Phil to get the Troop together and briefed us up on what was afoot.

'Right, fellas,' he began, 'here's the score.' John paused and nodded towards Phil before he continued. 'We are now part of a small naval task force, which has been detached from the main Task Force and ordered to proceed further south into the Atlantic, rendezvous with *Endurance* and recapture South Georgia.'

*Bloody hell*, I thought to myself, *hadn't foreseen that one. Thought we were going to the Falklands.*

John went on, 'The force is under the overall command of *Antrim*'s CO, Captain Brian Young, and includes the Type 12 frigate HMS *Plymouth* and the RFA *Tidespring*, which has the bulk of M Company from 42 Commando embarked. Along with the Bootnecks, D Squadron and some SBS patrols form part of the land component, which is commanded by a Marine major called Guy Sheridan. The operation is being called Operation Paraquet.'

'That's a pretty small land force,' remarked Sid.

'Yes, I know,' said John, 'but I think that's why the brass back home were keen to get us involved, and the boss has been told by both Young and Sheridan that having sixty-odd extra blokes from the Squadron is a welcome boost to the numbers.'

'Paraquet,' mused Binsy, 'sounds like some form of weed killer.' He was thinking of the well-known brand of herbicide called 'Paraquat'.

'Actually, it's a variation of the spelling of "Parakeet",' James said with a slight sneer.

'Whatever it is, it sounds bloody daft to me,' Binsy sniffed back.

There is no logic to how the British military selects the codewords for its operations, other than that they are given random names that will not risk portraying the nature of their intent. Not surprisingly, the sense of the ridiculous, which runs strong among the more junior ranks of military personnel, meant that the name of the toxic chemical became the preferred term for the endeavour that we were about to embark upon. However, the actual operation had a more serious purpose and was conceived against a backdrop of intense diplomatic activity.

Retaking South Georgia would demonstrate early success, and Thatcher's government also saw the advantage of attaining leverage in the American-brokered negotiations with Argentina by a quick win. But it also meant that 'Paraquat' came with caveats. The island was to be retaken with the minimum of force, minimum casualties were to be incurred by either side, and very little collateral damage was to be caused. The term 'minimum' also applied to available intelligence about Argentine forces and defences on the island. It also applied to the resources allocated to the operation.

What we did know about the enemy was that on 2 April a small party of Argentine Marines had occupied the abandoned whaling station at Leith harbour on South Georgia in support of the scrap-metal workers who had landed there illegally in March. The next day, Lieutenant Keith Mills and his twenty-two Royal Marines had put up a plucky defence at Grytviken against an enemy force that was twice their size and backed up by helicopters and a naval corvette.

John passed on what little updated gen he had been given on our potential enemy.

'The Argentine naval vessels have been withdrawn, but it is assumed that their troops in Leith and Grytviken are still there, which indicates that there could be anywhere between seventy to upwards of one hundred Argentine personnel present. What we don't know is whether they have been reinforced or what defensive positions they have adopted. It looks like our role might be to find that out and either deal with what we find or cue in the rest of the land force.'

'Looks like OP ops,' Phil cut in. 'Sounds good.'

'Yes, but getting on to South Georgia is something we have got to work out, and it looks like the terrain is pretty demanding where we are going,' John replied.

With M Company, the SBS and D Squadron, we could muster a combat force of around 250 fighting personnel, backed up by the punch of naval gunfire from *Antrim* and *Plymouth* and supported by two Wessex Mk V troop-carrying helicopters aboard *Tidespring*, *Antrim*'s own Mk III anti-submarine variant of the Wessex and three much smaller Wasp helicopters from *Plymouth* and *Endurance*. If the Arg forces on South Georgia hadn't been reinforced, then we outnumbered them, but not by much, and they would hold the advantage of being in defence. As the Royal Marines had already shown by shooting down the Arg Puma and holing a corvette with an anti-tank weapon during their defence of Grytviken, troops assaulting by helicopters, supported by naval vessels coming close in shore, were vulnerable to a well-dug-in and determined enemy, however small. Therefore, it became essential that we confirmed the type, number and disposition of any troops that we would be facing before any plan of attack could be decided.

It was agreed between Delves, Sheridan and Young that the SBS would conduct covert reconnaissance of Arg dispositions at Grytviken and that we would concentrate on confirming their presence around Leith. The key question that remained unresolved was how to get on to the island undetected. While we hunkered down in the lower decks of the ship, hot bunking as best we could, and tried to get used to the worsening weather, Cedric and the rest of the command triumvirate of the 'Paraquat' task force began to lay their plans in the admiral's day cabin on *Antrim*, which had been set aside for the task.

The mission was not going to be an easy one. Located just over 800 miles from the Falkland Islands and little more than the same distance again to the outer edges of the Antarctic Circle, the island of South Georgia is a harsh, remote spot. Uninhabited, except for a team of twenty or so British Antarctic Survey scientists at King Edward Point near Grytviken, colonies of king penguins and sea lions, it is an unforgiving place of extreme terrain and weather. Often blasted by the Roaring Forties to its north and fed by arctic storms to the south, it is a land of steep, forbidding mountains, ice crevasses and blizzarding snow, driven by unpredictable katabatic fall winds, which can rush down the sides of its ridges and peaks at hurricane-force speeds. Most of the potential insertion sites lay close to the island's coves and fjords, which were occupied by long-abandoned whaling stations at places like Grytviken and Leith. But they were obvious places to land and easy places to be seen by an alert enemy.

It was a quandary that would occupy our commanders in the days ahead. But in truth we saw little of the command team and had only an outline idea of the operational intent. Instead, we were preoccupied with adjusting to our alien lower-deck environment of a forest of confused terminology, maritime practice and the impact of increasingly worsening weather. Walking in a straight line became a thing of the past, as the ship was hit and slapped by the rising swell and crashing waves, making movement along a passage a zigzagging affair. If we found a vacant bunk space, we had to learn to sleep in a braced wedge position, jamming feet and arms against fixtures to avoid being tossed out of it by the violent motion of the ship.

Fortunately, I did not suffer from seasickness, but others did. I often came across Binsy groaning on a bunk, when he wasn't heading to the heads to throw up. 'Mate, I am in bloody clip and I can't keep anything down,' was all he could manage to say, before he staggered off to heave up what little he had left of the contents of his stomach.

Even some of *Antrim*'s crew were suffering and they were also having to adjust to our presence. We were a scrum of anonymous faces competing for the onboard scarcity of space. Our kit was strewn along the ship's corridors, mess decks and in the junior ratings' galley. Piles of ammunition boxes, along with crates of 66 mm anti-tank launchers, grenades and mortar ammunition, littered every conceivable nook and cranny, which shifted about hazardously unless lashed down securely.

Like the rest of the ship's company, we were issued with thick white cotton anti-flash hoods and gloves, to protect our faces and hands against blast burns and fire if the ship was hit by an enemy torpedo or missile. We had to carry them everywhere, which seemed a little surreal, given that we were soldiers and were not yet at war. Storm-blown, cramped and uncomfortable, we were beginning to get used to the ceaseless motion and confines of our new world, when we were told that 19 Troop would be moving to another ship.

Down to only two days' supply of food, HMS *Endurance* had made the rendezvous on 14 April. Since delivering the Mills party of Marines to South Georgia just before the invasion, she had remained in the vicinity, hidden among the large, tabular icebergs, trying to gain intelligence on Argentine activities on the islands. Mountain Troop were being sent on board to tap into that information in preparation for making a possible landing from the ship to conduct the recce of the enemy position at Leith. Quite how she had remained undetected was beyond me.

Known as '*The Red Plum*' on account of her bright-red-painted hull, she must have stood out among the ice and white snow-capped mountains of the shoreline like a sore thumb. All other Royal Navy vessels were painted in drab battleship-grey, but *Endurance* was a very different kind of ship in both purpose and nature. Bought from a Danish shipping line for her ice-resistant hull and fitted with a couple of Oerlikon cannons and a brace of Wasp helicopters, *Endurance* was the only permanent naval presence stationed in the South Atlantic before the crisis. The government's announcement that she would be withdrawn from the area at the end of the year and would not be replaced was perceived by Argentina as a lack of British commitment to the Falklands. Consequently, it was a major trigger in their decision to invade.

Although half the weight and size of a destroyer, *Endurance* possessed more space to accommodate passengers. Her eight-man hydrographic team had been left in Stanley to create extra room to transit Mills's reinforced Marine detachment of twenty-two Bootnecks to Grytviken. As both elements had subsequently been captured, it meant that we could utilize their vacant quarters. However, Sid and I ended up being accommodated on Army camp beds in a chain locker storage compartment in the forward part of the ship, and, as it lacked the deep steadying keel of a warship, we suffered for it.

Each time the bows plunged down into the trough of a large wave, we skittered in our camp beds across the steel checkplate decking. As they rose up, we skittered back again to where we had started, which made for a unique sleeping experience.

There was also a difference in attitude aboard *Endurance* compared to *Antrim*. While they largely observed the Royal Navy's routines and traditions, *Endurance*'s crew appeared to be more relaxed in their application of them. It meant that we were left undisturbed by the minor tyranny of constantly broadcast meaningless instructions and didn't have to keep asking the crew what they meant and what we were expected to do. The one stipulation was that we were on no account to go up and out on to the main deck, which seemed a sensible order, as the chances of being swept overboard were high. While we generally kept to ourselves, stayed below decks, cleaned weapons and wondered when the seaborne agony of our steel-entombed confinement would end, John Hamilton was up on the bridge, looking at options of how we might get on to South Georgia undetected.

John pored over maps and charts with Lieutenant Commander Andrew Lockett. As *Endurance*'s meteorological and hydrographic officer, he had expert knowledge of the waters surrounding South Georgia and its prevailing weather conditions.

'What about inserting by parachute?' John asked.

'It's an absolute non-starter,' Lockett replied. 'You say anything above a 15-knot wind makes jumping hazardous? Well, what you have to understand is that the katabatic winds up in the mountains can reach 100 mph. If you didn't break your necks on landing, you would be blown miles off course from any drop zone.'

John wasn't deterred. 'What about putting helicopters down on one of the glaciers?'

'Maybe less dangerous than parachuting, but helicopters are inherently unstable in the wind conditions up there, and I would also advise against it.' He admired John's pluck, but the experienced naval officer felt that the young SAS captain was a little naive when it came to appreciating the savage nature of the prevailing weather conditions.

As a troop, we were surprisingly ignorant of any detail of what might be afoot. As Binsy would often say, we were 'mushrooms: living in the dark and fed on shit'.

The only thing that seemed certain was that we would be going somewhere that was going to be cold, as we had been issued white camouflage overalls and were about to be offered more arctic kit.

In March *Endurance* had picked up a joint services expedition team from South Georgia, which had just finished a four-month foray on to the island. Extracted before the invasion took place and dispatched back to the UK, the expedition had left a pile of their kit on board the ship. We were invited to help ourselves to it. We selected some old fibreglass pulk sledges and a couple of ropes. Some of the blokes found the odd pair of mittens, as well as a few fur-trimmed hooded parkas and some stiff-soled mountain boots, but there wasn't much else. Other useful items, like snowshoes and skis, either weren't part of the expedition's inventory or had been taken with them when they returned to the UK.

With the modest supplement to our own kit, we were then moved back to *Antrim* again by helicopter. Space on the destroyer remained at a premium, and we swapped places with 16 Troop, which was an indication that use of their specialist freefall capabilities had been ruled out as a method of insertion on to the island.

In the three days that we had been away on *Endurance*, the planning on *Antrim* had advanced. Taking his meals in the small planning cell and sleeping slumped in a chair, Cedric had rarely ventured out of the admiral's day cabin on the ship as he wrestled with the issue of getting his patrols on to the island to recce Leith. He wanted Mountain Troop back on *Antrim*, as he needed our specialized skills for the one option that he could find for getting us on to the island.

Any landing site would have to be sufficiently far enough away from the target area for the patrols to be inserted undetected in daylight. Due to the nature of the terrain and weather, flying in at night wasn't an option, and the risk of the helicopters being heard or seen had to be avoided. What information could be gained from scant map coverage, limited air photography and local knowledge gleaned from *Endurance* suggested that there might be one place. However, it was risky, and there were others who advised strongly against it.

## 8

Flanked by jagged mountain ridges and extending for a length of 3 miles, the mile-wide Fortuna Glacier flows northeast down towards Cumberland Bay on the northern coast of South Georgia, 5 to 6 miles from Leith. As a mass of imperceptibly moving ice, compacted and consolidated by year after year of freezing layers of snow, it is fissured with deep crevasses and snow bridges caused by the combined pressure of its sheer weight and the forces of gravity.

Cedric had also been cautioned against its use by Guy Sheridan. As an experienced mountain and arctic warfare expert, Sheridan believed any landing on Fortuna would be too hazardous in bad winter weather. While John Hamilton had received similar advice from Andrew Lockett on *Endurance*, he felt that it was our only option. The mountainous terrain would mask the sight and sound of any helicopter approaching. Additionally, if a landing was made halfway up the glacier at around 1,000 feet, it was hoped that the worst of the crevasses could be avoided.

Cedric was also influenced by the fact that the legendary explorer Ernest Shackleton had crossed the glacier successfully with three other men in 1916. Weak from hunger, at the end of an epic 1,600 mile journey to reach safety after their ship had been trapped and crushed in the ice of the Antarctic, Shackleton's small group had made the traverse with little more than 50 feet of hemp rope and a ship's carpenter's adze between them. Cedric's sense of mission and history was strong, and he felt that if Shackleton could do it, so could we. He was also aware of the pressure of time. London wanted a quick win, which he factored into his thinking. Though not keen on the option, both Young and Sheridan agreed to go along with the boss's plan.

The date of the insertion on to Fortuna was set for 21 April. John had warned us about the impending mission when we arrived back on *Antrim*, as the plan was developed and refined by Cedric and his planning cell. On 20 April we received a set of formal Squadron orders in the format of what the Army calls an 'O', or 'orders group'. Everyone from D Squadron on board *Antrim* attended. Crammed into a storage room amidships, we sat on pallets and boxes to listen to the boss, as he confirmed his plan.

The boss started by covering relevant points concerning the terrain and what he knew about the enemy, which was short on detail. He then confirmed our mission.

'John, 19 Troop is to land on the glacier, set up an OP position overlooking Leith in order to report on any enemy dispositions, then either deal with what you find, if you think you can handle it, or cue in the rest of our available forces.' Cedric repeated the mission twice, and John responded with a simple:

'Got it, boss.'

'The conditions are on the margins up there and are going to be challenging. But Shackleton managed it without the kit we have and he was in pretty poor clip, so I need you to give it a go, Cedric paused and looked at each one of us, as if to acknowledge the significance of what he was asking us to do.

There weren't any questions when he asked for them. If any man had doubts about what we were being asked to do, they didn't show it. The general view was that it was feasible, and we were up for giving it a go.

We broke up and collected as a troop on the junior ratings, mess deck with John and Phil to thrash out the details of how to deliver the mission Cedric had given us. With his considerable mountaineering experience, Lofty Arthy's input was crucial.

'I reckon that we can do it, boss. The key thing is that we make it to the rocks on the ridgeline above the glacier before it gets dark. That way we can move by daylight and get into cover before the temperature drops during the night.'

John looked to Phil, who nodded and said, 'Lofty is right. With the heavy kit in the pulks, we can take tents with us, and I reckon that we can make the distance, shelter for the night and then move into the OPs just before first light.' Phil glanced at the rest of us and we nodded.

*Yeah, 'KISS' – keep it simple, stupid*, I thought. *It will all be about the Met*, which was looking pretty minging.

'Right, that's the plan,' John confirmed. 'Once we get eyes on Leith from the OPs, we can then take the call on whether we deal with any Argies ourselves or call in the rest of the Squadron and Royal if it requires more firepower.'

That night, under the cover of darkness, our small force of ships approached to within 30 nautical miles of the coast of South Georgia and drove headlong into the onslaught of a screaming storm coming up from the Antarctic.

Dawn broke to the gathering ferocity of a force 10 gale, which lashed the ships with mountainous waves driven by the increasing fury of a 60 knot wind. That under-stated word 'margin' was used again, and at first light a decision was made to test fly the route in and assess the conditions up on the glacier using *Antrim*'s Wessex Mk III to confirm whether the mission was a 'go' or 'no go'. Cedric and John went with the helicopter crew. Below decks we wedged ourselves in against any fixed point in the junior mess area and waited. Holding on as best I could, to avoid being thrown against the rising and fall-ing bulkhead, I listened to the creaking and groaning of the ship all around me. As *Antrim* twisted and rolled like some great metal snake in the surging water and batter-ing wind, I half wondered if the superstructure could take the strain. Occasionally, Binsy groaned out in misery from the bunk below me.

An hour and a half later, *Antrim*'s Wessex was back, and we loaded our kit and boarded the two Wessex Mk V's from *Tidespring*. During the recce up on the glacier, the crew of the Mk III had found a gap in the weather and confirmed that the operation was just within the capabilities of the helicopters. Cedric and John had also discussed the conditions 1,000 feet up on Fortuna over the helicopter's intercom while they looked down on it. They were still far from ideal.

John expressed some doubt. Their headsets crackled with static and interference, as the two men discussed the situation. 'You've got to get on John.' said Cedric, the intention being that John had to make a decision – Cedric knew that it had to be his call. However, John may have taken what Cedric said as an order. He paused for a moment, looking back out over the icy terrain below him and then replied, 'OK, we'll do it.'

If John had any concerns, he kept them to himself when he got back. The recce confirmed that the mission was a 'go', and we flew out in a formation of three helicopters line astern, only to be forced to turn back to the ships by thick low storm clouds and a driving blizzard of snow, as the weather gap closed.

Another two hours passed. The Met was improving, and we tried again, six men in each of the Wessex Mk Vs, which followed *Antrim*'s Wessex Mk III carrying John and the remainder of the Troop. Coming in from the north, the helicopters flew into the more sheltered waters of Possession Bay, shifted south and lifted to cross a spit of high, rocky ground. Dropping down over the other side into Antarctic Bay, we then began making the climb up on to the Fortuna Glacier. The clouds parted as we flew into the first bay, to reveal a landscape straight out of *The Lord of the Rings*.

Dark, granite-black mountains rose up steeply from the coastline. Every gully and ravine was stuck fast with ice and snow, and their high peaks were clagged in by thick cloud that robbed the sky of its horizon. It looked forebodingly ominous, and we were constantly being buffeted sideways by high winds. As I contemplated the four days we planned to spend in such a forbidding place, I thought to myself, *Let's get up there, get it done and then get the hell out*. My next thought was *Shit!* followed by *What the fuck was that?* as the Wessex was side-slapped violently by a sudden squall of blizzarding snow, and the world outside the fuselage window suddenly turned into an impenetrable murk of thick, milky whiteness.

Minutes of blind elevation passed, but they seemed to stretch for an eternity. It was only logic that told me that we must still be climbing, when the pitch of the engines changed and the clattering chatter of the aircraft's blades indicated that we were about to land. The crewman slid open the helicopter's compartment door a few feet off the glacier, and an icy blast immediately stabbed its way into the inside of the cab.

We scrambled out as the wheels touched down and the crewman yelled for us to go, before helping us manhandle out our pulk, weighed down by ammunition, machine guns, tents, radios, batteries and food. A momentary jet of heat discharged from the aircraft's large exhaust ports, which curled round the outside of the door. Then the full temperature shock hit home, with a savage penetrating force, knifing through several layers of clothing, including the white camouflage nylon snow suits we wore. It felt as if we were naked. The wind competed with the noise of the engines, meaning we had to shout to be heard, but it also sucked the breath out of our lungs.

I glanced across at Bilbo as we wrestled with the pulk. His face had *I don't want to be here* written all over it. *Too right*, I thought. *I don't want to be here either, mate!* We turned from the helicopter and knelt to shield ourselves from the sharp, stinging ice crystals thrown up by the downwash of its rotor blades as it lifted off. The snow bridge it had landed on suddenly crumpled in on itself and collapsed into the crevasse it had been momentarily covering. Then all the helicopters were gone, as if sucked up and swallowed by the swirling snow, the noise of their engines suddenly absent, leaving us alone with the vicious howl of the shrieking wind. After picking ourselves up, we began shaking out into single file.

'Keep together. Keep the pace and make sure you watch for the hidden crevasses,' Lofty shouted out above the wind. 'We'll swap over and take turns on the pulks as we get higher.'

Then we bent forward into the gale and started to climb.

The glacier was not overly steep, but without snowshoes or skis, our standard-issue boots sunk us knee-deep into the snow with each energy-sapping step. If we broke through a thin snow bridge, we went up to our waists or shoulders and had to claw our way out through the crumbling snow, cursing our misfortune, but acknowledging our luck that the crevasse could have been considerably deeper.

Everyone ported their rifle and belt order, which was heavy with ammunition and added to the 50 lbs of weight we carried in the bergens on our backs. We took it in turns to pull the overloaded pulks allocated to each patrol. Visibility was down to zero, and we climbed blind into the surrounding whiteness, following a compass bearing and trying to count our paces, as the biting wind whipped up ice crystals the size of course-grain sugar, which slashed raw against any exposed skin. The spindrift that caught in the weapon parts immediately froze solid. Progress was painfully slow, but it generated the much-needed heat our bodies craved.

We trudged relentlessly upwards but had already lost precious daylight hours due to the delays in getting on to the glacier. As the remaining light began to fade, the weather deteriorated further. The wind picked up, and the sharp spindrift of ice crystals turned into a constant air-blown wall of driving snow. Our leg muscles screamed in protest as we continued to slog up Fortuna, but in the two to three hours of back-breaking effort we had travelled little more than half a mile. It was beginning to get dark, and the weather continued to worsen. Still well short of the shelter offered by the rocky ridgeline at the top of the glacier, we would have been mad to continue, and the decision was taken to stop for the night.

'Get the tents up,' shouted Phil. 'We have to get into shelter fast.'

We didn't need further encouragement, as each patrol began battling against the blizzard with flimsy aluminium poles and heavy cotton flysheets. Our patrol's tent was plucked from our grasp as we struggled to set it up and it was sucked away into the white-blown night.

*Fuck this for a game of soldiers*, I thought. I looked around and spotted a small lee by the curving edge of a crevasse slightly above us. Shouting over the wind to be heard, I pointed it out to Paddy Armstrong, whose patrol had also lost their tent. 'Paddy, up there. Let's dig ourselves into the snow.'

'OK, mate, I'm with you,' Paddy shouted back, and we made our way over to the small lip of ice and snow and started to dig snow graves into the scant shelter it offered.

Others also gave up the unequal fight between the inadequate tents and the storm. Bilbo capitalized on his

93

size and climbed into a precious civvy Gore-Tex bivy bag Binsy had brought with him, which he buried under one of the pulks. Binsy was 6 feet 4 inches, and it made for a tight squeeze, but by cuddling together they shared their mutual body heat, as a better alternative to trying to survive the night in the open.

Chris Seakins got into one of the two tents that the other patrols had managed to set up by substituting the useless poles with their own bodies. To keep the tent up, they had to sit upright and use their backs to brace the flysheet. Chris was sitting closest to the entrance and periodically had to get out to shovel the snow that built up around the tent to reduce the pressure of its weight on the human tent poles inside it. 'My fault for being a crow,' he later recounted.

Once we had established a modicum of shelter, exhaustion overcame the cold to induce a fitful, uncomfortable night of sleep. We were in enemy territory, but no one gave a second thought to posting sentries. To do so would have run the risk of someone freezing to death. But our real security lay in the fact that no one in their right mind would be out on a night like the one that we were enduring.

I awoke in my hole covered in several feet of snow, sodden and frozen to the core. As I dug myself out through the crush of weight that had built up over me during the night, it was readily apparent that the coming of morning had brought no abatement in the weather. If anything, it had deteriorated further, and it was so cold that my teeth hurt. I tried to stamp back some warmth into my chilled body. At the same time, I flapped my arms and willed my blood to start flowing back to my hands and feet. I then dug out Paddy, who was still fast asleep.

I looked around. Visibility was down to less than 20 metres, and I could make out one misshapen tent half buried in snow. Around it, other members of the Troop began to emerge from underneath the pulks like punch-drunk, shivering moles. I headed down towards them, as our sorry little encampment began to stir back into life. A small group of figures huddled around a map, and I caught imperceptible snatches of shouted conversation as I approached. John Hamilton was in deep discussion with the senior NCOs. Everyone had survived the night, but it was clear that our position was untenable. Progress up the glacier had been negligible, we were soaking wet, and the conditions were worsening. The temperature had dropped to below minus 25 degrees centigrade. With no chance of drying out and an increasing wind chill factor, we were already on the edge of hypothermia and frostbite.

Lofty was leading the discussion. 'If we spend another twenty-four hours out here in the open, there is a real chance that people will die. This is worse than anything I ever saw on Everest, and we need to get off this glacier.'

'He's right, boss,' said Phil. 'We need to request an evac ASAP or we are going to start to lose people.'

As the boss on the ground, it was John's call, and he knew that it would be foolhardy to continue.

'OK. Let's break radio silence and put out a request to *Antrim* for an immediate extraction.'

Phil acknowledged John and got someone to get on the radio.

'Phil.'

'Yes, boss?' Phil looked back at John.

'Tell them to hurry.'

# 9

The urgency of the situation was not lost on anyone on board *Antrim* when the coded Morse signal was picked up by the SHQ signallers in the ops room. During the night the ship had been smashed by 100 knot winds and towering waves that had crashed across the deck. The captain had invited people up on to his bridge to witness the full force of the storm, so they would have a tale to tell their grandchildren about its nature and fury. What we must have been going through at 1,000 feet up on the glacier wasn't lost on Cedric, who climbed into *Antrim*'s helicopter, which would once again lead in the other two troop-carrying Wessexes that had been tasked to pick us up.

The wind had dropped, although not by much, when we heard the clattering approach of the helicopter, invisible but somewhere out in the milky whiteness. The accuracy of our navigation the previous day had paid off, and the crew of the Wessex knew where to find us. We popped a signal grenade to help pinpoint our exact location, but the brightly coloured smoke was immediately whipped away and washed out in the snow-driven wind.

Then we heard the noise of the engines begin to recede and then fade away into nothingness. *Had they failed to see us? Or was it the weather? Yes. It must be the weather. Surely they will come back and make another attempt?* Such questions and thoughts were on everyone's mind. But all we could do was huddle closer together, as we shivered and waited, our lips and noses flecked with ice crystals and frozen beads of moisture, making us look like some forgotten team of polar explorers.

Another hour passed before the beat of an approaching helicopter filled the air around us once more. The visibility had suddenly improved out to about half a mile, and we saw the three helicopters break out of the clag and popped more smoke to attract their attention. They picked up the wisps of multi-coloured smoke fizzing out of the small canisters and made straight for our position. The Troop was packed and ready to go; no one expected them to hang about and risk the weather closing in again. The helicopters touched down, the doors slid open, and we started to clamber into them. Five to six men to each aircraft. Further up the glacier, a snow squall kicked up and chased down towards us, as if desperate to enclose us in invisibility and prevent us from leaving. I felt a profound sense of relief as I buckled in and the Wessex Mk V began to lift us from its clutches. But something was wrong, and we were beginning to turn. I looked out of one of the windows and then I saw what had happened to the other Wessex Mk V.

We hover-taxied across the short distance to the crash site. The helicopter lay bent and crumpled on its side, engulfed by the swirling squall of snow. Blinded, disorientated and with little altitude to play with, the pilot had lost all visual reference points, and the helicopter had slide-piled into the slope of the glacier, the tips of its rotor blades biting into its surface and then thrashing themselves to fragments in the snow and the ice. The weather had almost immediately cleared again, and our own Wessex landed offset 20 metres away. We jumped out and made our way over to the stricken airframe.

It had impacted on its left side, allowing the crewman and passengers to scramble out of the upturned troop door. The pilot was stuck in his cab, so Chris Seakins and I climbed on to the edge of the cockpit and started battering open his crew door.

'Can you smell that?' Chris said.

'Yes,' I replied, 'avgas, leaking all over the snow from the engines, which are still red hot.'

There was no fire, but the rich stench of aviation fuel pooling below compelled us to work quickly to free the pilot. Like the rest of his crew and passengers he had sustained nothing more than cuts and bruises, as he had managed to get the nose of the helicopter up just as it stoofed in, which lessened the impact. However, Phil Currass had a nasty gash on his head. 'You all right, mate?' I asked. Phil nodded, and droplets of blood dripped red on to the whites of his arctic camouflage suit. We split ourselves up between our own Wessex Mk V and *Antrim*'s Wessex Mk III. I piled into the Mk V with Phil, and we prepared to lift off again.

The crash demonstrated the dangerous nature of flying off the glacier in the prevailing weather conditions and the success or failure of escaping from Fortuna's grip would be critically determined by the skill of the two-man crew who flew the helicopter and *Antrim*'s Wessex Mk III. Nicknamed 'Humphrey', the Mk III aircraft was an older variant of the Wessex helicopter. Unlike the troop-carrying twin-engine Mk V types, Humphrey had only one engine. However, it was designed to find and kill submarines, so it was fitted with a radar optimized for operations over sea, and not suited for collision avoidance among land features. It also had an automated flight-control system, which, coupled with its radio altimeter, enabled the helicopter to maintain a stable hover without external visual references. These were the characteristics that might help us navigate a safe route off the glacier, as the capricious visibility closed down again.

The remaining two helicopters lifted with Humphrey in the lead. With two pilots, an aircrewman and an observer officer in the back to provide collision avoidance, manage the navigation and direct the pilots in both aircraft, *Antrim*'s Wessex had a better chance of finding a way back down the glacier. If the single pilot in the following Wessex could keep Humphrey in sight, it would provide him with an airborne visual reference point, when those on the ground were obscured by shifting cloud or blizzard.

With the extra weight of more passengers from the downed Wessex on board, Humphrey struggled into the air. Buffeted by the wind, the helicopter started to make its way down the glacier with its wheels travelling little more than 30 feet off the ground. As it lifted to clear a raised ridge of ice, the flight path was suddenly obscured by another pillar of squalling snow. Travelling three helicopter lengths astern, the trailing Wessex simultaneously lost sight of Humphrey in the whiteout, robbing the pilot of any chance of seeing the elevated lip of ice he was about to hit.

His visual reference suddenly gone, our pilot instinctively pulled on the power and lifted the nose up, but it was too late. His starboard wheel clipped the side of the crevasse, tipping the Wessex sideways, digging the tips of the main rotor disc into the side of the glacier. It was a miracle that the flailing blades didn't thrash the cab to pieces with us inside it, but the ice and snow had acted as a shock-absorbing energy damper. If the helicopter had impacted on hard ground or rock, the blades would have snapped back, and the bent metal would have chopped us into mincemeat. It all seemed to happen in slow motion, like being in a car crash, as we half slid and half bumped into the glacier's slope. No doubt the reduced impact was due to the skill and the reactions of the pilot and the fact that the crewman had insisted that we had all strapped into our seats before take-off. Regardless, we landed on top of one another as the airframe pitched on to its side and slewed to a halt in a blur of fragmenting ice and shrieking metal.

This time the helicopter landed upturned with the troop door facing down hard against the ice. The crewman who had narrowly missed being thrown out of the aircraft when the helicopter went in popped open the bubble-shaped escape exit panel on the other side of the fuselage and ushered us out. He urged haste. 'Get out! Get out! And get away from the cab. It might go up at any moment.'

We didn't need encouragement, as the now familiar strong odour of fuel piss-pooling yellow under the sizzling hot engines reached our nostrils.

We surveyed yet another scene of twisted metal carnage,

as the last vestiges of the squall that brought us down died, almost as suddenly as it had started. Mercifully, no one was badly hurt, although Phil picked up another gash on his head. I checked him out briefly. 'Fuck me, Phil, everyone gets out without a scratch, except you, and you pick up two.' Phil responded with a stoic grin. 'Cheer up, mate, at least they're evenly spaced out, one on each side of your forehead in exactly the same place.'

Through the gloom we heard Humphrey coming back. Then, once again, the noise of helicopter engines receded beyond the periphery of visibility, and we were alone again, stuck up on the glacier. Given the events of the previous day and the condition we were in, walking off Fortuna was a non-starter. The downed aircrew were insistent that *Antrim* would be doing everything possible to recover us, although it would take some time. So the only option was to wait it out in the freezing wind.

Survival mode kicked in, and we dragged out the ten-man survival rafts and recovered the pulks from both crashed aircraft. Inflating the dinghies, we got out of the biting wind, got a brew on and settled down to wait. The sound of approaching engines returned sooner than expected – a couple of hours after the first crash. It was Humphrey, but the weather and cloud had closed back in again, and they were unable even to approach, let alone to land. The downed pilot managed to speak to the crew on a handheld radio and confirmed that everyone was OK. Humphrey's observer told us to hang in there and that they would be back for us.

I looked across at Bilbo. His face bore two days of stubble and was freckled with crystals of ice. He looked back. There was no need to say anything. Last light was less than three hours away, and the prospect of spending another night out on Fortuna was a forbidding thought. I wasn't the only one who was beginning to wonder whether we would make it down from the glacier at all.

# 10

At 1630 Zulu, Humphrey took off once more from *Antrim* loaded with blankets and medical supplies. It would be the last possible attempt to lift us off before nightfall. The weather was worsening again. Battling back up Fortuna, the crew used the helicopter's radar and dead-reckoning navigation to find its way through swirling cloud and savage katabatic winds, which threatened to snatch it out of the sky and dash it against the ridges of rock that towered above the edges of the glacier, seemingly close enough to reach out and touch. For the crew, it was like driving a car at night at 90 miles an hour along the streets of Manhattan in thick fog and without lights. But by means of leveraging the technology on board, skilful dead reckoning and pushing higher, they found a gap in the clouds and spotted the Day-Glo orange inflatables beneath them.

Packed with heavy anti-submarine sonar gear, consisting of electronic boxes, radar screens, hydraulic systems and winches, a Wessex Mk III is designed to carry two crew members in the back, with the capacity to take three or four extra passengers at a push. Consequently, the aircrewman and observer began packing us into the back of the helicopter, as if they were arranging a Chinese puzzle. I curled into a floor space near the tail-pylon with Bilbo sitting on my lap. He had his weapon but wasn't wearing his belt kit.

Others were stacked like cords of wood on top of men already lying prone on the floor; some with their arms and legs sticking out of the side door. One of the blokes had to lie across the observer's and crewman's double seat and then became a human cushion. There was no room for our kit, and a debate had ensued about what the crew would let us take with us. Ditching your bergen, belt order, machine guns and personal weapon does not sit easily with any soldier, and there was a brief but lively debate at the door between the aircrewman and some of the blokes still waiting to get in.

The crewman was saying, 'Fellas, you can't come in with your kit. We are already way overweight.'

'We are not leaving it behind, mate,' someone replied.

'Well, it's either you or your kit. This is the last bus off the mountain, and we need to go now. You've got a choice to make.'

The blokes relented, and the crewman compromised by letting them keep their rifles, but everything else – bergens and belt kit – was ditched.

With sixteen extra men on board, even denuded of most of our kit, the helicopter was grossly overweight. The single turbine wound itself up into a screaming whine of protest, as the pilot sought out the torque from the gearbox by pulling on the power in an attempt to lift. The airframe vibrated violently with the effort but only managed to sink lower into the snow.

Then, as if suddenly unstuck, we lurched up uncertainly before bumping back down again. The pilot kept the power on, and we staggered into the air on the lifting force of a gust of wind, which the pilot had deliberately timed his next attempt to meet. We shifted skywards and forwards, as an unseen bridge of ice beneath the aircraft collapsed under its lifting wheels to reveal a deep cavernous fissure big enough to swallow the helicopter into the abyss.

I was thankful at the time that no one had told me about the crevasse. As far as I was concerned, we were finally off the blasted glacier and making good speed down its slopes to the warmth and safety of HMS *Antrim*. Someone even cracked open a packet of fags and passed them round the cramped interior, which filled with a celebratory fug of smoke. What I couldn't see in the clag was just how close we were to the steep ridges flanking the ice, which flashed past on either side of us. Even the slightest miscalculation by the observer or deviation by the pilot from his instructions would cause the blades to clip the jagged edges and send us to our doom.

A combination of wind speed, velocity, gravity and denser air at higher altitude was keeping us in the sky, but only just. As we cleared the bottom of the glacier and began to turn out to sea, the lower altitude and warmer air at sea level meant that the challenges of defying gravity were becoming markedly greater. At the time, the principles of flight meant nothing to me, but both Bilbo and I could sense that the flight characteristics of the helicopter had become more sluggish as the overladen aircraft struggled across the top of the water and attempted to stay in the air long enough to make it back to the ship.

In a normal landing sequence, a warship provides a favourable relative wind for landing, usually within about 30 degrees of the ship's heading. It then comes into a controlled hover alongside the port side of the flight deck, slows to match the speed of the ship and then moves sideways until over the centre of the flight deck before touching down. Humphrey didn't have the power for any of that. The helicopter would have to fly an approach that put us straight smack down on the deck in one go.

Based on a hasty air speed/distance calculation, it would be a one-shot affair. If the pilot got it wrong, we would smash into the back of the ship in a mess of shattering metal and fire. If we overshot, we would land in the water. Packed tight inside, we would be lucky to get out, and if we did, we could not expect to last more than ten minutes in the freezing water without an immersion suit, which only the aircrew were wearing. We could tell from the grim, set faces of the aircrew among us that the landing was going to be dicey, and in those final few minutes of flight the atmosphere in the aircraft became tense.

Through the port window I could see the white wave tops skimming beneath us. I watched the distance above them reduce as we closed with the ship. We seemed perilously close to the water when the stern of the ship came into view. I could make out the flight-deck officer frantically waving us off. We were coming in too fast, the angle was all wrong, and he was telling the pilot to abort. The pilot ignored him. Suddenly the deck was rushing up to meet us, and we thumped down on to it in undercarriage-jarring fashion.

The flight-deck crew were all over the helicopter like ants, furiously lashing Humphrey to the deck with thick nylon straps. In an instant I could hear the engine winding down, as the power was shut off. Suddenly it seemed quiet. The first man stumbled out on to the deck, while

Bilbo and I waited as the pile of wedged humanity between us and the door disentangled themselves. 'Fuck me,' Bilbo said. 'That was fucking mental.'

'You're not wrong there,' I replied. 'I've never been so fucking terrified in my life.'

'Me too,' said Bilbo, 'but you can stop hugging me now, Splash.'

'Oh yeah, sorry, mate,' I said, as I released my grip, and we made our way to the door.

Cedric was there to meet us, along with Lawrence, who said in his understated way, 'Sporting landing, chaps.'

The boss said little, but he was clearly counting us in as we made our way into the hangar deck, and his face was stitched with the relief of a concerned commander.

Hypothermic, frost-nipped and bruised, we were sorted out by the ship's medical team in the wardroom, which had been set up as a casualty reception facility. The surgeon's relief matched ours when he realized that his more intricate skills were not required, beyond the application of a few stitches for those who needed them, blankets and hot brews. The sailors were shocked by our appearance and what we had been through. The matelots gave up their bunks so that we could get a night of unbroken rest, but not before the ship's deputy supply officer announced over the ship's intercom that their previous night's film, *Hawk the Slayer*, would be replayed for the benefit of what he referred to affectionately as 'our trees and shrubs', by which he meant us.

Over 8,000 miles from home, having survived one of the most inhospitable places on the planet, this double breach of the ship's strict routine meant the world to us. While we watched John Terry prancing around with a magical sword in some fantasy nonsense on the ship's close-circuit TV system, John Hamilton and the senior NCOs sought out Humphrey's crew with a bottle of whisky to thank them for saving our lives.

In many ways 19 Troop had been lucky. We had survived by the skin of our teeth. However, our joy at making it through the experience of Fortuna was soon replaced by a feeling of near embarrassment. As an SAS unit, the Squadron came with a reputation, and we had muscled our way into the party. We had been seen to have ignored advice, failed to deliver our mission and written off two expensive helicopters worth millions of pounds in the process. In short, it had turned into a cluster.

Everyone had made it through the ordeal, although getting off Fortuna in one piece had been a close-run thing, and disaster had only been avoided by the slimmest of margins. The game was also up. The activities of the ships around South Georgia had not gone unnoticed by an Argentine Boeing 707 surveillance aircraft. But, in war, the wheel of fortune can turn quickly, and it was about to rotate again in the most unexpected of directions.

On operations in Northern Ireland, prior to going to the Regiment.

My time as a jungle warfare instructor in Belize, in 1976.

Receiving my Greek Parachute Wings in Greece, about nine months prior to the Falklands.

HMS *Endurance*, nicknamed the 'Red Plum' due to the colour of her hull, which makes her stand out against the dark, forbidding backdrop of South Georgia.

The first Wessex Mk V troop-carrying helicopter to crash on the Fortuna Glacier lies on its side. Chris Perkins leads a group of us making our way to get the pilot out of his cab. I am just behind him. Minutes later, our other helicopter also piled in.

One of the helicopters' survival life rafts, which was set up to provide shelter while we awaited rescue from Fortuna.

The Wessex Mk III helicopter known as 'Humphrey' on the flight deck of HMS *Antrim*. Elements of 19 Troop emplaning prior to the assault on Grytviken. Binsey is on the far left of the photo, behind John Hamilton, who has a 66 mm slung across his back.

Members of Mountain Troop piling into the two Navy Lynx helicopters sent from HMS *Brillant* to pick us up from *Antrim* and fly us on to South Georgia to assult Grytviken.

D Squadron's Sergeant Major Lawrence Gallagher standing in front of the disabled Argentine submarine *Sante Fe*, which was moored at the quay at King Edward Point.

Mountain Troop at King Edward Point after its recapture on 24 April. Six weeks later, six of those in the photo would be dead and three would have been evacuated due to injury. I am sitting in the middle of the front row, with Bilbo on my left. The faces of those shown from the left are Lawrence Gallagher, Lofty Arthy, Sid Davidson and Phil Currass, who were killed in the Sea King. John Hamilton, who was also killed in action at Port Howard, is on the right of the photo.

A commando Sea King approaching the crowded deck of HMS *Hermes*. Some of the ship's Sea Harriers are lined up along her starboard side.

Inside the flight deck of HMS *Hermes,* looking from the flight elevator. Sea Harriers are packed in tight in front of Sea King helicopters. Another Sea King sits up on the deck and has its rotor blades folded.

The mess deck similar to where we were accommodated on HMS *Hermes*, which provided the relative luxury of an allocated bunk space. In most other ships we served on, we hot-bunked or bedded down on any available piece of deck space.

Inside the hanger deck of HMS *Hermes* just before we launched the raid on Pebble Island. I am on the very left of the picture, with my AR15 Armalite assault rifle in my right hand. The trooper in the foreground was fortunate enough to be able to afford to buy his own footwear. Most of us suffered with issued boots, which were bloody dreadful. Left to right: me, Sid Davidson, Lofty Arthy, Bilbo Drake.

Pebble Island, looking from west to east, showing the route in from the insertion point at Phillips Cove. The airfield is in the near foreground of the photo, just above the rocky bluff on the nearside coastline.

HMS *Glamorgan* providing naval gunfire support from its 4.5 inch guns during D Squadron's raid on Pebble Island.

The aftermath of D Squadron's raid, showing three types of the eleven Argentine aircraft we destroyed. It also shows the line of three craters of the blast, which caught us when it was detonated by the garrison as we began to withdraw.

Members of D Squadron on a Sea King. The large helicopter was roomy, but were often dangerously overloaded with troops and kit, as we found out to our cost.

The flight deck of HMS *Intrepid* during the cross-decking operation from *Hermes* (shown in the background) on 19 May. Some of the Squadron's stores are piled up in the foreground with some of the blokes who had already made the trip over. This picture was taken during daylight, an hour or so before tragedy struck.

# 11

The episode on Fortuna had not been our finest hour. The imperative to get eyes on the Argentine dispositions on South Georgia remained, although the loss of the two troop-carrying Wessex Mk V helicopters had reduced the options. It was Boat Troop's turn to try a more direct approach. The plan was as simple as it was risky.

It entailed HMS *Antrim* having to leave the relative safety of the open sea and steam close inshore into Stromness Bay. Using the cover of darkness as her only protection, the ship would come within 2 miles of Leith. 17 Troop would then cover the final distance to the shoreline in five Gemini boats. Landing at a place called Grass Island, they would observe any enemy movements ashore, before crossing on to the mainland to conduct a more detailed reconnaissance of the old whaling station. Dark or not, no captain wants to take his warship anywhere near the more vulnerable waters of an enemy coastline. What had happened to the Argentine navy corvette during the Royal Marines' defence of Grytviken was on everyone's mind.

In the pitch-dark early hours of the next day, 23 April, *Antrim* came to action stations, as she began her run into Stromness Bay. Mountain Troop's respite from the hot-bunking routine ended, as we were shaken out of our sleep and told to get dressed. There would be no role for us; this would be a solely Boat Troop affair, and the Navy's job to get them there, but when a ship closes to action stations everyone must be awake. We stayed out of the way on the mess deck, while around us *Antrim* became a blur of purposeful activity with serious intent.

The internal lighting system was dimmed to red, as watertight hatches around the ship were clanged shut and clipped home. Gun crews closed up ready to fire, and damage-control teams took up emergency positions, ready to fight any fire and keep us afloat in the event of the ship being hit. The tannoy system went silent, and we were told to keep our voices down and avoid making any unnecessary noise as the destroyer slid into the flat, calm waters of Stromness Bay powered by its silent steam propulsion.

The stormy weather of the previous day, which would have provided more cover for the ship's approach, had abated. It had been replaced by a tranquil sea state, absent of wind. Although it was a pitch-black night, the tension on the ship was palpable. As we sat and whispered among ourselves in the eerie red half-light of the mess deck, the ship slowed to a stop, and 17 Troop put their boats over the side. It was still punishingly cold, and they had trouble starting their outboards. Old and knackered, the engines were reluctant to start in the icy waters and freezing temperatures.

Two of the Geminis eventually coughed into life, and, taking the other three non-starting boats in tow, the Troop motored out into the inky blackness, heading for the shoreline a mile or so distant. Oblivious to the events on the deck above us, we felt the ship begin to turn as it headed back out into the greater safety of the open sea. We also felt a dramatic change in the weather, as the ship started to roll against a rapidly rising swell. A sudden gale had kicked up and had come out of nowhere.

'Oh Christ, here we go again,' groaned Binsy, as the once-quiet confines of the ship were filled again by the sounds of grinding metal and the increasing noise of *Antrim*'s engines as she cranked up her power and pulled away from Stromness Bay. I lay on my bunk above Binsy, thinking, *This is no night to be out at sea in a small inflatable boat.*

As *Antrim* left them in her wake, Boat Troop's attempts to make landfall were turning into an epic every bit as challenging as the near disaster that had befallen Mountain Troop up on the glacier. During their stormy passage inland, the three Geminis under tow broke loose in the growing fury of waves and wind and were swept out to sea. One was recovered, and the patrols from the three surviving boats made it to Grass Island, where they were able to get eyes on the Arg positions at Leith during the final hours of darkness. But as daylight broke the next morning, the other two boats were reported as missing.

Once again, Humphrey was pressed into action to find them. After a long box search of the ocean along likely drift routes, one of the inflatables was picked up at the very limit of the helicopter's duration. The Gemini was already 62 miles out to sea and the three-man crew were stiff with ice by the time they were winched to safety by the Wessex. But the search failed to find the second missing boat, and three members of Boat Troop remained unaccounted for. It was bad news. We all knew that there was a high chance that their inflatable had capsized in the storm and, even with the dry suits they would have been wearing, their chances of surviving in an angry, freezing sea would have been minimal. Part of the mission had been achieved. We had finally got some patrols ashore to observe the target at Leith. But the likely loss of comrades, and another mishap, compounded a mood of growing despondency among the Squadron, which we all felt.

The SBS's efforts to recce the enemy at Grytviken had also run into trouble. During the night, HMS *Plymouth* and HMS *Endurance* had attempted to reinforce the element of the SBS reconnaissance troop which had already landed on the foreshore at Hound Bay with more men and two of their own Geminis. The boats would enable the SBS to get closer into Cumberland Bay and Grytviken. One of the inflatables was damaged when they were flown in by the ships' Wasp helicopters. The surviving Gemini attempted to make the crossing but was driven back by high winds and gathering sea ice, which forced the operation to be abandoned, and the SBS party was evacuated.

In the eyes of the Navy, the Special Forces element of their task force was not covering itself in glory. The initial task the embarked SAS and SBS personnel had been set had been only partially completed and at significant cost. We had failed to set the conditions for a quick victory in recapturing South Georgia, and the operation was losing momentum. However, whatever the commander of the Task Group thought about his SF troops' performance, the captain of *Antrim* now had a more pressing concern of a very different nature on his mind.

On 18 April, the Argentine submarine *Santa Fe* had put to sea from its naval base at Mar de Plata in Argentina, and British intelligence had assessed that it was likely to be heading for South Georgia. With much of the morning of 23 April having been spent recovering and searching for SF patrols, at 1400 hours Zulu, *Endurance* picked up a high-frequency radio transmission from the submarine 100 miles to the northwest. It could only have been the *Santa Fe*. Argentine air activity had also picked up. About the same time, an Argentine C-130 Hercules was spotted and reported by *Plymouth* with the deduction that it could be sending our location to the submarine.

The first we knew of the unfolding situation was when the main broadcast started to blare and *Antrim* went to action stations for the second time that day. The ship also seemed to be picking up speed and steering in an erratic fashion. Dealing with the threat posed by the *Santa Fe* was core naval business compared to the previous distractions of trying to get us ashore. The matelots became fixated and set to it with impressive professional purpose. We again got the sense that we needed to stay out of their way and loitered on the mess deck, where the bunks were noticeably free of any occupants.

I stopped a passing matelot to ask what was going on.

'The ship is zigzagging to reduce the chances of being hit by a torpedo,' he answered in somewhat alarming fashion.

'Shit,' I replied.

'Yep,' the matelot said. 'The captain is dispersing the

ships, so we can get away from being trapped against the coastline and conduct ASW against a possible Arg sub that might be heading our way.'

'ASW?'

'Anti-submarine warfare, mate,' he said with a look that suggested I might be a bit simple.

As we steamed hard further out to sea, *Endurance* was being left behind. The engines of the ice patrol ship were too slow to keep up with the *Antrim* and *Plymouth*. Additionally, her diesels generated too much noise, which is a bad thing in ASW, where acoustics in the water matter. So the ship, with 16 Troop on board, would have to take her chances and hide as best she could among the icebergs around the island.

The next day, an Arg Boeing 707 overflew *Endurance*. Nige said, 'It was close enough to shoot down, and the bugger was clearly reporting our position. But we weren't allowed to, as the bosses on board said we were still not at war with Argentina.'

However, it demonstrated that things were getting serious, and the initiative was passing to the Argies. The gravity of the situation was not lost on our senior commanders back in the UK, who were concerned that the mission to capture South Georgia was unravelling. HMS *Brilliant* was dispatched at best speed to head to South Georgia from the main naval Task Force still heading to the Falklands. Equipped with two anti-submarine weapon-carrying Lynx helicopters and sonar radar, the frigate would boost the *Antrim* group's capability to respond to the presence of the *Santa Fe*, and orders were given from London to search for the sub and destroy it.

The next morning, *Antrim* and *Plymouth* turned back to South Georgia. Armed with two depth charges, Humphrey closed towards the coast to search for the submarine. Assuming that the sub might also be coming to drop off troops and supplies to the Arg garrison at Grytviken, the crew of the Wessex hoped to catch her on her way out of Cumberland Bay. Homing in on a brief contact on their helicopter's ASW radar, they spotted the *Santa Fe* on the surface and attacked and damaged the submarine with their depth charges.

Humphrey's observer then called in *Brilliant*'s Lynx helicopters to use torpedoes to prevent the sub from diving. One was dropped, but missed the submarine, but the crew had clearly had enough and they turned to limp back towards the safety of Grytviken. As they did so, the submarine was continually strafed with machine-gun fire from the Lynx helicopters and rockets fired by Wasps from *Endurance* and *Plymouth*, which had joined the fray. Some of the action was captured in broadcasts made over *Antrim*'s tannoy.

'Dye hear there. Dye hear there . . .' it blared. 'Contact with the enemy submarine has been made and it has been hit and damaged.'

The matelots went mad with jubilation. The euphoria of the moment was not lost on us down on the mess deck, but the pitch of own our excitement suddenly shot up when we were told to grab our weapons and be ready to make an immediate assault on Grytviken.

Phil came running into the mess deck area, yelling, 'Grab your kit and get your weapons out of the armoury. We've got a shout and we are going in. Once you've got your weapons get to the flight deck as fast as you can.'

I rolled off the bunk and snatched up my belt order, as the rest of the Troop tumbled from their pits around me and grabbed their stuff, then headed for the weapon lockers at speed.

'What's the brief?' I shouted at the back of Sid's head, as we charged down in an urgent throng along a narrow passageway, dodging boxes piled on the deck and matelots coming the other way.

'Dunno, Splash, reckon we will find out when we get topside,' he replied.

With the attack on the *Santa Fe*, everything had changed. There had been a lively debate between the *Antrim*'s captain, Royal Marine commanders and Cedric about exploiting the situation and seizing the initiative. With the sub crippled and clearly out of the game, the view of some was that the Argies would be reeling, and a hasty assault on Grytviken should be mounted before they had time to recover from the shock of losing their key military asset.

The downside was that the major land forces, in the form of the 150 men of M Company, were still 200 miles away on RFA *Tidespring*, which had been dispatched further out to sea when the presence of the *Santa Fe* was reported. A quick estimate of force ratios had established that, by combining D Squadron HQ, Mountain Troop and the SBS troops and the Royal Marines ship detachments aboard *Antrim* and *Plymouth*, we could muster a scratch force of just over 110 men, half of it SAS. This also included the command element of M Company, with one 81 mm mortar and a small party of naval gun spotters from 148 Battery, who were also aboard *Antrim*.

The force would be lifted in by *Antrim*'s Wessex and *Brilliant*'s two Lynx helicopters in several waves, while being supported by gunfire from *Antrim*'s and *Plymouth*'s 4.5 inch guns. The downside was that we were likely to be outnumbered by over two to one. We would also be landing into an area where we had no intelligence on what we might be facing and would be going in blind. With no recce and no eyes on, similar maritime risk also applied to the ships.

Cedric was aware of the dangers but had been all for launching the assault and getting on with it quickly. There were few precious daylight hours left, and the weather could change any moment. Others shared his opinion, including Humphrey's aircrew who had attacked the sub and watched it limp back into Cumberland Bay. The view of the hawks eventually won out after some heated debate. It was decided that we would land on a flat area of moraine known as the Hestesletten feature. It was just over a mile to the south of Grytviken and masked by a ridge of high ground called Brown Mountain.

Brown Mountain would provide some cover for the helicopters too as they flew in and landed, if it was not dominated by Arg defensive positions, which was a big 'if'. We suspected most of the enemy would be centred around a small cluster of buildings belonging to the British Arctic Survey station at King Edward Point on the northern side of Cumberland Bay. But first we would have to advance round the headland of Brown Mountain and then push through the abandoned whaling station at Grytviken itself, which would provide plenty of opportunities for an enemy ambush and would be difficult to fight through if they were prepared to defend it. Again, what Keith Mills's Marines had managed to do a few weeks previously with only twenty-two men was on everybody's mind.

We grabbed extra GPMGs from the ship's armoury to beef up our firepower, along with our own personal weapons and 66 mm light anti-tank weapons, which we referred to as 'LAWs' or just as '66s'. Familiar from *Rambo*-type films and containing a rocket in an extendable half-metre-long tube, they were easy to sling over a shoulder and would be handy against any dug-in infantry. We stuffed spare ammunition and as many grenades as we could into our belt kit. Although what we wore on our waists, carried in our hands or slung across our shoulders weighed around 50 lbs, we would be going in light.

There would be no room for bergens, which was just as well, as they had been left on the glacier. We also left the Squadron mortar behind, as the Marines would be bringing their own 81 mm and dedicated people to crew it. It was a heavy piece of kit, but the MILAN anti-tank missile system was the one enhancement we took for some added punch – and partly because Nobby Clark insisted on bringing it.

Nobby was part of Graham Collins's logistics team and worked with him and Wally in the stores. He was a fully badged member of the Regiment and an Oman veteran too. But he was coming to the end of his time in an Army where, at the age of forty-two, you are considered over the hill and discharged from service. Most of us were pretty sure that Nobby had received his demob papers just before we left Hereford, but suspected that he had ignored them in order to get down south. With that on his mind, he wasn't about to miss out on what we were about to do. His willingness to carry the MILAN probably reflected his enthusiasm to be included. It was additional clout,

Nobby was a good bloke, and we needed the numbers, so he was more than welcome to come along.

Tooled up and ready to go, we went aft and mustered on the flight deck at the stern of the ship. Just inside the helicopter hangar, John and Phil gave us an outline brief on the mission. We gathered round, dropping to one knee so we could look at the map John had laid out on the deck in front of him.

'Right, guys, the Lynx helos from HMS *Brilliant* are inbound to pick up and fly us in here.' John pointed out the landing site on the map. He was keyed up, but his direction was clear and concise.

'*Antrim* and *Plymouth* will cover our fly-in and lay down a barrage to support our advance once we land. The plan is to move round the coast under their fire, clear through the old whaling station at Grytviken and press on to take the Arctic station at King Edward Point.'

Phil nodded his approval and added, 'Remember, folks, this is an advance to contact, and we could be pretty exposed. If you see a target, we need to make sure we win the firefight, and the first few seconds will be vital.'

He looked back at John, who emphasized the point that we were to use minimum force if possible and prevent any unnecessary damage to the British Antarctic Survey property.

'Any questions?' he asked.

Sid and Lofty both said, 'No questions, boss.' We were clear on the mission. We were set to go.

'Good. Let's make it so.'

# 13

We collected on the flight deck and waited for the helicopters. *Antrim*'s battle ensign was stiff in the wind as the ship surged forward, leaving a foaming white-grey wake as she steamed hard at over 30 knots. To her stern, HMS *Plymouth* was making similar speed, her ensigns also snapping taut in the breeze. The headlands of Cumberland Bay were off the port bow. Then the captain's voice came through the external speakers: 'Gentlemen, you are about to see a sight you are unlikely to see again: two British warships bombarding an enemy position ashore.'

With that there was an almighty crack, as the twin 4.5 inch guns opened fire from the ship's forward turret. The air around the deck was instantly engulfed by the caustic tang of burned cordite. The more distant boom of *Plymouth*'s guns also started to echo across the water, and we could hear her shells splitting the air like tearing paper as they headed inland.

I was standing next to James. 'Bloody hell,' he said. 'British gunboat diplomacy at its best. This is one for the history books.'

'You're not wrong there,' I laughed. 'I wouldn't fancy being on the receiving end of that lot.'

Both ships kept up a steady rate of fire and were putting rounds into the air every two to three seconds. Large empty brass shell cases clanged and piled on to *Antrim*'s shot-matted deck. The two sailors charged with tossing them over the side into the ship's wake were working like the devil to keep up with the rate of fire. It was heady, exhilarating stuff. We were pumped with adrenaline and eager to get going as the helicopters started to come in.

'OK, here come the birds. Let's get ready,' Phil shouted above the din of shellfire and aircraft engines.

Mountain Troop was in the first lift with the Squadron head shed. I climbed into one of the blue-painted Lynxes, avoiding the tail rotor and ducking low under the spinning blades. Its anti-submarine weapons had been removed from its racks so that it could lift the maximum number of people. We managed to squeeze in half the Troop, including John Hamilton's patrol. I was wedged in between Alex and Chris and looked across at James. His face was a picture of the keyed-up thrill that we all felt. No doubt masked behind it was the same tinge of apprehensive anticipation that I felt mixing with my own flush of excitement. A hardening knot, somewhere deep in your belly. Fear reminding you of the reality of what you were about to do. *Would it be a hot LS? Would we get shot to pieces when we landed, or even before we got there?* We had all been in at least one helicopter crash, and the sea looked cold. I banished the dark thoughts as we lifted and started the fly-in, doors open, fast and low, 30 feet above the waves.

The shoreline was rushing towards us, the brownish-green smudge of what I took to be Brown Mountain looming up on the right. The helicopter banked round and flew back out to sea. I noted the Wessex in front and the second Lynx to the rear do the same thing. *What the fuck?* John must have been thinking the same thing. I couldn't hear what he was saying, but he was talking energetically into the microphone of the headset he had plugged into – no doubt asking what was going on, as the aircraft seemed to adopt a holding pattern out to sea.

There was nervous tension on the faces around me. Something seemed wrong. Waiting for combat is worse than engaging in it, and not knowing what you are waiting for is even worse. A minute passed. John started gesticulating and shouting at the same time to make himself heard. Something about fire control coordination. Another minute, and then we were running in again towards the landing site. I made a final last check of the magazine housing on my rifle, and that the safety was on, as I tensed leg muscles, ready to jump out of the cab as soon as it landed.

The wheels touched. 'Let's go!' shouted John, as he dumped his headset and followed the first of the blokes out of the side door. Our boots hit the ground, and we fanned out into all-round defence, thumping down into the prone position, watching our arcs surrounding the helicopter, which was only there for a moment before it headed back for the next lift. The 4.5 inch shells from *Antrim* and *Plymouth* were screaming overhead, accurately being called in by the 148 Battery team spotting the fall of shot from a Wasp helicopter hovering out to sea. Forward of us, the heavy rounds crumped in on the other side of Brown Mountain, reverberating around the bay.

I noticed that the newer blokes in the Troop, me included, got into cover with greater gusto than the old sweats from Oman. Lawrence Gallagher was on his feet strolling around like he owned the place. 'Guys, get off your belt buckles,' he raised his voice only enough to be heard over the din. 'We ain't under effective fire, and you will know when we are, because the bullets will be bouncing off your webbing.' We pushed ourselves up on to one knee.

Once more the air filled with the sound of returning helicopters, as our tiny force built up. The radio started to get busy, and I heard Cedric in my earpiece, instructing the Marines' mortar to start registering targets on Brown Mountain, which loomed above us. There was little cover on the wide-open moraine valley of the long-dead glacier we had landed on, and if the enemy had us in their sights, then we were finished. The boss wanted the Bootnecks to drop ranging rounds on it, so that accurate mortar fire could then be provided and adjusted in an instant to land where we needed it if a threat materialized on the higher ground. However, the Marines seemed to be preoccupied and were taking an age.

Cedric started to get impatient. There were a few choice words on the net and then a decisive 'Sod it, let's go' cut through the static.

'Right,' shouted Lawrence, 'everybody up. Let's go.'

We shook out into our assault groupings and started advancing to contact, heading south towards the sea. Mountain Troop were the right-hand troop, with a troop of SBS on our left and Cedric and SHQ slightly behind. The weather was still and slightly overcast, but compared to what we had been used to, it was a good day for a fight. With split moraine rocks and spongey moss and grass underfoot, the going was easy, and the pace steady. Every man scanned the ground ahead, ready to react to any movement by acquiring a target and then winning the firefight.

We kept advancing, with nothing to our front. The formation started to swing round to the north, so that we could follow the shoreline around Brown Mountain, which would bring us on to Grytviken. Ahead, there was a series of sand dunes close by the sea. Suddenly a head popped up, wearing what looked like a balaclava, and then another, movement clearly responding to our approach.

'Contact to our front!' somebody shouted.

We dropped down and started engaging targets with a withering weight of GPMG and semi-automatic fire. No effective enemy return fire – in fact nothing at all – came back at us.

Another shouted order: 'Cease fire!' The firing died away. 'Push on.'

We resumed the advance over some dunes and discovered that we had engaged and enraged a colony of elephant seals. Some of the great beasts had been hit, and the sand was smeared red with their blood. Ignoring them, we pressed on; we had to keep moving. The wounded animals, each weighing as much as a small car, started to fight among themselves. We had to edge past tons of thrashing flesh and snapping teeth to get on to the shingle of the shoreline. It was surreal and awful, but there was no time to dwell on it.

Another target was called out by Cedric: a suspected enemy bunker, with what looked like a radio antenna sticking out of it, up on the higher ground in an obvious place for an OP.

Cedric shouted forward to John, 'Get a missile into that position.'

'Right, boss. Nobby, hit it with the MILAN.'

Nobby set up the MILAN firing post and launched a projectile, the bright glow of its rocket motor weaving a path uphill towards the target before it exploded in a satisfying shower of earth and rock debris. It turned out to be a mound of earth with a piece of angle iron sticking out of it, but no one was taking any chances. Some of the troops started pushing up on to the higher ground, with Cedric and SHQ. We continued along the shingle and passed the carcass of the downed Argentine Puma helicopter lying forlornly on its left-hand side, with its back broken. *Hell*, I thought to myself, *we chose a good place to land. Any further forward of Brown Mountain and that could have been one of our helicopters that got the good news.*

As we rounded the headland, the rust-red buildings of the old whaling station suddenly came into view a few hundred metres in front of us. Across the water of the bay to its right we could see the cluster of white BAS buildings at King Edward Point, with their red- and green-capped roofs. The dark-black shape of the *Santa Fe* languished forlornly at the jetty in front of them. The mountainous range of snow-capped peaks surrounding the bay was a background of exploding ordnance as the ships pulverized the rocky ridgeline above Grytviken. A brace of shells landed every few seconds; they were being walked on to King Edward Point from left to right, getting steadily closer to the buildings with each salvo. To add further demonstration to the intent, *Antrim* steamed close into the shore to demonstrate its ability to start engaging with direct fire.

With the likely positions of any enemy in sight, it must have been possible for the Argies to see us. We were advancing out in the open, our movement constrained by the narrow foreshore. I braced myself to receive incoming fire. We were well within the effective range of any machine gun, and I started looking for likely positions of cover, which were scant on the gently sloping shingle.

Nobby had the MILAN set up and was in the process of getting ready to put a missile through the *Santa Fe*. The Navy wanted to be certain that she was finished, and it would reinforce the message that we meant business to the Argentine garrison. GPMGs were also loaded and recocked to make sure that they could pour a stream of fire into any points of resistance. But instead of the snap and whine of bullets, our appearance round the headland was met with a flurry of white, as sheets began to drape from the windows of the buildings around King Edward Point.

A white flag was run up the BAS flagpole and fluttered in the wind next to the pale-blue stripes of the Argentine national flag. Chris saw the flags first. 'Fuck me. They have thrown the towel in.' John was on the net trying to tell Cedric that the Argies clearly had no intention of putting up a fight. Focused on finishing off the *Santa Fe*, he hadn't seen the flags and was about to order Nobby to fire.

John, seeing what was about to happen, yelled over to Lofty, 'Lofty, get up to the boss and tell him that the Argies are surrendering.'

'Right, boss,' Lofty shouted back as he legged it up on to the high ground to tell Cedric there was no need to fire the MILAN.

Cedric initially ignored Lofty, and the missile was about to be sent on its way.

'Boss, boss, listen to me,' Lofty implored.

Cedric snapped back impatiently, as commanders do when they are fixated on the job in hand. 'What the hell is it?'

'They have surrendered.'

The boss looked up, incredulous. 'Bloody hell. They have.'

The voices in my earpiece were busy with how we should react to the surrender. Sheridan wanted Cedric to halt his advance but wasn't in direct comms with the boss. *Antrim* had received a garbled radio message from the Argie commander, reinforcing his desire to surrender. There was talk of wounded, some mention of a minefield. It was a potentially confusing picture, but Cedric was the man on point and saw the imperative to crack on and to maintain the momentum by getting to King Edward Point and securing the position as fast as possible by accepting the surrender.

Cedric told John Hamilton to stay firm in a covering position and to be ready to react if the Argies started anything while he pushed forward with Lawrence and the rest of his four-man tactical signals team. Cedric took Sid Davidson with him, as he spoke Spanish, apparently, which was news to me. I pushed up to my left to get on to some elevated ground with Bilbo and Alex Brown. Alex set up his GPMG, and we watched Cedric's small party move forward. Pushing through the abandoned buildings of the old whaling station, they moved on round the bay to the BAS buildings. We continued to watch and wait.

They got there safely: no mines, no resistance. Cedric had read the ground and the tactical moment correctly. He took the initial surrender, and Lawrence pulled down the Argentine flag, took out a neatly folded parcel of material from the inside of his smock and ran up the Union Jack in its place.

# 14

By the time we were called forward, about 100-plus Argentine Marines and sailors sat quietly on the ground in three ranks in front of one of the buildings. Cedric had got them to stack their weapons. There was no hostility on the part of either side, and they were compliant. The Argies seemed somewhat bemused and awkward, as if they were a little embarrassed at being caught somewhere they should not have been, but they also seemed to be relieved that it was all over. They had been attacked by armed helicopters, lost their submarine and witnessed an encroaching naval firepower demonstration that could have been brought down on to them at any moment.

Though disciplined, they were dishevelled and hungry. The Arg sailors from the sub were particularly smelly, clearly having had no access to showers for a couple of weeks. Lawrence told us to take charge of the prisoners, and we moved them into the shelter of a BAS communal dining hut and set about feeding them from a large store of pre-prepared meals which had been stocked by the survey team. Bilbo, James and I found huge tin trays of lasagne and heated them up in the kitchen, before serving them to our prisoners. Eight trays of food did the whole lot, and we did it again the next day to give them breakfast.

It was a bizarre experience. As we served out pasta to

men in blue naval coats and olive-green field jackets, amidst steaming mugs of tea and the cosy fug of humanity feeding together, it dawned on us that, moments earlier, we had been prepared to kill these men. They were appreciative, civil and nothing like the stereotypical misperception we had had of them up until that point: something akin to Manuel in *Fawlty Towers*.

Later that evening, I sat down at the supper we provided and chatted to the skipper of the *Santa Fe*. Captain Bicain was a decent, cultured man, who had been trained at the Royal Naval College at Dartmouth. He spoke good English, and we talked about places he had visited in England.

'Your country is beautiful,' he told me. 'I saw much of it when I was not training at the academy and I liked going up to London: so much to see and do.'

'I have never been to Argentina,' I said, 'but I bet it is a beautiful country too.'

'It is, and a very far cry from all of this,' the captain replied.

He also expressed his gratitude for the treatment of one of his crew, who had been wounded during the helicopter attack on his submarine. The man would lose his leg, but his life was being saved by the surgeon in the sickbay aboard *Antrim*.

The following morning, M Company arrived in Cumberland Bay from *Tidespring*. They were clearly pissed off at having missed all the action and were detailed to take over from us. With the Royal Marines looking after the prisoners, we were free to explore our surroundings, and I headed off to the whaling station at Grytviken with James and Bilbo.

Laid along the shoreline at the mid-point of the bay, the collection of wooden huts and storage tanks stained orange with the corrosion of time had been abandoned in the middle of the 1960s. 'Wow, this place is straight out of *Moby Dick*,' James said.

He was right about that. It was like stepping back in time. The place had been left untouched due to its remoteness and preserved by the cold. Chandlery stores were still full of ropes and shackles for the ships that now lay forsaken and derelict along the shore. Great stacks of oxidizing chains, with links as big as your fist, were piled like cairns. Along with the tall, rust-stained tubular chimneys of the oil-melting workshops, they stood testimony to an age long since past.

A small white timber-framed church with a sharp pointed black spire, built in the early 1800s, stood sentinel to it all at its centre, framed by the panorama of ice-covered peaks behind it. The neatly kept cemetery containing Ernest Shackleton's grave was located away from the church, close to the route of our advance into Grytviken, so we walked back along the foreshore to visit it. Seeing the dark, rough-cut granite pillar of the man who had had a bearing on our attempt to traverse Fortuna enhanced the sense of the history of the place.

'To think he crossed that glacier with little more than a piece of rope. That's quite something,' remarked James.

We turned and headed back through Grytviken to King Edward Point. Passing the post office, some of the blokes got hold of first-day-issue cover stamps and had them marked up and stamped with the date of the Argentine invasion to take home as souvenirs. Bilbo noted the safe behind the counter in a corner, which had been left untouched by the Argies.

'How about using a 66 to look inside?' he said half-jokingly.

'I think we'd better be getting back to the Point,' I suggested, before temptation could get the better of us.

By the time we got there, the once-untroubled atmosphere of civility and collaboration between ourselves and the Argentine prisoners had evaporated.

Now firmly in charge of things, the Royal Marines had wanted the damaged sub moved from King Edward Point, as they claimed that it was in danger of sinking and fouling the jetty. Captain Bicain was happy to oblige and sent a few of his men on board to help some sailors from HMS *Brilliant* move the *Santa Fe* to deeper water. In the process the sub suddenly listed to one side, and an Argentine petty officer threw a ballast tank lever to correct the sub's trim. A lone Bootneck who was standing as a guard to the prisoners thought the Arg sailor was trying to scuttle the submarine and shot him several times with a pistol.

Captain Bicain was beside himself with anger. As he saw it, a willing act of cooperation and assistance had met with an unnecessary act of violence. I was sitting next to him when one of his men brought news of the tragedy. There was a heated exchange in Spanish, and I made myself scarce. When Sheridan entered the mess hall, Bicain made an immediate beeline for him and didn't hold back from telling the Marines commander what he thought about the death of his man. The good feeling that had grown up between the two sides had been well and truly shattered.

It was the saddest of notes on which to be leaving Grytviken, but we had been called back to *Antrim*. On arriving on board, we heard the news that Leith had also fallen without a shot having to be fired. Although initial radio calls inviting the small garrison of twelve Arg Marines to surrender had been ignored, the threat of receiving a bombardment from *Plymouth*, which steamed aggressively offshore, combined with an assault by the troops from the SBS and the Squadron's 16 and 18 Troops, which were still aboard both the frigate and *Endurance*, had eventually been enough to convince them to give up. So the Arg troops and thirty-nine scrap-metal workers went into the bag as well.

The Arg force was led by a notorious character called Lieutenant Commander Alfredo Astiz. He had overseen an interrogation centre during Argentina's dirty war in the 1970s. Hundreds of Argentine dissidents were alleged to have met a grizzly end under his charge, including a Swiss woman and two French nuns. Astiz lived up to his slimy reputation and was a complete contrast to the sailors we had looked after at Grytviken. When he agreed to surrender, Astiz had indicated that a football pitch at Leith would be a good place for the helicopters to land. Suspicious of his motives, 17 Troop recommended a more offset location for the Navy's aircraft. When a detailed search of the area was conducted after the surrender, it was discovered that the Argies had put an IED on the pitch, which Astiz had failed to mention. Nige got to guard him, and his conclusion that he was a 'nasty piece of work' was spot on.

Air Troop supplied guards to watch the Arg POWs,

who were placed in *Endurance*'s hold until they could be transferred over to the care of M Company at Grytviken. The blokes in 16 Troop started noticing that every time the guard shift changed, one of the prisoners asked to use the ship's heads. They assessed that it might have been part of an escape plan and were certain that Astiz had put the POWs up to it. After that, Astiz was separated from the other prisoners and ended up being confined in the surgeon's cabin on *Antrim*, where he also proved troublesome. He spoke good English, though, so he was given a book about the SAS to keep him busy, which I am sure was just what he wanted.

The other piece of good news was that the Navy had picked up our missing boat crew from the one remaining Gemini that had been set adrift and was still missing when we took Grytviken. The three members of Boat Troop had made it ashore through the storm and landed in Stromness Bay. Keen to avoid capture, they hadn't activated their search and rescue beacons. Unaware of the events unfolding around them at Grytviken and Leith, they had remained hidden until they caught sight of HMS *Plymouth* and flashed out a distress signal. She spotted it and picked them up.

The efforts in South Georgia had eventually come good and delivered the quick, bloodless victory that Margaret Thatcher's government had been looking for. It was captured in Captain Brian Young's signal that had been sent from *Antrim*, which was then relayed back to the UK by the main British Task Force: 'Be pleased to inform Her Majesty that the White Ensign flies alongside the Union Flag in Grytviken, South Georgia. God save the Queen.'

It was emotive stuff, although there was no mention of the fact that it was Lawrence's Union Jack that had been run up the BAS flagpole. Back home, Thatcher came out of Number 10 Downing Street, on the evening of 25 April, into the glare of camera lights and flashbulbs with her secretary of state for defence and had the news read out to a pack of TV cameras and journalists. When the defence minister finished reading his announcement that Grytviken was back in British hands, there was a bevy of questions from the media about what was going to happen next. Maggie cut them off and told them to 'Just rejoice at that news.'

In truth, I suspect that she had no better idea about what was going to happen next than we did.

The topic of whether Argentina would now relinquish the Falklands without a fight, having seen that we meant business, was on everyone's lips. The Argies' response to the retaking of South Georgia was full of indignation and defiance. The buzz on *Antrim* was that their government had said that they would fight for the islands 'to the last drop of their blood' and that they now considered that they were at war with Britain. But our side was still publicly seeking a peaceful solution to the crisis. Al Haig's diplomatic marathon had also continued throughout the South Georgia episode, and a proposal was on the table, waiting for a response from Galtieri's junta. There was even talk on the mess deck among the matelots that we might be sent home, but I, like most of the rest of Mountain Troop, wasn't so sure.

On 28 April, we were cross-decked to HMS *Brilliant* from *Antrim* by the remarkable crew who flew Humphrey, the Wessex that had played such a key role in everything that had unfolded. Without them, 19 and 17 Troops would have undoubtedly suffered significant losses at the mercy of the ferocious weather both on land and at sea. Along with *Antrim*, they would be staying on for a few more days to support M Company, who would now garrison South Georgia. D Squadron had been ordered to sail north with *Brilliant* and join the main Task Force of British ships converging on the Falkland Islands.

Two days after we left *Antrim*, a detachment of sailors from the ship's company buried Chief Petty Officer Felix Artuso with full military honours in the frozen ground of the cemetery not far from Shackleton's grave. The death of the Argentine sailor shot by the Royal Marine was on my mind as we sailed back out into the open sea of the South Atlantic and left South Georgia behind us. We had given the Argentines a bloody nose and we nearly did it without shedding any blood. But my sense was that the real fighting was about to begin and was likely to be a damn sight bloodier.

## 15

With the events of Operation 'Paraquat' behind us, we headed north back into the vast emptiness of the South Atlantic in the full grip of the oncoming winter. The dramatic South Georgian landscape of ice-bound fjords and jagged snow-capped peaks was now replaced by an endless grey monotony of heaving, mountainous seas and driving rain. As a missile-armed Type 22 frigate, HMS *Brilliant* weighed 2,000 tonnes less than *Antrim*. The difference in size between the two vessels meant that we felt every moment of the weather-inflicted torture aboard the smaller ship as she plunged relentlessly through the waves and rolled against the howling wind.

There was a distinct lack of space on the mess decks on board *Brilliant*. Hot bunking became a faded memory of comparative luxury, as we made do with finding any spare bit of deck among the ship's storerooms and passages on which to bed down. Despite the squeeze, *Brilliant* was a happy and friendly ship. The captain, John Coward, made a point of seeking us out in our ad hoc quarters and apologizing for the cramped conditions in which we found ourselves. His convivial nature set a tone that extended to the rest of the ship's company. His officers and ratings also made us feel welcome, despite the fact that our presence must have disrupted their well-oiled routine. Queues for the galley increased, as did competition for the washrooms and the heads. While a reflection of a crew that enjoyed high morale and strong personal leadership, our reception was also influenced by the role D Squadron had played in the retaking of South Georgia. However, any hope that what had transpired on the island might have encouraged Argentina to accept a diplomatic solution to resolve the issue of the Falklands had faded.

On 29 April, Buenos Aires formally rejected the American proposal offering Argentina an internationally backed stake in the islands' administration, and discussions of their future sovereignty, in return for a withdrawal of all Argentine forces. In any event, such an accommodation would have been equally unacceptable to Thatcher's government, but the junta's rebuff brought an end to several weeks of US-backed attempts to avoid war.

The next day, Britain announced the imposition of a 200 mile Total Exclusion Zone, or TEZ, around the Falklands. It amounted to a declaration of intent to initiate hostilities, as any Argentine ships, forces or aircraft within the TEZ were now liable to attack by British forces. The same day, the Reagan administration imposed military and economic sanctions on Argentina. By the time we cross-decked from *Brilliant* to HMS *Hermes* and joined the main Task Force on 30 April, sides had been chosen, and the battle lines drawn.

'Looks like war,' I said as we sat in the galley and listened to the announcement of the exclusion zone on the tannoy.

'Hmm,' Alex responded, as he held his plate, which was in danger of clattering off the table with the motion of the ship, 'we are heading right into it, and I am not sure I want to be on board a warship when it kicks off. The Argies have their own navy, and the news reports suggest they have got plenty of stuff to send one of these things straight to the bottom of the ogin.' He gestured to his surroundings with one of his diggers.

'Yeah,' I agreed, 'a bloody great battleship, an aircraft carrier, and Exocet missiles courtesy of the Frogs.'

'French bastards,' chipped in Bilbo. He looked at Binsy. 'You all right, mate? You look a bit peaky.'

Binsy was feeling below par again and wasn't eating. 'I just want to get off this bloody thing and on to dry land. A muddy shell-scrape in the sodding rain has got to be better than this.'

Fortunately for Binsy, he didn't have long to wait to get off *Brilliant*; but we would only be heading for another of the Navy's ships.

We were lifted off from the frigate's stern during the late afternoon by a series of Sea King helicopters, which shuttled the Squadron and all our stores to HMS *Hermes*. The 'Junglie', a troop-lifting variant of the Sea King, was much larger than the Wessex Mk Vs that had crashed attempting to take us off Fortuna. Designed to replace the ageing Wessex, they could carry up to thirty fully laden troops in their cavernous interior and were equipped with two powerful Rolls-Royce Gnome engines, which produced a distinctive sound like a buzz-saw. Along with the ASW version of the helicopter, the Sea Kings were the workhorses of the Royal Navy.

The Junglies flew us across calmer seas, which, without

the power of the fierce wave-driving winds, had abated to a heavy, rolling swell. As we climbed higher, I could make out the silhouettes of other ships dispersed far across the ocean under an intermittent clag of drifting thick grey banks of mist. This was the Task Force, an array of vessels of all different types, but devoted to the one purpose of retaking the Falklands. They had left ports along the south coast of England under spring sunshine and to an enormous fanfare of cheering crowds, with sailors lining their sides and helicopters and Harrier jets bright and shiny on their flight decks.

'Blimey, look at that lot,' Binsy shouted over the noise of the engines. He seemed to have perked up with the sight of so many ships below him.

'They look like they have taken a battering from the weather on the way down here,' I shouted back.

The hulls were streaked orange with rust, and their decks were devoid of crew and aircraft, which were battened down inside the ships against the harsh ocean environment of the South Atlantic.

'Look, that must be *Hermes*, the flagship.' James pointed out towards the massive ship at the centre of the battle group through one of the helicopter's windows. 'Admiral Woodward must be on board her,' he added, referring to the Task Force commander. 'The smaller carrier must be HMS *Invincible*.'

The other ships appeared to be arranged in a layered defence around the two aircraft carriers in the ensemble of maritime power that lay stretched out across the sea below us.

Type 42 destroyers steamed far out on the horizon, often beyond the line of sight on the furthest fringes of the fleet. Equipped with longer-range Sea Dart surface-to-air defence missile systems, they were stationed to provide protection against incoming hostile missiles and aircraft. Further in, the County Class destroyers and smaller frigates held positions within a few miles of the centre of the Task Force, each one ready to catch any enemy leakers that might make it through the outer defence perimeter. With their shorter-range Sea Cat and Sea Slug missiles, their job was to prevent anything getting through to the flat-tops and the larger tankers and assault ships that rode in their wake.

The sight left us in little doubt that we were about to embark on the serious business of war. 'I am not sure I fancy the Argies' chances against that lot,' Bilbo said, as the pitch of the Sea King's engine began to change as it slowed into its final approach.

We came in to hover off her port side, and the superstructure on the right of the flight deck loomed up to fill our starboard window. The pilot matched the speed of the ship and then crabbed right over the deck. The wheels of the Sea King put down with a slight bounce of its undercarriage, and we piled off with the engines still running. Working under the downdraught of the main rotor, we formed a human chain and set about offloading the stores. Shouting to be heard above the noise of the wind and the helicopter's engines, while gesticulating vigorously with his arms, a member of the flight-deck crew set about directing where to put the boxes and containers we were offloading. Following his instructions, we placed them on a part of the deck which the yellow-jacketed sailor referred to as being the 'elevator'. With the stores unloaded, we turned to shield ourselves from the blast of the Sea King's rotor blades as the pilot pulled the power back on and lifted off to make the return trip to *Brilliant* to collect the remainder of the Squadron.

## 16

The afternoon light was already beginning to fade on the invisible horizon, somewhere out across the sea to the west, when the mechanical whirr of the motors of the aircraft lift kicked in with a jolt and we began to descend from the flight deck. As we dropped into the hangar deck, the platform lowered us into an abstract world of glaring strip lighting, which revealed an unforgettable scene of the *Hermes'* twelve Sea Harriers and half a dozen Sea Kings packed tight between the bulkheads and running the full length of the ship.

The harshly lit air was musky and heavy with the distinctive smell of aviation maintenance. The synthetic mix of aviation fuel, blended with the odour of oils, plastics and greased metal, immediately assaulted our nostrils. Our other senses were overwhelmed by the noise of generators, the high-pitched whine of power tools and the echoing ring of metal striking on metal, as our eyes took in the blur of engineers and armourers working among the jam of airframes like a small army of ants.

At 28,000 tonnes in weight, 750 feet in length and with a crew of over 2,000 souls to man her, the rest of the ship was equally impressive. Compared to *Endurance*, *Brilliant* and even *Antrim*, *Hermes* was like a small floating town adrift in the inhospitable wasteland of the sea. Apart from possessing her own mini airport, the aircraft carrier was equipped with a hospital, briefing rooms, water treatment plant, laundry, shop and a huge galley, which could double up as a large cinema to put on films for the ship's company.

Apart from her size, the other instantly noticeable thing about *Hermes* was her stability. A deeper draught, combined with the ship's overall length and weight, reduced the impact of bad weather. The need to wedge yourself into a bunk or anchor down a camp bed during a storm now looked like it would be a thing of the past.

I looked across at Binsy.

'This will do,' he said, as he took in our surroundings, and the elevator came to a stop with a slight bump. We stepped out into the main hangar space.

'Happy now, Binsy?'

'You bet, Splash, and I am starving too.'

We saw Wally and Graham waiting for us over by a bulkhead near one of the Harrier jets. Responsible for the Squadron's admin, they had been flown on to *Hermes* in advance of the rest of us. 'Right, lads,' Graham said, 'welcome to *Hermes*. You'll find her very different to the other ships. There's a lot more space, but also a lot more people too.'

'Where can we get some scoff?' asked Binsy.

Graham let the laughter subside and then continued. 'The flight deck above us is known as Zero Deck. The ship has six other decks below it, and each one has a corresponding minus number. This is 1 Deck. The galley is on 3, one deck above where you will be living. So you should be happy with that, Binsy.'

'Roger that,' Binsy beamed back.

'OK, grab your kit and follow Wally. He'll show you to where you're dossing.'

The various departments and decks of the ship were connected by a maze of passages and ladders. Consequently, finding your way round the ship would have been a considerable challenge without Wally to guide us to our accommodation on Minus 4 Deck.

We followed Wally through a myriad of passages and ladders, festooned by a bewildering array of pipes and tubes and interspersed by watertight doors, which were held back against the bulkhead. Each of the heavy white metal doors was marked with red lettering, which seemed to indicate when they should be shut or left open. We proceeded further down into the bowels of the ship, and an increasing sense of depth enveloped us.

'Hey, Wally,' I asked, 'just how far down are we going?'

'Down to Deck 4, Splash,' Wally said over his shoulder, no doubt wondering if I had been listening to Graham.

'Yes, I know, mate, but just how far down is that?'

'He means, are we going to below the waterline, Wally?' James cut in.

'Oh, yes, mate. Well below.'

'OK, thanks,' I said, trying to sound as nonchalant as possible.

Even as soldiers, we had enough knowledge of ships and enough of an imagination to know that if the shooting war started and we were hit, the chances of survival reduced the deeper we went into *Hermes*.

Although far below the waterline, when we eventually got there, the accommodation we had been allocated was in a league of its own. It was ample and spacious, as it was usually earmarked for an embarked Royal Marines commando unit. Each of the thirty-man mess decks was generous enough to accommodate two of our undersized troops with ease. With dedicated washrooms and heads, they were fitted with three-tiered bunks and furnished with a decent amount of locker space, as well as a communal area with a TV and benches.

'This is the dog's bollocks,' Binsy exclaimed as he threw his kit on to one of the top bunks.

I stowed my stuff on the middle bunk underneath his and looked about, wondering whether there would still be sufficient space to accommodate all of Binsy's kit once he started spreading himself and his possessions around the place. 'Yeah, it's bigger, and at least we have got our own grots for once, but it still has that same smell about it.'

'I know what you mean,' Bilbo said, as he squared himself away on the bottom bunk. 'Rancid feet, sweaty bodies, stale food and farts. Fancy a brew before we go and get some scoff?'

'Good idea,' Binsy agreed. 'Make mine a standard NATO, mate: milk and two sugars.'

There were numerous scalding hot water points around the ship, which were a godsend for thirsty Toms used to making do with a hexamine cooker in a trench. Bilbo waited for Binsy to locate his mug among his kit and then set off to find one.

*Hermes'* galley, when we got there, was equally as impressive as the rest of the ship. It looked like it could accommodate half the ship's complement in one sitting, seemed to operate round the clock and offered a huge variety of different dishes. The three of us helped ourselves from a long stainless-steel hotplate and found a vacant Formica-topped table. Lofty came over to join us, his plate groaning under a mountain of food.

'This is fucking gleaming,' he said, nodding in the direction of Binsy's similarly stacked plate.

'Beats eating compo babies' heads and arctic,' Binsy grinned, referring to the small cans of steak and kidney pudding in our compo rations and the freeze-dried cold-weather rations.

'Looks like you have got your appetite back, Binsy,' I observed.

'You can say that again. Died and gone to heaven.'

Binsy was clearly back on form. And just as well.

*Hermes*' sheer size, and the responsibility heaped upon her as the Task Force's principal aircraft carrier and flagship of the commanding admiral, made her seem impersonal, devoid of the warmth we had enjoyed on board *Brilliant*. The chilly atmosphere was compounded by a palpable sense of mounting tension as the carrier entered the TEZ. Almost as soon as we went on board, the crew started coming to action stations.

The alert was piped through the carrier's main broadcast and provoked a flurry of activity as sailors stopped what they were doing and rushed to their alert points and began to shut fast watertight hatches to maintain the integrity of the ship if it was hit. As alarms sounded and fire-fighting and damage-control parties formed up, we headed to our muster position in a storeroom lower down in the bowels of the ship towards the stern known as the '2 Sierra Flat', although none of us had a scoobies why it was called that.

Grabbing our anti-flash gear and leaving our grots, we passed sailors donning fire-resistant suits and breathing apparatus, conscious of the fact that we would at least be above the waterline, as heavy metal doors were clipped shut above and behind us.

The Argies were thought to have a couple of operational submarines, and their own navy was reported to be at sea and to pose a credible threat to the Task Force. But the biggest fear stemmed from the risk of being hit by an Exocet. The French-made anti-ship missile was a potent weapon and was on everyone's lips. It was widely believed that the Argentine naval air arm had several of them, which could be launched from their Super Etendard jets.

Our own Navy had Exoccts, which could also be launched from ships, and every matelot knew what they were capable of. If a missile hit you, it was likely to turn your ship into a raging inferno. If the blast of the exploding projectile didn't kill you, the fire it generated probably would, or you might drown, trapped in a flooded compartment of buckled metal if the Exocet destroyed a critical bulkhead.

Among the younger sailors, it was a major topic of conversation in the ship's galley. Not least as *Hermes*, carrying the bulk of the Task Force's aircraft, which were critical to our ability to take back the Falklands, was the Args' target of choice. It was a real fear, but for the time being all we could do was make the most of our new surroundings. And wait for it all to begin.

# 17

On 1 May, the war for the Falkland Islands began. It was still dark when the Sea Harriers started taking off from *Hermes* to conduct ground attacks against the airport at Stanley and Arg aircraft at Goose Green. Even several decks down, we could hear the whine of their engines as they built up take-off speed and then accelerated across the deck to launch themselves from the Harrier ski-jump at the bow of the ship into the sky.

It was light when they returned, and I went up on to the flight deck with Bilbo and James to watch them land from a viewing position out of the wind at the bottom of the ship's control tower. James saw them first. 'Here they come.' I looked to where he was pointing out across the stern of the ship.

'Got them,' I replied. 'They are coming back in pairs.'

'There are two more over there,' Bilbo added, picking out another brace of jets as they appeared on the horizon.

At first, they were distant specks against a surprisingly clear blue sky. Then they became more visible, as the jets circled round the carrier, waiting for a spot on the deck and clearance to land. Each aircraft slowed as it came in to hover offset from the ship. Then they wobbled over the deck, still in vertical flight, before touching down with a thump and slight bounce as the main wheel undercarriage made contact with the surface.

They shut down their engines as flight-deck crews in brightly coloured jerkins moved out from the control tower area to attend them. Yellow, blue, red and green, each colour worn to designate a particular deck function round the aircraft.

We knew that the Sea Harriers had been busy as their bomb racks were empty of the ordnance they had dropped on enemy positions. We also knew that they had received some attention from the Arg air defences. 'Look at the back of that one,' Bilbo said, as one jet came in with a hole the size of a large fist knocked out of its tail. It was clearly a bit of a surprise to the pilot, who had just climbed down the red movable steps that had been put up to his cockpit by the guys in the blue jackets. We were close enough to hear him exclaim 'Fucking hell' when he walked round to the rear of his aircraft to inspect it and saw the damage a cannon shell had inflicted.

Their missions complete, individual fighters were moved on to the aircraft lift and then lowered into the hangar deck area below like some mythical bird of prey. The first Sea Harrier strike against Arg positions on the islands was a follow-up to an air attack made by a single RAF Vulcan bomber, which had flown all the way from Ascension in an attempt to drop twenty-one 1,000 lb bombs on the runway at Stanley during the hours of darkness.

The news of the attack was reported on the ship's broadcast. It was apparently the longest-distance bombing raid in history and took seventeen Victor air-refuelling tankers to provide enough fuel for the one Vulcan to make the 8,000 mile round trip.

'Typical bloody crabs,' remarked Binsy when we heard

the news of the raid over the broadcast. 'They fly all the way down here, drop a couple of bombs and then head home to their nice, cosy, warm beds. Lucky buggers.'

While the rest of the Task Force remained in the open sea, around 100 miles to the east of the Falklands, a destroyer and two frigates had been detached to sail close in shore under the cover of the night to bombard the airport at Stanley with their 4.5 inch guns. The ships attracted a response from the Args. When daylight broke, they were initially attacked by Mirage jets sent from airfields 400 miles away on the mainland in Argentina and then by four Turbo Mentor light attack aircraft which had taken off from airstrips on the Falklands. The small propeller-driven aircraft were chased off by Sea Harriers, which then managed to shoot down two Mirages from a second sortie made against the ships.

Later in the day, the Argentine air force got close enough to strafe two of the ships with cannon fire, which caused some slight damage and a minor injury to a sailor. But two bombs narrowly missed the destroyer, and one of the attacking Dagger fighters was shot down by a Sea Harrier. Another Sea Harrier also managed to shoot down an ageing Canberra bomber later that day. Listening to it all, as snippets of information were piped over *Hermes'* internal broadcast system or passed on at the Squadron daily briefing held in 2 Sierra Flat, was heady stuff.

Although the action was taking place a hundred miles away, it was a clear indication that the shooting war had started in earnest. The Task Force was beginning to take it to the enemy. Pounding their positions ashore and shooting down their aircraft was part of the process of softening up the Argies on the islands and writing down their air capability before eventually making an amphibious landing somewhere on the Falklands.

There was no detail on how subsequent operations would unfold, as the senior commanders were still formulating their plans. We were all assuming that a landing would eventually come, we just didn't know when or where. But while we were beginning to take the war to the enemy on and above the islands, we were in no doubt that the Argies would be wanting to hit back. It made the threat of air attack and the prospect of being hit by an Exocet all the more real, and the air raid warnings started to come in thick and fast.

The Navy's air raid status alert system was based on a series of colour codes. 'Air raid warning – white' indicated that there was no immediate danger of enemy aircraft and was taken as being an 'all clear'. 'Yellow' meant that there was an imminent threat of an enemy attack developing, and 'red' meant that incoming hostile aircraft were heading for you. The subtle distinctions between 'yellow' and 'red' didn't make much difference to us. If you were at air raid warning – white, you were OK. Anything else meant something was inbound: it might have your name on it and it was bad.

During those first days in the TEZ, yellow and red attack warnings were near constant. The repetitive, robotic voice would blare out over the ship's tannoy, 'Air raid warning – red! Air raid warning – red! Air raid. Take cover! Take cover!' as klaxons sounded and bells rang throughout the ship. Sometimes the words, 'Brace! Brace, came over the system, which was more alarming, especially when it was followed by a bang, which would provoke a sudden frantic fumble of activity as people scrambled out of their bunks, threw down their cutlery and stopped eating, or cut their ablutions short, as they rushed for the nearest safe area or simply hit the deck where they were.

We were asleep when one particular warning came in, and the waking world was suddenly alive with the cacophonous noise of alarms, urgent alert instructions and the drumming of running feet along passages. I moved faster than Bilbo: although he was in the bottom bunk below me, I got under it before him, and then Binsy piled on top of both of us, bringing half his kit with him.

'What the fuck was that?' I said as the concussion of an explosion reverberated around the ship.

'Dunno,' replied Bilbo. 'Could it be a hit?' Other blokes, also under their bunks, were thinking and saying the same thing.

'Should we stay here or head to the muster point on the flats?' I asked. No one had the answer, and we spent the next fifteen minutes lying on the cold steel of the deck. Eventually, the stand-down was announced over the tannoy, and I told Binsy, 'You can get off me now, mate.'

We asked a passing matelot whether we had been hit. 'It's chaff, mate,' he told us. 'Stuff we fire off to decoy any incoming missile.'

Initially, responding to alerts and coming to action stations were alarming affairs. You would be lying or sitting there on the deck, knowing that there was nothing you could do except wait it out, pray, bite your nails and hope that nothing would come piling through a bulkhead. As time passed, though, we became more used to it, and, as well as the threat of attack, whether it came from the sea, or above or below it, boredom became something to add to the list of our enemies. We were eager to get stuck in.

Having joined the carrier when she sailed from Ascension Island, G Squadron were already on board *Hermes* by the time D Squadron cross-decked from *Brilliant*. They had been given the task of covertly inserting on to the Falklands to conduct surveillance operations against Argentine positions ashore. It was a classic SAS task. Gathering strategic intelligence behind enemy lines was our main war role in the event of any conflict with the Soviet Union on the central European front.

The SBS was the other element of SF troops on *Hermes* and had been tasked to reconnoitre the island's beaches and shoreline as possible landing points for the amphibious and ground force elements of the Task Force. Patrols from both G Squadron and the SBS had begun to be inserted ashore by Sea King helicopters after dark on 30 April in conjunction with the Task Force's air attacks and naval bombardments. For the men of G Squadron, it would mean four weeks of continuous patrolling. Digging hidden observation posts into the wet peat by night, they would spend the daylight hours motionless and concealed as they watched Argentine positions around the main settlements on the islands. Using weighty 320 high-frequency radios and Morse code to send back information on numbers, dispositions and equipment, the patrols would provide the Task Force with vital intelligence on the enemy to inform the British plan of how best to attack and to defeat them.

It was dangerous work. The moment a patrol of between

four to six men landed on the ground, they were on their own. Deep inside enemy territory, they would be far from help if they were discovered and attacked by Arg forces, which were bound to be looking for them. At best, they might get air support from a Sea Harrier. But even if one of the precious aircraft could be made available, the pilot would have to be briefed, fly up to 200 miles to get to the target area and then locate the patrol on the ground. All of which would take time, and there was a good chance that any jet sent to assist a patrol in trouble would arrive too late to make a difference.

The conditions that G Squadron were operating in were also austere and arduous in the extreme. Virtually everything they needed for a month of unsupported operations would have to be carried on their backs. As well as hefty radios and the heavy spare batteries needed to power them, enough rations, ammunition and long-range viewing devices would have to be man-packed in bergens, along with sleeping bags, camouflage netting and ground sheets.

Constantly moving at night to avoid detection and lying still and alert by day, they would be permanently exhausted. With nothing more than the scant cover of a shallow scrape in the sodden earth and a thin, taut-stretched jungle poncho, they would be exposed to the driving rain and the biting cold. Their feet would become soggy and white-sore with the blight of trench foot from the lack of circulation and from being permanently wet and frozen. When they needed water, they might be lucky enough to find a stream that was safe enough to draw it from. But often they would have to squeeze filthy sheep-fouled liquid from the peat, which would be likely to give every man who drank it diarrhoea, as well as making them sick.

The SBS faced similar conditions, but they would be lifted in and out frequently by helicopter to recce a particular beach or landing area, as the nature of their task required them to report their findings to the planners back on *Hermes* in person. There was no such respite for the men of G Squadron, who were in for the duration. They were the unsung, and unseen, heroes of the war. However, while our comrades evaded Arg patrols, reported back on the enemy's movements and froze their butts off on the windswept hills and boggy peat moors of the Falkland Islands, we were still kicking our heels aboard *Hermes*.

Events on South Georgia had consolidated our position in the Task Force order of battle, and it was agreed that D Squadron would have responsibility for conducting any SF direct-action attacks. But while Cedric and Danny scoured intelligence data coming from G Squadron and maps in the operational planning rooms somewhere above us in the ship's superstructure, looking for a suitable target to raid and attack, the admiral and his staff had more pressing concerns.

## 18

While Arg forces on the islands were being bombed and bombarded, their high command were laying their own plans to strike back at the British Task Force. We knew from the daily update briefs we received that Argentine naval forces had put out to sea to attack the Task Force. A carrier group led by the aircraft carrier *25 de Mayo* was reported as being somewhere to the north of the TEZ. The intelligence updates also indicated that another group of three warships, led by the cruiser *General Belgrano*, was operating to our south, and that both groups of enemy naval vessels were intent on attacking the British fleet in a pincer movement.

The intricacies of maritime operations were lost on most of us. The potential threat posed by the Arg aircraft carrier and a heavy cruiser were real enough and added to the other risks of air attack and submarines, but dealing with them was a matter for the ships and crews of the Task Force. Around us, sailors and naval aircrew went about their business of operating defensive missile systems, manning weapons, conducting ASW sweeps and launching air patrols. As soldiers, we were idle bystanders, and the monotony of underemployment began to take hold as time progressed and began to blur into a seemingly endless dullness of eating, sleeping, reading, responding to alerts, coming to action stations and waiting.

Occasionally, mail arrived from the UK. Flown out from Ascension and airdropped to the ships in the Atlantic, the thin blue-paper envelopes that folded out into a page of writing, known as 'blueys', had a dramatic effect. Familiar handwriting giving news of loved ones and events at home became a morale-boosting high point in a sea of tedium and threats. Opening one of those cheap, crisp airmail-thin letters took you momentarily out of the alien environment of metal, confined humanity, constant noise and alerts. For a brief moment, you were back home in Hereford, as you read about family matters, the spring weather, your garden and how the grass needed a cut.

In one letter, Liz wrote to me:

> I watched more of the ships leave on the TV yesterday. There were lots of people to see them off. Mum rang me after last night's news. She asked after you and I think she is worried about you. I am too, so please take care and come back safely.

The tone of Liz's letters revealed that she had softened. The departure of the fleet from places like Portsmouth and Southampton, amidst a glare of publicity and the fanfare of bands and TV coverage, had stood in stark contrast to our own discreet departure. But I think it had brought home to her what we were about, and I detected in what she wrote that she was caught up in the national fervour of the cause, as well as being concerned for what we might be facing.

By 2 May, D Squadron had been aboard *Hermes* for four days, although it felt a lot longer. Nothing marked out the day as being any different to the others. We attended the midday briefing, went to the galley, took some air on the deck and watched Sea Harriers and ASW variants of the Sea Kings as they launched on their missions. Sheltering against the strength of the wind in the lee of the ship's towering superstructure and watching the aircraft take off from the deck provided a respite from the humdrum life below decks and a chance to experience daylight. Then the news about the *Belgrano* was piped through the broadcast system, and the ship's company went mad.

The announcement that the ageing Argentine cruiser of Second World War vintage had been hit and sunk by two torpedoes fired by the Royal Navy submarine HMS *Conqueror* was greeted by a frenzy of cheering sailors on every deck of *Hermes*, as if a World Cup-winning goal had just been scored.

The controversy that surrounded her sinking never touched us on *Hermes*. Had we been asked for an opinion, our view would have been simple: the *Belgrano* was an enemy warship, which had put to sea with the intent of doing us harm and was located only a few hours' steaming time away from the Task Force. Equipped with 6 inch guns, and with thick armour-plating that could stop most Royal Navy surface weapons, the cruiser was a significant threat, and it was right to take her out of the equation, however tragic the consequences. The decision to sink the *Belgrano* was further justified by the fact that the rest of the Argentine navy returned to their home waters after the sinking and never ventured out to sea again during the rest of the conflict. A very real threat to the Task Force had been removed at a stroke. However, while a necessary evil of war, any jubilation at the sinking of the *Belgrano* was short-lived. Two days later, the Argentine navy struck back, and the dreaded threat of the Exocet became a stark reality.

I was lying on my bunk, absorbed in *Far from the Madding Crowd*, when the news that HMS *Sheffield* had been hit came in. It was before lunch, after a morning of interminable air warnings had ceased. All had been false; our patience had been stretched thin, and it was good to be immersed in the bucolic calm of the Wessex countryside. I was lost in the bit where the thriftless Sergeant Troy gets pissed with the farm workers during a storm, when Phil came on to the mess deck and told us what little he knew about the tempest that had just engulfed one of the Royal Navy's Type 42 destroyers.

The details were scant. HMS *Sheffield* was one of three destroyers on picket duty far out on the fringes of the fleet to our west. Well up-threat from the carrier battle group, the destroyers' job was to act as the next line of defence after the Sea Harriers in protecting the carriers *Hermes* and *Invincible* against any incoming aircraft or missiles with their longer-range Sea Dart surface-to-air missiles. The two Arg Super Etendard jets had been picked up on the radar of one of the other destroyers but was missed by *Sheffield* and dismissed by *Hermes*. We were at air raid warning – white when it happened.

'Splash, Bilbo, grab your patrol med kits and get up to the galley, which is being set up as a casualty clearing point. The boss has heard that they are expecting a lot of casualties from *Sheffield* and he is standing all of the Squadron's medics by to help.'

'How bad is it?' Bilbo said.

'I am not sure, but it sounds bad. There is a real flap on, so you need to get up there ASAP.'

I looked at Bilbo, and then we both grabbed our medical packs and went up to the galley as fast as we could. Like me, Bilbo had done a stint with an A and E department as part of his training so as to become a squadron medic. By the time we got there, most of the other D Squadron medics were gathering in the dining facility, including Sid Davidson, the other medic in 19 Troop.

The green plastic chairs had been cleared and stacked, leaving the fixed dining tables to act as treatment platforms for the wounded, when they started to come in. We were paired off, two medics to each table under the overall direction of a naval surgeon. Bilbo and I stood over our allocated table and started to empty out the contents of our packs on to the Formica surface: bandages, drip-receiving kits, scissors and morphine. Then we waited and wondered what was about to be brought through the door.

'What do you reckon we are in for?' said Bilbo.

'Who knows? I suppose it depends on how they triage the casualties. The worst ones will go to the sickbay, but if there are a lot of them, we might be dealing with some pretty badly hurt people.'

As we stood poised in the galley, 20 to 30 miles away the crippled *Sheffield* was fighting for her life. Fire-fighting teams and damage-control parties fought desperately to keep the ship afloat and rescue sailors trapped below decks in smoke-filled passages and compartments, as the ship rapidly became a raging inferno of burning fuel and flammable fittings.

It didn't take long before the first of the casualties were landed on the flight deck above us in a relay of Sea Kings. Their arrival was piped over the broadcast system, and we braced ourselves. Above us, badly burned men were stretchered from the helicopters. Others walked, assisted, with bandaged faces and hands. The announcement of the arrival of more casualties was kept up as a running commentary on the intercom, but our tables remained clear.

As horrific as it was, the number of injured among the ship's crew was lower than expected. After a couple of hours, the helicopters stopped landing, and we were stood down. Twenty men had died, and, although we were not required to treat them, scores more had been wounded. *Sheffield* was eventually abandoned by her crew, and her burned-out hulk was taken in tow. Six days later, water poured in through the mortal wound in the destroyer's side caused by the missile strike, and she sank in heavy seas.

It would be an understatement to say that the impact of losing *Sheffield* was sobering. The more serious casualties remained in the sickbay, where horrific burns had been treated with thick white pain-soothing and antiseptic Flamazine cream. Badly burned hands had been placed in plastic bags, and surgery had saved the lives of many. At breakfast the next morning, we saw some of the less severely injured, and the comparison of the burns suffered, or not, to their faces and hands reinforced the importance of wearing anti-flash hoods and gloves properly to protect exposed extremities from the immediate flash and heat of an explosion. If you weren't wearing your hood properly at the moment of detonation, there would be no time to pull it up or get your gloves on. Those that had not, suffered for it. Still etched with shock, their faces were red-raw with blistered skin, their hair singed to the scalp and their fingers swollen pink and sore, looking like the anaemic compo sausages Graham and Wally served up to us on Ascension.

The tension aboard *Hermes* increased noticeably, and the Exocet threat became the topic of everyone's conversation.

'Apparently, it took just two minutes for the Exocet that hit *Sheffield* to close the distance to the destroyer from its launch point,' James said, as we sat on our bunks and discussed the previous day's events later that evening. 'I doubt the poor bastards had a chance to do anything about it, especially as they were out on a limb protecting the rest of the Task Force.'

'So that means if an incoming missile is detected we are going to be lucky if we get three minutes tops before it hits us,' I said, noting the fact that *Hermes* was stationed in the centre of the fleet.

'That extra minute isn't going to make any difference,' retorted Binsy. 'If one of those Frog missiles has got your name on it, there's not a thing that you can do about it, and you can kiss your arse goodbye.'

'That's helpful, Binsy,' James said, 'but you're probably right. Best we get off these floating coffins ASAP.'

Everyone nodded in agreement.

There was not a man among us who wouldn't prefer to

take our chances ashore. On dry land, as a soldier, you could choose where you positioned yourself, you could dig in, take cover behind something solid and, most importantly, you could shoot back. And our ability to do so was about to improve substantially.

# 19

The C-130 flew in slow and level with its tailgate open as it headed towards the ship on the horizon. The pilot maintained a steady 110 knots, just fast enough to prevent the aircraft from stalling, but slow enough to give what he carried the best chance of hitting the target. The pilot acknowledged the location of the British frigate lying 3 miles dead ahead. On the ramp at the back of the plane, Paddy O'Connor from G Squadron clipped his static line into the wire cable running above his head, his eyes fixed intently on the red jump light that burned brightly to his right as his peripheral vision caught the sea rushing past a few hundred feet below him.

The red light flicked off. In the same instant the light below it glowed green, and several bundles were pushed off the tailgate. As the last one left the aircraft, Paddy followed it out into the void. For a moment he felt the familiar sensation of falling, then his parachute canopy snapped open. Half a minute later his feet hit the surface of the sea; despite wearing an immersion suit, he immediately felt the impact of cold-water shock. He floated on the swell with the aid of his life jacket and checked the location of the gifts that he had brought with him, which had splashed down under their own parachutes just before he landed. He counted the containers, which bobbed between the waves. *Good, all there*, he thought to himself.

Now all he had to do was wait for the boat from the frigate to come and collect him and his stores. He hoped that it wouldn't take long.

One of the gifts was a green 5-feet-long coffin-shaped box, which a few hours later sat on the floor between the bunks of the mess deck accommodation and looked ominously intriguing. Made of smooth pressed aluminium, it had the words 'Rocket Ammunition with Explosive Projectile' stencilled on it in white lettering. The box contained a shoulder-launched man-portable heat-seeking Stinger anti-aircraft missile. Designed by General Dynamics, it had only recently entered service with the American military and was an ideal fire-and-forget air defence weapon for small units and troops on the move. Along with 40 mm underslung grenade launchers for our M16 rifles and a few sets of tactical satellite radios, the Stinger was another present from US Special Forces, which had been rushed out to the Regiment when it joined the Task Force.

Later that day we sat round the container, as the short, stocky Irishman flipped open the catches and pulled out a long, slim black missile tube, which had a grill-edged firing box attachment at its front end. Although he was a G Squadron man, Paddy had been sent out to Fort Bragg in America at the start of the Falklands crisis to learn how to use the Stinger. Now he was passing on his instruction to us.

Paddy had returned briefly to the UK from the States, but there had been no time to return to Hereford to say goodbye to his wife Iris and their two young children. Instead he boarded the RAF C-130 Hercules, which flew him via Ascension out to the Task Force, where he made his parachute jump into the sea with several crates of Stingers and other American equipment.

Paddy made no mention of his arduous journey south as he talked us through the operating concept of the weapon. 'This, gents,' he said, holding up a fist-sized canister, 'is argon gas, which cools the missile's infrared seeker-head, which in turn allows it to home on to the hot engine exhausts of an enemy plane or helicopter.'

He fitted the canister to the front of the launcher and then went on to explain that the Stinger, once locked on, emitted a high-pitched tone, which allowed the operator to align the sights in the weapon's aiming eye piece and then fire the missile, which would then automatically track its way to the target.

'No tone, no lock-on,' he continued. 'Fire it before you get the change in tone, and the missile will cream itself into the ground. Savvy?'

'Sounds a bit complex to me,' one of the blokes said.

'Not if you listen for the tone,' Paddy assured us. 'It's a fierce bit of kit, and the next best thing to sliced bread for shooting down enemy aircraft. I hit the remote-control target aircraft every time on the test ranges in the States, but you have got to be sure to wait for that change in tone before squeezing the tit.'

Weighing 35 lbs, the Stinger was two-thirds the weight of the Army's own Blowpipe shoulder-launched anti-aircraft system and had over twice the range, being able to bring down an aircraft at 5 kilometres. Unlike the British missile, the Stinger didn't need to be guided to the target by the operator using a radio-controlled system, which made for human error. The Regiment weren't issued

Blowpipes, but, compared to the Stinger, I am not sure that we would have wanted them.

As we passed the Stinger around and lifted it on to our shoulders, Paddy talked us through the firing sequence, and I wondered whether we would be able to grasp in a couple of short, informal training briefs what it probably took a US forces operator weeks to learn.

As we familiarized ourselves with the missile's operating procedures, a more traditional means of dealing with Argentine aircraft was being discussed two decks above us in the small annexe off *Hermes'* wardroom.

Located just a few hundred yards off the northern tip of West Falkland, Pebble Island is one of just over a score of outlying islands occupied by settlers of the Falklands' sheep-farming community. Measuring just under 20 miles in length and 5 miles across at its widest point, Pebble Island shares the same topographical features as the rest of the archipelago. Devoid of any natural tree or shrub cover, its open terrain undulates in a mix of low-lying peat bogs, large ponds and rocky elevated ground, carpeted by a thick mix of fibrous grass and clumps of 3–4-inch-high heather-like scrub called 'diddle-dee'.

Like the rest of the Falklands' isolated settlements, Pebble Island is served by a grass airstrip capable of handling short-take-off turboprop aircraft, which, combined with its geographical location, was a feature that made it attractive to the enemy. During the last week of April, Argentine engineers and a company of Marines landed on the island with the intention of rendering its small airfield capable of handling light military aircraft and to defend it from attack.

Initially providing an operating base for a clutch of Argentine navy Turbo-Mentors, the airfield was later reinforced by six twin-engined and heavily armed Pucara attack aircraft, which were dispersed to Pebble Island after the Task Force air attacks against the airstrips at Stanley and Goose Green on 1 May.

Enemy activity on the island attracted attention two days before the raids on the other airfields, in the brief engagement with the flight of Mentors over Falkland Sound on the first day of air attacks. None of the small Argentine planes was shot down, but the encounter reinforced intelligence from signals intercepts of enemy communications, which had picked up the presence of the engineers and Marines at the settlement. When likely numbers of ground- and aircrew were taken into account, estimates suggested that the garrison on Pebble Island consisted of around 100 enemy personnel.

The reports had also caught the attention of Cedric and the head shed planning team in Wardroom 2 located on 2 Deck. An annexe off the main wardroom for *Hermes'* officers, Wardroom 2 had been made available to D Squadron when the unit joined the carrier. As we fumbled with American anti-aircraft technology, Danny West, Lawrence Gallagher and the boss pored over maps and charts of the island. On paper, as a target for a direct-action raid, Pebble Island looked ideal. More detailed information on the enemy dispositions was limited, but the planning team were able to draw on the local knowledge of the Squadron's Royal Navy liaison officer.

Lieutenant Commander Roger Edwards was a thirty-five-year-old Fleet Air Arm pilot who had ferried an additional Lynx helicopter out to HMS *Brilliant* when the frigate first joined the Task Force. He had also previously served on HMS *Endurance* in the Falklands and was married to a Falkland Islander called Norma, whom he had met in the UK. *Brilliant* already had a sufficient aircrew complement to fly two aircraft, and Roger found himself without a job. It was a situation which, when combined with his intimate knowledge of the islands and his maritime experience, made him an attractive prospect to D Squadron.

Never one to miss an opportunity, Danny West had seized upon this when the two men met on board the frigate during the passage north from South Georgia. Danny and Roger struck up an immediate friendship, which led to an informal arrangement of Roger joining the unit as the Squadron's Royal Navy liaison officer for the duration of the campaign. Roger was able to confirm that the presence of Argentine aircraft on Pebble Island constituted a significant threat to the Task Force, particularly if San Carlos Water became the preferred location to make an amphibious landing.

The significance of the Pucaras at Pebble and the risk they posed to the landing was not lost on Cedric. Situated 30 miles to the northwest, the airstrip is less than ten minutes, flying time from San Carlos and its northerly entry point of Falkland Sound lying between West and East Falkland. The Argentine-built Pucara was a nasty little ground attack aircraft which, if it caught the landing force as it entered the narrow straits, would wreak havoc.

We learned just how deadly the Pucara was from the

RAF forward air controller attached to the Squadron. Flight Lieutenant Garth Hawkins's job was to call in any supporting air strikes from our own jets and direct them on to a target using a laser designator. An expert at his job, which he carried out with boyish relish, he was popular with everyone, not least as he was thick-skinned and could take a joke about being a crab.

Garth was also responsible for teaching us how to recognize enemy aircraft and he knew all about the Pucaras and what they were capable of. Sitting among the bunks of the mess deck one morning, he went about describing the enemy aircraft's capabilities with enthusiasm.

'Right, gents, this is the Argie aircraft we need to really worry about,' Garth said as he held up a photograph of a Pucara. He went on enthusiastically, 'The Arg jets are a concern, but the Pucara is specifically designed for striking enemy troops from the air. The Daggers and Skyhawks will be flying so fast if they come at you, their pilots will hardly have time to line you up in their sights before they are past you . . .'

He paused for effect.

'But the Pucara is a very different kettle of fish. It has a maximum speed of 311 mph, but it can slow itself down to just 90 mph without dropping out of the sky, which makes it an ideal platform for shooting up things from the air.'

He paused again, pointing out the armament points on the aircraft.

'Making an engagement at such slow speed, they can offload almost all their ordnance in one pass to deadly effect. Armed with two Hispano automatic cannons in its nose, capable of firing 270 20 mm rounds apiece and four 7.62 mm Browning machine guns along its fuselage, loaded with 900 bullets each, that's a devastating rate of fire.'

He beamed back at us.

'The helicopter boys are absolutely shitting themselves about it. While they might be able to evade the jets, by hunkering down in the low ground between the hills and watching them sweep past, there is no hiding from the Pucara, which is why it's the real bogeyman out there.'

In addition to its guns, the Pucara also had extra teeth in the form of two rocket pods mounted under the wings. Each contained nineteen 2.75 inch rockets. The size of a milk bottle, a single warhead could blast a hole in the side of a ship or shower troops with red-hot shrapnel. They weren't overly accurate, but at slow speed and low height against ships or troops concentrated together, they didn't need to be.

If they caught the landing force as it made its way into San Carlos, they could chop a landing craft packed full of over a hundred Brit soldiers to pieces in a matter of seconds. Even if the troops made it to the shore, they would be out in the open, grouped close together and with nowhere to run from the Pucaras. If they weren't cut down in the first few passes, the aircraft could make tight turns and pounce on them again and again until they ran out of ammunition.

The Argentines nicknamed the Pucara the 'Fortress'. As it was fitted with armour-plating it could take punishment and keep flying and killing. Even if some of them were shot down by the ships' air defence systems and the

Sea Harriers, the rest of the Pucaras were bound to get in among the amphibious landing craft. Cedric was convinced that D Squadron could stop that from happening.

The boss planned to insert Boat Troop by canoe to conduct a reconnaissance of enemy positions on the island. The recce party would then report back and cue in an assault force made up of the Squadron's three other troops using Sea Kings to get them on to the island. However, it was a concept that entailed risk, not only to D Squadron, but to the Task Force as a whole.

The Sea King helicopter had an operating radius of 600 miles, but fully laden with troops, on a tactical insertion at low level made against prevailing winds, its range was considerably reduced. In order to launch the raid, *Hermes* would have to steam closer inland for the helicopters to make the round trip from the carrier to Pebble Island. In doing so, she would expose herself to a much greater threat from enemy submarines and Exocet-carrying jets from mainland Argentina. Consequently, Cedric's bold and ambitious proposal would need the clearance of the Task Force's commander.

He put his plan to Sandy Woodward on 5 May. But just a day after HMS *Sheffield* had been lost, the admiral wasn't prepared to subject one of his critical aircraft carriers to additional risk and rejected it out of hand.

# 20

The radar warning receiver located in the tail of the Sea Harrier squawked once. The high-pitched tone in the pilot's earpiece indicated that the aircraft had been 'painted' by an enemy radar. The onboard computer system logged the bearing and elevation of the likely source. The Sky Guardian system fitted to the Sea Harrier was notoriously unreliable and was often switched off by the Navy's pilots, due to the distraction of its constant false alarms. But on this occasion, the jet's warning receiver was switched on, and the report of the brief radar contact was taken seriously.

When the recorded data was analysed back on *Hermes*, it tracked the likely source back to an area around Pebble Island. If the Argies were going to place a radar anywhere to track British aircraft and the approach of the Task Force from the north, Pebble was an obvious place to put it. On the lookout for suitable Argentine targets to strike on shore, the Regiment's CO had already considered the likely location of enemy radars. Lieutenant Colonel Mike Rose fed in his own assessment that the island was an ideal location to station a radar. Combined with the Sea Harrier report, it caused profound concern, changing the nature of how the threat of Argentine presence on the island was viewed. The admiral now developed an urgent imperative to deal with it. He called a meeting to discuss the issue on 10 May.

Woodward thought he had two options; neither was ideal. A naval bombardment or air attack on Pebble Island might destroy and damage some of the aircraft, but not all. There could also be no guarantee that the radar, if located, would be taken out. Additionally, bombs or gunfire risked causing civilian casualties among the local population. D Squadron provided him with a third option. While a direct-action attack entailed risk, it offered precision, avoidance of collateral damage and certainty if successful. But, despite the need to neutralize the threat posed by the Argentine presence on the island, the admiral turned down D Squadron again.

Woodward and his key staff officers knew that the landings on the Falklands were scheduled for a window between 16 and 25 May. If they went in any later, the onset of winter and worsening weather would preclude an amphibious operation and jeopardize the subsequent land campaign. The option of using D Squadron had first been flagged up to the Admiral by G Squadron's boss, who suggested that it might take three weeks to plan, organize and execute a raid against Pebble. It was time the Task Force commander didn't have. When Cedric found out, he got back in front of the admiral with G Squadron's commander and told him it could be done within three to four days. Woodward responded by saying, 'Make it so.'

At the time, most of us were unaware of the impending raid. As SF personnel, we had 'prone to capture status', which meant that plans were kept a closely guarded secret until the last safe moment when we could be briefed. However, in Wardroom 2, the OC of Boat Troop, along with his troop senior NCO and the Squadron head shed, went into planning overdrive. By first light the next day the plan was set, and *Hermes* began steaming west to get close enough to Pebble Island.

Later that night, eight men of Boat Troop and four rubber-coated collapsible canoes were inserted by two Sea King helicopters into a sheltered cove on the northern shore of West Falkland. They landed with the intention of unfolding the two-man kayaks then paddling through a narrow strait of water and across Whale Bay, which separated West Falkland from Pebble Island. It was nearly 10 miles, but by sticking close to the coast, it was hoped that the canoes could avoid the worst of the weather and strong seasonal tides to make landfall on Pebble undetected. Once ashore, the patrol would split up into four-man teams. One would recce and secure a helicopter landing site for the subsequent fly-in of the rest of the Squadron. Moving on towards the settlement under command of the troop commander, the other half of the patrol would recce routes to the settlement and establish an OP to observe the airfield by daylight. As well as reporting back on the location of aircraft and the presence of any radar, the OC of Boat Troop was also responsible for refining a detailed plan of attack.

Based on a conceptual outline that Cedric had thrashed out with the head shed the previous night, the Squadron's mission included killing or capturing Argentine aircrew living in the settlement. But then the South Atlantic weather had its say.

The onset of a full gale created a raging rip tide through the narrow confines of Purvis Gap, which provided access to Whale Bay. The troop commander and the rest of his patrol watched the foaming, surging water from the shore on West Falkland. Even the cover of night did nothing to diminish its raw power from men that had already felt the full force of an angry sea during their attempts to make landfall in South Georgia by motorized boats. Realizing that they would have to adapt and adjust their plan of getting on to the island, they began dismantling their canoes.

When stripped down and packed into their large shoulder-strapped oversized holdalls, each half of a kayak weighed in excess of 50 lbs. With all the other equipment to carry as well, the patrol would have to make the tortuous overland journey to a different departure point, further along the coast, three times. Having stashed their bergens in a hide, and weighed down with the heavy stowed canoes on their backs, the men of Boat Troop looked like bent beasts of burden as they set off to cover 6.5 kilometres over rocky high ground and stream-cut gullies to circumnavigate the narrows on foot.

Dumping the canoes at the other end, they then turned back to pick up the rest of the kit and then set out once more for the alternative launch area. Having humped their kit for a total of 20 kilometres over difficult terrain, they were still going to have to paddle around the shoreline of Whale Bay, make landfall on Pebble, patrol the 8 kilometre route to the settlement and establish the OP. However, the weather was still against them, and the wind whipped the water lying between them and Pebble Island into a wave-torn fury, forcing the patrol to delay launching their canoes until the following night, when the storm abated.

The Stinger went back into its box when we found out

about the proposed raid. If everything went right, the sophisticated missile system wouldn't be required. The aircraft D Squadron would be targeting would be on the ground. A few pounds of well-placed plastic explosive would do the job. But first the exact location of the aircraft had to be identified, a plan had to be confirmed, and then we had to get to the airfield, get to the planes, destroy them and then get out again.

Weather would clearly be a factor, as would the enemy defences on and around the island. But the biggest enemy was time. If the admiral wanted to get the attack in before the earliest opportunity to launch the main Task Force landings, the Squadron would have to complete the covert reconnaissance of the island, develop a refined plan of attack and execute it within four days. The clock began to tick.

The absence of half of Boat Troop was our first indication that something was up. But once confirmed, the plan to attack the airfield generated a buzz of excitement and a flurry of activity.

'Bloody hell,' James said, 'if we pull this one off it will be an epic. The Regiment hasn't done anything like this since the last war.'

'If this comes right, it will be a fucking wet dream,' Binsy said, grinning from ear to ear.

'No shit,' I said.

'Yeah, I know. Beware what you fucking wish for,' replied Binsy, his grin beaming back at me.

He was excited. We all were. *Fuck, we are really going to do this*, I thought and felt a rush of adrenaline through my veins.

And James was right. This was the type of mission that had made the Regiment famous four decades earlier, during the Second World War. The series of behind-the-lines attacks against German and Italian airfields in North Africa in 1941 by David Stirling's 'Originals' had destroyed hundreds of enemy aircraft and was the stuff of legend. It was a history that the modern-day Regiment lived and breathed.

At midday on 13 May, the message finally came in from Boat Troop. The weather had slackened and they had made it across to Pebble Island by 0400 hours Zulu. In the remaining hours of darkness, the OP overlooking the airfield had been established. The information they sent meant that we were about to tread in the footsteps of men like Paddy Mayne and Jock Lewis.

Confirming the presence of eleven aircraft and suggesting an immediate attack, the message came in too late for *Hermes* to get the Squadron in position close enough to the shore to make the attack that night. There was also no mention of an enemy radar, but the threat posed by the Arg aircraft was clear. Sitting in cramped rows on the deck of the storeroom in the bowels of the carrier, Cedric laid out his plan of attack.

He told us what he knew about the enemy. It wasn't much, but he reminded us that we shouldn't underestimate them.

'It will be a full squadron attack,' he continued, 'but we are going to be quick about it, time is going to be short, so focus on destroying the aircraft.'

Cedric covered off the coordinating points, regarding how we would launch by Sea King helicopters once

*Hermes* was in range of the enemy coastline, which would then fly us to a landing site at Phillips Cove, located just under 5 miles to the southeast of the airfield. We would be met by Boat Troop, who would then guide the rest of the Squadron to its assault positions, having led them in through a squadron RV point 1,000 metres short of the airfield.

The simultaneous assaults by 16 and 18 Troop would be backed up by the Squadron's own 81 mm mortar, as well as naval gunfire support from HMS *Glamorgan*. As a heavy County Class destroyer, *Glamorgan* carried the same guns that had been used by her sister ship HMS *Antrim* in the shelling of Grytviken. The warship's 4.5 inch shells would deliver a mix of HE and star shells. The high-explosive rounds would be directed on to a mountain feature known as First Mount to the north of the airfield, which would act as a fire reference point, from which the shells could then be adjusted in closer to the airfield. The illumination projectiles would be fired to pop parachute flares high over the airfield and would provide the assaulting troops with the necessary light to make their attacks.

'17 Troop are already ashore and will act as the guides; 16 Troop will go for the settlement; 18 Troop will attack the airfield; 19 Troop . . .' Cedric paused and looked at John Hamilton, 'you are in reserve.'

I glanced across at Bilbo and Binsy as Cedric finished his orders and asked if there were any questions. I noted the look of disappointment in their faces. No doubt mine and that of every other man in Mountain Troop sitting beside us said the same thing. We thought, *Crap, in reserve. Air and Mobility Troops had been allocated the plum jobs, while we have to sit back and wait and hope we get called in as reinforcements.*

The allocation of tasks was based on the fact that 19 Troop had been the lead sub-unit in retaking South Georgia, and the other troops now deserved to have their share of the action. But fairness and sound tactics weren't much consolation. None of us wanted to be in reserve on a once-in-a-lifetime job like this one. If the attack went to plan, it was unlikely that Mountain Troop would get to fire a shot. It bothered us, but we would just have to suck it up. Being part of a squadron is a team sport, so there was no point in bitching about it when the orders session broke up. Anyway, even as the reserve, we had too much to do.

As the contingent element of the plan, we would have to be prepared to do everything, in the event that one of the other troops was unable to complete its task, needed help, or something else unforeseen cropped up during the mission. After the O group, each of the troops collected separately to start crafting their own plans to deliver the intent and tasks that had been given out by Cedric. Mountain Troop got together with John and Phil back up on our mess deck.

We talked through the options and possible eventualities, each one of us able to point out potential strengths and weaknesses, until the plan solidified, and everyone knew their part in it. But it was John who took the lead. At the end of it, he summed up and put his mark on it as the troop boss.

'OK,' he said, 'if we are in reserve, that means we need to be prepared to reinforce or take on one of the other troops' tasks.'

'Right, boss,' agreed Phil and I noted a greater sense of deference in his response. The new troop commander had proved his mettle on South Georgia and Phil was acknowledging that.

'That means we need explosives as well as firepower. Paddy and Alex, you are the dems experts, so you knock up the charges.'

'Right, boss,' they replied in unison.

'Good. We've got a plan. Let's get cracking with the battle prep. Phil, you sort the ammo.'

'Roger that,' said Phil, and with that we broke up and got cracking with the battle prep.

As the Troop demolitions experts, Paddy Armstrong and Alex Brown set about constructing the charges in case the chance to blow up the radar or any aircraft came our way. I watched them as they puffed away on their fags and kneaded PE4 plastic explosive into shape, inserting slim silver detonators and crimping home lengths of black initiating cord into the explosive, ready to be ignited by brown grip switches. A small pile of black-taped destructive power began to build up in a pile next to them. They were men absorbed in their work, blissfully unaware of the furtive glances they attracted from the odd passing matelot, who seemed to hasten their step when they spotted the rollies clamped into the side of their mouths.

Firepower meant drawing extra ammunition to supplement our personal weapons. As well as additional 5.56 mm rounds for my M16, I drew 200 rounds of linked 7.62 mm for the patrol's GPMG, which would be carried by Chris Seakins. I also selected two 66 mm light extending anti-tank rocket launchers. Another American weapon, the 66 was already on general issue to the British Army and we held plenty in the Squadron armoury. From the information we had received, we didn't expect to come up against armoured vehicles, but aircraft were also made of metal, and the logic suggested that a 66 would provide another means of destroying them. Furthermore, they were good against enemy dug into bunkers.

I also packed two fragmentation grenades and two white phosphorus canisters into my webbing. The WP were designed to create covering smoke screens, but burning phosphorus was also good for clearing trenches and setting things on fire, like aircraft. Almost everyone drew at least one green plastic carrier containing a brace of 81 mm mortar bombs. Weighing nearly 18 lbs apiece, they would be dropped off with the mortar crew at the Squadron RV. We would go in wearing belt order, but with all the extra ammunition and weaponry, I also got hold of a daysack, to stow the 66s, extra link for the GPMG, my radio and patrol medic's kit. The mortar bomb 'greenies' had a carrying strap, which fitted over the shoulder, although those issued with two of the heavy containers would have to carry them with one in each hand like suitcases.

Bilbo stood up with a groan. He had his belt order on, his Armalite across his chest and a greenie in each hand. 'I must be carrying 70 to 80 pounds with this lot.'

'You look like you are on your way to catch a train,' I said.

'Very funny, Splash, but I ain't got much choice. If I strap both across my shoulders, the straps will cut off the blood supply to my arms, and they will stop working, which will be a fat lot of use when it comes to firing my gat.'

Time becomes compressed during battle preparation, and as we packed and repacked our kit, the most immediate enemy ticked by on our wrist watches, but by the middle of the next day, 14 May, we were set, and the raid would go in later that night. Troop plans had been discussed, debated and formalized. Kit had been drawn, issued and prepared. On Pebble Island, Boat Troop remained concealed and watched and waited for our arrival.

Now it was up to the Navy to get us to the release point for the helicopters. With the rest of the Squadron, a small naval gunfire party from 148 Battery to call in the shells from *Glamorgan* and Roger Edwards coming with us to provide local knowledge and liaise with any civilians, the assault element constituted forty-six men. We expected to face Arg forces numbering at least twice the size of the troops we could muster, so success would depend on achieving surprise and speed, and using darkness to complete the mission and get off the island before first light the next morning. *Hermes* could not afford to wait for us so close to the enemy shoreline without the cover of night. If we were still on the island at dawn, she would have to head back out to sea before first light risked exposing her.

With such a small force and no place to hide, being left on Pebble Island in daylight hours would also make us extremely vulnerable to any Argentine follow-up. If we were to have the time needed to complete the operation, it meant that *Hermes* had to be at the helicopter launch point by 2300 hours and ready to steam away again by 0600 hours. Allowing for an hour to fly each way to and from the island by Sea King, once we inserted on to the island we would have six hours on the ground to get the job done. All timings were given in Zulu. Being four hours ahead of local timings, it meant that *Hermes* would be heading back out into the open sea well before the sun rose at the local time of 0730. However, despite our best-laid plans, a familiar enemy was on hand to frustrate us.

## 21

It would take five hours for *Hermes* to steam nearly 150 miles away from the Task Force to get to the launch position 70 miles to the north of Pebble Island. At 1800 hours Zulu, the carrier detached from the main group of ships with *Glamorgan* and HMS *Broadsword*. While *Glamorgan* would sail closer towards the island to provide D Squadron with gunfire support, the smaller frigate would stay further out to sea with *Hermes* as a goalkeeper, providing protection with her Sea Wolf anti-aircraft missile system.

As the detachment of ships turned west to begin their journey towards Pebble Island, they ran into a southerly gale, which had grown up during the afternoon. The bows of the ships plunged through crashing waves as they sought to make headway through strong winds and a pitching sea. We felt the change in sea state below decks. *Broadsword* suffered in the heavy weather and was struggling to keep up. The waves breaking across her bows also damaged her Sea Wolf launchers, and the small flotilla was forced to slow its passage so the frigate could repair them and catch up. We were kept informed of the progress of the ships and were aware that we were already slipping behind schedule.

Hours passed. We had grabbed a last meal in the galley. We had checked and rechecked our kit, and now there was nothing to do but wait. We sat about on the mess deck or lay on our bunks. Some dozed fitfully, dressed and ready to go with kit packed and weapons stacked on the floor by our bed spaces. I tried to read, but focusing on anything other than the mission eluded me. Like everyone, my mind was on what awaited us on Pebble Island. The word went around: another delay. The reason was not given, but the agony of waiting continued.

Up on the bridge of *Hermes*, the confounding weather conditions were forcing a recalculation of the time and distance to the launch point. Buffeting headwinds meant the helicopters would burn more fuel, which meant the carrier would need to move closer to the shoreline than originally estimated to bring them within range of the insertion point.

The gale was also causing problems in getting the helicopters ready as the Sea Kings had folded blades. The wind howling across the flight deck threatened to wrench the blades from the rotor-head housings before they could be locked into place. Consequently, one by one the helicopters had to be taken back down into the hangar deck. Then, sheltered from the wind on the aircraft lift, each of the Sea Kings' blades had to be spread, locked into place and the engines started before they could be raised back up to the deck and moved to their take-off positions. The flight-deck crews were working in overdrive. But it took time, burned fuel and meant the Sea Kings' tanks had to be topped up again before they were eventually ready for us. We finally got the call to assemble on the hangar deck. By the time we were directed to climb on to the aircraft lift to ascend to the flight deck, it was 0100 Zulu, and we were now running two hours behind schedule.

The lifting mechanism whirred. The artificial light of the hangar's shelter disappeared below us as we drew level with the flight deck. Then the full fury of the storm met us in a shock of wind and water, which sought to snatch the breath from our mouths. Sea spray burst over the sides of the ship, crashing across its pitching deck, which made for perilous purchase. The strength of the gusts whipping across the bows threatened to drive us to our knees. Encumbered with in excess of 60 lbs of kit, we bent into it like old hags as we tried to maintain our footing and began to make our way forward to the helicopters.

The four Sea Kings sat line astern, their rotors spinning and the roar of them competing with the howling gale. The helicopters were lashed to the deck by nylon straps to hold them fast to the heaving deck and prevent them from being driven overboard by the pounding storm. Arranged in sticks, each troop was detailed off to its allotted Sea King. We instinctively bent a little lower as we moved under the rotor blades that thrashed the air in a spinning blur of energy above us, their downwash noisy and savage.

We scrambled into the large helicopters through the starboard side door. Though the interior was roomy, we filled it with men and equipment. The fold-down canvas seats in 19 Troop's Sea King had been tucked away. We would make do with floor space and sat on daysacks or the greenie mortar bomb carriers. Positions and kit were shuffled in the darkness, as more people piled in and we created additional room for them. The faces of the men were smeared with camouflage cream and merged into the blackness, but the excitement was palpable, and the edge of nervous anticipation equally keen.

The frame of the helicopter vibrated as the rotors thumped hard just above our heads. This was the moment that we had been waiting for; we were tooled up, keyed up and ready to go. But something was wrong. Something was being said at the door by a crewman whose feet were clearly still on the deck. Why wasn't he getting in? He was talking with urgency into the microphone attached to his helmet and reaching into the cab. His touch was relayed forward by others towards John Hamilton. John looked back and worked his way to the door. Shouted words, again, unheard, and suddenly we were being told to get off the helicopter.

'Fuck.'

We reassembled back down in the hangar. Now the aircraft had *too much* fuel on board, which made them too heavy. They would have to lift from the deck and dump it over the sea before landing back on *Hermes* to pick us up. I looked at my watch again. It was 0200 Zulu. Three hours behind schedule.

Like everyone else, I now doubted that we would get this one on. *The boss must be feeling it too*, I thought. More so, as it would be his call as to whether we had enough time left to complete the mission or whether the risks were now too great and it should be called off. Time and darkness were critical 'go' criteria for the operation, and they were both becoming increasingly close to 'no go' limits. Cedric loitered in the crew-ready room off to one side of the hangar with Danny, Roger and Lawrence. Smoking cigarettes to the butt, drinking brews, no doubt cursing the Navy internally and agonizing over the decision he might have to make. The rest of the troops kicked their heels in the hangar, sitting about, also smoking fags up by the hangar deck.

A few chatted, but most of us were silent, dealing with a mix of emotions: disappointment, anticipation, apprehension and fear, the latter compounded by the delay and doubt, as waiting for what might unfold in combat is generally far worse than actually engaging in it, when minds are focused and there is a job to be done. Another quarter of an hour, maybe less, passed, and then we were back on board the helicopters, our kit stowed and ready to go. The airframe vibrated and rattled as the twin Gnome engines screamed for power and the gearbox transferred torque to the rotor blades. The crewman of our Sea King was now inside the open door, and this time he slid it shut as the helicopter lifted and banked into the wind.

# 22

The four Sea Kings headed south towards Pebble Island in line astern. They flew into the storm, fast and low, a few feet above a heaving sea. I could make out John Hamilton up front in the space between the two pilots, framed against the barely perceptible faint green up-light glow which cast back softly from the instrument panel in the cockpit. Plugged into the intercom, John could listen and talk to the aircrew, although he would have been able to see little through the windscreen of the helicopter as the wipers thrashed backwards and forwards to keep it clear of the driving rain.

The pilots were flying on night vision goggles. Passive night vision technology was in its infancy, and the seven sets of NVGs fielded by the Sea King aircrews of the Navy's 846 Squadron were another gift from the Americans. Clamped to the front of the pilots' helmets and adjusted down over their eyes, they looked like a *Star Wars* face mask. Designed to capture tiny photons of ambient light and intensify them, they could produce a visible green image of significant objects, such as a person or a tree line, up to 200 metres away in pitch darkness. They were state-of-the-art technology and used by 846 Squadron for Special Forces missions, facilitating low-level flying at night that could never have been contemplated without them.

The two pilots up ahead in the cockpits of the Sea Kings were working hard. Flying nap of the earth just above the surface of the sea required them to be on their mettle. Radar altimeters were engaged as part of the helicopters' flight control system, but the lead pilot's left hand remained glued to the collective, the right grasping the cyclic stick, each one making tiny adjustments to accommodate for the changing wave height and heavy turbulence.

One slip or misjudgement, and we were going down. It was like driving a Formula 1 racing car in bad weather, at night without lights, and compounded by the fact that they were doing it all on NVGs that robbed them of their peripheral vision and sense of depth. Clad in thermal underwear, cotton overalls, one-piece flying suit and rubberized survival suit, they sweated like pigs, each pilot having to concentrate like the devil with effort beyond focus.

Without goggles, the world outside the helicopter was a deep, velvet blackness. I didn't need NVGs to know that we were flying low, as I squatted on top of my daysack in the cramped blackness of the troop space behind the pilots. Glancing out of one of the square Perspex windows, I could make out the white peaks of cresting wave tops, rising high enough to lick the wheels of the helicopter. It made me think of the what ifs: *What if the pilot makes an error and stoofs us into the waves? What if the Argies pick us up on the way into the target and shoot us down over the sea? What if the enemy are waiting for us?*

I thought of the mangled mess of the Arg Puma at Grytviken and wondered whether some of the fuel we dumped would make any difference if we began taking fire and crashed. Fear on the advent of combat is a curious phenomenon that people feel differently. For some, its fingers claw at their belly; for others, they jab at the base of their throat. I felt it most in my gut. But my biggest fear was of letting the men, who nestled close around me, down. At that moment, Queen and country hardly mattered, but my mates in 19 Troop, the Squadron and the Regiment, in that order, did.

In the blackness, I could hardly make out the faces of the men around me, but I knew that they were there, sitting, like me, backs pressed against the sides of the aircraft with rifles facing muzzle down against the floor. Each man feeling the bump and rock of the helicopter as we beat our way through the turbulent air.

Sid was sitting next to me on my left, and Bilbo and Chris on my right, huddled towards the tail-plane among stacked greenies with the patrol GPMG on its bipod at their feet. Alex and Binsy sitting somewhere by the door and James up near John and Phil. All of us alone with our thoughts, hidden and lost in the dark and the noise of the engines, contemplating what might lie ahead.

I ran through the plan in my head, mentally ticking off a checklist of tasks and forcing myself to focus on the 'actions on' responses to the possible what ifs. I thought of dealing with casualties and subconsciously felt for the shape of my patrol medic's kit packed into the top of my rucksack between the two protruding 66s. I ran through the drills for extending and firing the rocket launchers, something I had done a hundred times in training but was determined not to botch in the heat of battle.

Ahead of us in the cockpit of the lead Sea King, the

pilots picked up the red flash of a handheld right-angled army torch. Shielded and filtered, it would have been near invisible to the naked human eye, but through NVGs would have been a bright beacon of briefly flashing white-green light against the dark shadow of the shoreline. John and the helmet-clad crewman turned and shouted in unison as the message came through the intercom in their headsets.

'Two minutes.'

It was the warning order that we were making the final approach to the landing site. I glanced at my watch. I let the luminous second hand tick round the face once, then tensed my thigh muscles and lifted myself up on to one knee, grabbing the straps of my daysack and slinging the greenie over my shoulder as I prepared myself ready for the exit. Sixty seconds to go. Around me, others were doing the same, and the inside of the aircraft became a jumble of motion. The crewman slid the troop door open, and I noticed the slight shine from the surface of the ocean being replaced by the darker shade of coastline as we crossed over the threshold from sea to land.

The sound of the engines changed as the Sea King flared to bleed off speed and height. The pilot pulled on the cyclic lever to bring the nose of the helicopter up, working the pedals with his feet at the same time, while pushing down on the collective to prevent the aircraft from climbing and striking its tail rotor on the ground. Making a rapid tactical landing in a tight space was the bread and butter of the Navy pilots who flew the Junglies, and the Sea King came to a hover a few inches above the earth. *God, these boys make it look like a piece of piss*, I thought.

As I scrambled to the door, I pulled back the cocking handle on my M16 and chambered a round, thumbing the safety catch to ensure it was on and checking the housing of the magazine. Pushing off with my one free hand, leaving the warmth of the helicopter behind me, I leaped through the open doorway, knees bent as my feet searched for the ground. They found it an instant later: the softy, boggy earth of the Falklands. British territory, but in the hands of an occupying power.

The Sea King's blades still spinning above me, I moved out a few feet to the three o'clock position, where I threw myself prone and covered the arcs to my front over the sights of my weapon. The rest of 19 Troop fanned out into their all-round defence positions, as the down-draught of the main rotors beat the tufts of grass flat around us. I was aware of the other helicopters landing, disgorging the other troops to left and right.

The pilot of our aircraft was already pulling back up on his collective. I felt the intensity of the air pressure from the blade wash increase on my back and heard the power crank up as the Sea King climbed back into a ver-tical hover. It paused briefly, 10 feet above us, then turned and climbed, heading back out to sea with the rest of the empty helicopters. Suddenly they were gone. The noise of their engines receded into the nothingness of the night, leaving the small coastal gully where they had dropped us absent of sound, save for the wind howling over the tops of the surrounding bluffs. D Squadron's part in the retak-ing of the main Falkland Islands had begun.

# 23

It was bitterly cold. The wind cut through our thin clothing of smocks and the T-shirts worn underneath them. The drop-off point was a small cove on the south side of the island, which narrowed into a deep-cut re-entrant as it ran inland. With the flatness of its shoreline and steep sides to mask the noise of engines, it made for an ideal helicopter landing site. There was movement behind me as troop commanders gathered somewhere off in the darkness to receive confirmatory orders from Cedric. These would be heavily influenced by OC Boat Troop, as the man on the ground, as well as by the fact that we were well behind schedule.

There was soft murmuring off in the darkness, then John was back among the Troop to pass on what had been agreed with the head shed. He was short and to the point, 'Time is against us. The boss has decided not to assault the settlement – 16 Troop will just screen it instead. Main effort remains the airfield: 18 Troop will hit it and destroy anything they find there. Get ready to move.'

'Got it,' Phil whispered back.

We shook out into an SOP troop formation and waited on one knee for the troops ahead of us to start moving.

We set off in a rough double-filed order of march and pushed up the steep sides of the cove. It was good to be on *terra firma*, but the going was hard, and our hamstrings and calves ached in protest at the unaccustomed movement and effort after weeks of inactivity at sea. Breathing hard, I willed the muscle memory in my legs to return. It was also proving difficult to maintain formation. Marching in two columns offered a degree of tactical balance, but a precipitous terrain of rocks, pedestalled lumps of peat and low scrub of diddle-dee militated against the configuration. It was also too slow.

The ground underfoot and the need for speed forced us to break down into a single, twisting file, each man following the man in front. We continued to climb, and handrailed the coast. I could sense the sea off to my left, but my focus was on working my limbs to maintain a tactical bound of spacing behind Sid. I could see the back of his pack bouncing ahead of me and could make out the outline of two or three people beyond him forming the back of Phil's patrol. But John's team, who were leading the Troop, were lost in the blackness up ahead. 19 Troop were following 16 Troop, and 18 Troop were behind us. At the head of the winding snake of encumbered men, OC Boat Troop and Cedric were setting a cracking pace. Tactical navigation at night by a large body of men on foot moving at speed in single file over difficult terrain is no easy affair. It induces a concertina stop-start effect, which impedes ease of progress. It was hard enough for those in the middle of the file, but for the men in Mobility Troop at the back of the line it was turning into an absolute nightmare to keep up. They were forced to break into a jogging run to maintain station. If someone stumbled and fell, those behind him backed up and were brought to a stop. They then had to work hard to close the gap with the men in front of them who had been unaffected by the disruption, as we laboured on through the biting wind and the darkness.

The men around me suppressed curses as feet scuffed unseen rocks, stumbled over raised mounds of peat and tripped on spongey scrub growing a few inches proud of the ground, all of which made for an ankle-rolling hell. The thin plastic strap of the greenie cut into my shoulder, and the heavy carrier bounced uncomfortably against my hip as I tried to keep both hands on my weapon. But at least I was wearing my own belt order, with my self-tailored cargo strap keeping it snug around my waist.

Bilbo carried two of the mortar bomb containers by their carrying straps, one in each hand, with his rifle slung across his front. The hard edges of its metal slapped repeatedly against his chest, as he laboured behind me. He'd been forced to leave his personal webbing on the glacier in South Georgia, and his belt order was made up from surplus pouches taken from the Squadron stores and from what others in the Troop could spare. Now his ad hoc, make-do kit cut, flapped and chafed with every movement.

Sweat soaked the inside of my smock with the physical effort of maintaining my footing and keeping up. Mentally, I worked through the route I had memorized in my head from studying maps of the island on *Hermes*. The gradient of ground eased as we crested the top of the headland, at a point known as Shag Rocks. There was no pause to check our bearings, as the guides from Boat

Troop knew where they were going and turned inland, heading northwest. If anything, the pace increased, but the going was getting better as we headed downhill, and the scrub and rock became replaced by a carpet of thick tufty grass, although the stiff wind continued as a constant resistance to forward movement. We leaned into it and pressed on.

Stifled grunts were replaced by the monotonous rhythmic swish of one foot moving after the other through the long grass. Endless, but steady. Each step taking us closer to the final RV near a large pool of water marked on the map as the 'Big Pond'. I glanced at my watch: we had been going for over an hour, but my breathing had eased and my muscles had warmed up as the familiarity of physical effort returned. The ground began to flatten out and became boggier. Peaty water oozed through the leather and stitching of our boots.

The wind dropped, and the clouds parted to reveal a waning quarter moon, casting a haze of silvery light through the gaps. It was enough to reveal the dark outline of the high-banked sand dunes of Elephant Bay a mile or more out to our front, which curved round to the northern edge of where the map told us that the airfield would be. We continued towards the bay until we hit a fence line that ran to a junction of wire and posts at the northern end of the Big Pond, where it drained through the sand dunes and on to the beach. Located on our maps, the fences suggested that we were getting close to habitation. It was here that Cedric had decided to position the Squadron RV and the mortar baseplate.

The moonlight shimmered off the surface of the pond,

silhouetting the figures moving into the RV to drop off the greenies, while Nige Smith and the rest of the mortar crew were setting up the 81 mm weapon. We were counted into the RV by Lawrence; kneeling on one knee, he represented a bastion of calm authority and confidence.

'Right, blokes,' he whispered to us as we passed. 'Well done. Drop off your greenies and keep moving.'

It was a relief to be liberated from the weight of the mortar rounds, and 19 Troop pushed beyond the growing stack of containers and took up positions near the sand dunes. The cold began to seep back into our bodies as we lay prone on the wet ground. I looked at my watch. Dawn was not far off, and we would be racing the night if we were going to complete the attack and make the extraction off the island still under the cover of darkness. As the minutes ticked by, we lay motionless in the returning cold. Waiting. John had closed into Cedric's position, but I sensed something was amiss.

The plan had been to pass through the RV in a seamless movement, pausing only to drop off the ammunition for the mortar, then use the location to transition into our tactical assault formations. We should have been moving by now towards our reserve position ready to support 18 Troop's attack on the airfield, which we believed was located short of a mile to our west.

John came bouncing back to the Troop and called in the patrol commanders. I tagged on behind Sid to hear what he had to say.

'Mobility Troop haven't made it into the RV.' John didn't waste time elaborating why. He told us that Mountain Troop were 'now doing the airfield'.

'We'll make it up when we get there,' he added help-fully.

I darted back to Bilbo and Chris and had a moment to tell them of the change in plan. Bilbo acknowledged it by saying, 'Fucking right!' Chris was equally enthusiastic, but there wasn't time to catch his words. We were already moving.

Despite John's comments that we would be winging it, the benefits of a full Squadron brief were now playing out. As the reserve, we had planned how we would carry out 18 Troop's task. We had been jealous of it; now it was ours. Climbing over the fence line, we followed 16 Troop and conformed on their right flank as we turned north and shook out into a line-abreast formation, and started to advance towards where we expected the airfield to be. I could hear the waves washing gently against the sandy line of the shore behind the dunes of Elephant Bay to my right. Above us, the moonlight gilded the edges of scud-ding clouds, and a thin light played across the open ground in front of us.

Far off to my left beyond Air Troop, I could make out the dim shapes of what looked like buildings etched as barely perceptible shadows against the horizon of the night sky. I could hear the faint, distant, mechanical thump of what sounded like a generator coming from the same direction, which suggested that it must be the settlement. Apart from the generator, it was quiet, and there were no visible signs of any lights.

We stalked on through the half-darkness, cursing the moon and fretting about the absence of obvious cover. Ahead of us, the open ground sloped up towards a low plateau, which marked the forming-up point and start line for the attack. Beyond that, an elevated smudge of terrain loomed in the far background, marking the steep sides of First Mount. From the map estimate, its lower contours marked the end of the airstrip and the limits of our exploitation. There was no actual sign of the airfield, and the FUP still seemed a long way off.

There was a loud, explosive crack behind us, and then a mortar shell popped in the sky above our heads. The air on our right was split with the sound of tearing paper as a star shell zoomed in and burst in a brilliant dazzling globe of light. Trailing lazy meandering tendrils of smoke, the illumination rounds turned night into day as the flares, swinging under small drifting parachute canopies, cast eerie shadows across the ground. The sudden light also confirmed that the terrain was bare-arsed and devoid of any cover.

The forming-up point was still 300 metres off, and I scanned the terrain like a shit-house rat looking for any fold in the ground that might provide a sheltered fire position. *Surely, the game must be up, and the enemy must now know what we are about,* I thought as I imagined them tumbling out of their pits, cocking their weapons and rushing to their trenches as they slapped belted links of ammunition into the feed trays of their machine guns. We continued to advance steadily towards them. *Keep spread out,* I said to myself. *No bunching. Don't make it any easier for them.*

Still over 150 metres to go, the edge of the settlement was now more obvious 400 metres away on our left flank. *If they catch us here, out in the open ground, they will have us cold, and this is where we are going to die.* At any moment, I expected to see the dash of red enemy tracer rounds slashing out of the darkness towards us. *Perhaps they are waiting for us to get closer, waiting for the word from a steady commander who knows his business; waiting to see the whites of our eyes and all that.* I pushed the thoughts out of my mind, and we pressed on with our arses twitching.

More star shells popped above us, keeping up a continuous light. The mortar seemed to have stopped firing, but there was plenty of other indirect fire support. HE rounds from HMS *Glamorgan*'s guns joined the mix of illumination they were already putting up, each explosive shell landing with a mighty bang on the forward edges of the mountain. We made it to the bottom of the low plateau, which rose up as a short ridge of steep ground. A small white picket-fenced cemetery marked the start of the FUP. The ground was spotted with gorse bushes and, finally, a modicum of cover.

16 Troop peeled off left to screen the settlement, and we began to push straight on up the sloping ridge. It felt like we were about to go over the top, First World War-style. But still no response from the enemy. *Maybe they are waiting for us to top out on the crest before starting to knock us down?* Unanswered questions racing through my mind. *Still no sign of the damn airfield. Where is it?* I asked myself, willing it to be there.

My nerves were on edge. I glanced left. Sid was ghosting his movement against John's patrol in the centre of the Troop. James and Phil were beyond him, as the left-flank patrol. I looked to my right. Bilbo was keeping close to Chris, who cradled the GPMG ready to drop it down on its bipod and bring it to bear in an instant. Sid gave me a hand signal which said, 'Conform on me but push right with the gun group.' I flicked a thumbs-up.

Naval rounds continued to scream overhead, star shells popping above and HE slamming forwards of us. *Maybe it's the high explosive, that's what's keeping the enemy's heads down*, I thought, as my own head drew level with the top of the crest. My heart was in my mouth. *This is when it turns into a two-way range.* I braced myself for incoming fire to start chopping into us. Two steps further to go to the lip of the ridge, and then suddenly there it was, bathed in the light of burning aerial illumination. A flat, open airfield lined with Argie aircraft parked along the right-hand length of a main grass strip. Other aircraft were dotted on the opposite side of the runway along two intersecting alternative take-off strips.

*Fucking gleaming!* Nervous tension evaporated in an instant as I mentally rubbed my hands with glee.

There were no Argies dug in around the apron of the airfield. They may have missed their chance, but we were not about to miss ours. Parked in front of us, those aircraft were ours for the taking, and we were about to inflict the havoc we were born to wreak.

# 24

John shouted over to Sid, 'Take everything on the right of the runway. We'll do everything on the left, and Phil will give fire support.'

'Roger, boss,' Sid shouted back. 'Splash, start malleting that aircraft parked on the edge of the airstrip over with the GPMG!' He pointed to a Skyvan located 50 metres to our front. Alongside the smaller Mentors and Pucaras, the presence of the box-shaped Argentine transport plane was an added bonus.

Chris already had the GPMG down on its bipod with the butt tight in his shoulder and started firing long, killing bursts at the twin-engine transport aircraft. Not to be outdone, I pulled out one of the 66 mm rocket launchers from my daysack.

Dropping into a kneeling firing position, I pulled out the securing pin on the covering flap at the rear of the 66, dropped the flap and cracked back the extending inner tube, which locked into place with a satisfying click, as the sights popped up. With the launcher on my shoulder, I pulled the arming lever forward and ghosted the middle of the box-bodied aircraft with the rocket's 50 m sight graticule pattern and squeezed the firing button on top of the launcher with the fingers of my right hand.

There was a sharp retort and a *whoosh*, as the rocket burned out towards the Skyvan, hitting it square on, but nothing happened. I pulled out the second launcher and fired another rocket. Another hit, but again no explosion. What I didn't realize was that, while capable of burning through 12 inches of armoured steel, the kinetic jet of molten copper formed by the warhead detonating on impact was simply burning a neat hole through the thin-skinned sides of the aircraft and slicing out of the other side of the fuselage without causing any appreciable damage.

Chris was also hitting the Skyvan, raking it with fire from the GPMG, which Bilbo kept fed with belts of linked 7.62 mm rounds. They were having fun, lost in their task of destruction. Tracer punched more holes through the airframe, while the still-burning trace of ricochets danced wildly across the ground underneath the wings of the aircraft. One caught the avgas that leaked in a spreading pool on to the grass from the aircraft's fuel tanks. Suddenly the thing went up with a *woomph*, and a gigantic fireball of raging orange flame and filthy oil-black smoke billowed skywards. We felt the heat of the flames on our faces as we switched fire to the aircraft at the other end of the airfield.

'Fucking awesome,' I yelled over the noise of gunfire and explosions. 'Switch fire, 150 metres, at the aircraft on the left! Watch my tracer!' Bilbo spotted the rounds of tracer I was firing strike Pucara further up our side of the runway.

'Got it! On!' Bilbo yelled back. 'Switching fire.'

To our right, Paddy Armstrong was racing between the parked aircraft along the runway, placing the standard charges he'd made up in the cowls of the Pucara engines, where they would do most damage. He taped the charges in place, set the grip switches ready for firing and then moved on to the next aircraft, careful to select the exact same placement for the charges, to prevent subsequent cannibalization of the spares from one damaged aircraft being used to repair another. Around him, other members of the patrol were covering him and emptying magazines into the aircraft as they passed them.

The Turbo-Mentors also received explosive attention, from charges placed in the nose wheels and under the tail-planes. The machines Paddy was not working on were brassed up with machine-gun and rifle fire by John's and Phil's patrols. Those with underslung 40 mm launchers on their M16s were also firing off grenades at any aircraft within range. Other 66s were also being fired, no doubt punching more neat little holes through airframes.

The airfield was awash with a blaze of weapons fire, and another aircraft cooked off in a ball of flames, as tracer or grenades set off leaking fuel slicking in the grass. *Glamorgan*'s guns kept lobbing in shells, which were getting closer, as the naval gunfire spotter walked them in off First Mount towards the airstrip. I could see them landing not far behind two Pucaras on the edge of the airfield on our side of the strip, as we hammered away at them and a single Turbo-Mentor parked nearer to the burning Skyvan.

There was a lot of shit going down, and I am pretty sure that it was all ours. Cedric was pushing us on the radio to work with haste when another report came in that someone had been hit. 'Shit! Man down.' The call came in over the net from Phil; it turned out to be James. He had been struck by a splinter in the back of the leg. I caught something on the radio transmission from John back to Phil.

'Start extracting with your patrol and get the casualty back to the RV.'

'Roger out,' Phil replied.

Another voice on the radio. This time it was Cedric, ordering John to 'Break clean and fall back.' It was time to go.

'Sid, get your patrol back and follow Phil back to the RV as fast as you can.'

'Moving back now,' Sid shouted in reply and then to me: 'Splash, let's go.'

I relayed the order: 'Bilbo, Chris, cease fire, time to move.' They stopped firing and closed in on me, and then we doubled back the way we had come.

Paddy was racing back along the line of aircraft on the right-hand side of the runway, pausing at each of the charges he had placed to set off the attached grip switches. The brown plastic assembly ignited the black fuse cord crimped into the detonator, which Paddy had pre-inserted in each lump of explosive. Paddy had cut the fuses to allow for five to six minutes of burn time before the charges detonated. With the last of the grip switches initiated, it really was time to go, as the first fingers of dawn were already beginning to stroke at the darkness on the eastern horizon.

The remaining two patrols of the Troop began to close into John's position at the bottom of the main airstrip, as the rounds of naval gunfire began to creep across the airfield towards us. I was running to join them when the end of the runway seemed to disappear in a blinding flash of light and noise. BOOM!

The blast knocked me off my feet, and the air was filled with the acrid smell of burned explosive and falling debris. Chunks of earth and stone rained down on us, and everyone with a radio started shouting 'Check fire! Check fire!' I joined the chorus of alarm.

'Shit! What the fuck was that?'

'Must be a drop-short from the Navy,' Sid shouted as he picked himself up off the deck.

We were convinced that one of *Glamorgan*'s HE rounds had dropped short. In reality the Argies had finally sparked into life.

Remaining hidden during the assault, two Argentine Marines had concealed themselves in a trench dug into a gorse bush at the edge of the airstrip. Seeing us collect together, they must have fired off a set of command-wire-detonated explosive devices dug in across the runway. The buried explosive charges would have been placed to deny use of the airfield to enemy aircraft, but the opportunity to improvise and use them against us proved too good to miss. The rest of us shook ourselves off and got to our feet. One man from John's patrol stayed down. I heard him groaning. He was partially concussed when hit by a lump of rock thrown up in the explosion. Two blokes from John's patrol picked him up and began helping him back towards the RV.

Paddy emerged from the line of aircraft. He had also been blown off his feet by the blast, but not before he had managed to initiate the last of the demolition charges. He joined up with the rest of John's patrol as they started to withdraw. With ears still ringing from the blast, we followed. The extraction route back to the RV took us closer to the settlement.

The star shells and HE from *Glamorgan* had ceased. Other than the crackle of the fires from the burning aircraft and the sighing wind, the airfield had fallen silent behind us. The cluster of houses and farm sheds that made up the settlement was also quiet, except for the rhythmic hum of its generator. Darkness had returned, but the dawn was advancing. I could make out Phil's patrol ahead of us in the monochrome half-light, passing close to a large house on the forward edge of the settlement. James was limping as fast as he could, his arm across the shoulders of one of the team. We were hurrying to join them when all hell broke loose.

'Contact right!' someone shouted. 'Fucking get some fire down!'

Muzzle flashes, bright and angry, stabbed out towards us, as automatic fire ripped through what was left of the night. There were figures running and shouting in Spanish as they came round the side of the settlement. James went down. For a brief moment I thought he had been hit, then I noticed that he was returning fire. Everyone followed suit. Chris and Bilbo were quick on the Jimpy, and the reassuring thump of the machine gun joined with a cacophony of semi-automatic rifle fire. We were putting more rounds back than we were receiving. *Good, we were winning the firefight.*

There were more frantic shouts in Spanish. An Argie Marine waved his arms about – clearly the commander.

He attracted attention, and his shouts turned to screams when he was hit. Another one went down, and then that was it. As suddenly as it had started, it stopped. The surviving Marines dragged their wounded back with them as they beat a hasty retreat behind the cover of the buildings. There was no time to follow up after them. Now it really was time to go. Cedric's voice rang clear in the earpieces of our radios.

'Move out. Move out. Get back to the RV ASAP,' John shouted.

We dragged James and the other casualty back with us, across the vulnerable open ground of flat pasture with the settlement behind us. This was the time for the enemy to follow up against us properly, with their machine guns and support weapons, but there was nothing. We held our breath and pushed hard to get back to the RV, racing against the coming of the morning light and the passage of time. Both would expose us to a more concerted counter-attack from the enemy in the buildings behind us or from Argentine reinforcements arriving on the island.

As we put distance between us and the settlement, the humming sound of the generator receded, replaced by the noise of boots swishing through grass, now faster and more urgent than before. Then there was a crump of a small explosion from the direction of the airfield, followed by another and then another, as the fuses in Paddy's charges burned down into the detonators and set them off. I glanced over my left shoulder. The aircraft were obscured behind the ridge of higher ground, but balls of orange flame rolled above its crest into the fading night sky. Ammunition cooking off added to the growing sound of the devastation we had wrought. But there was no time to bask in the glow of satisfaction, the RV was still 200 metres away.

Lawrence Gallagher counted us in when we started to arrive. Still calm and reassuring, the big man offered some words of encouragement and ordered us into loading sticks by troop, ready to board the helicopters when they came.

'Come on, lads. Well done. Bloody awesome. Now shake out into your chalks and get ready for the aircraft.'

I noticed that he was covered in mud. The Squadron's mortar had dug itself almost up to its muzzle in the soft, boggy ground when it fired its first, and only, round during the attack, rendering it useless. Lawrence had spent most of the night helping Nige and the rest of the crew dig it out and had only just finished excavating it from the sticky, clinging peat. The pile of 81 mm bombs we had laboured so hard to carry in lay stacked in an unused heap. 'Those are staying behind,' Lawrence said to no one in particular.

*Thank fuck for that*, I thought.

The light was spilling in from the east as we crouched in lines ready for the pick-up. Our breath was visible as it condensed in the chilled air, before it was whipped away by a keen wind. But no one felt the cold. We were all buoyed up by the attack, adrenaline still pumping through our veins. Everyone had made it back to the RV. James had the thick wadding of a first field dressing strapped to his leg, and the other casualty was coming to. We had been lucky, but we weren't done yet. I glanced at my watch

213

for the last time that day; it told me that we were one minute to pick-up time.

Sixty seconds later, the sky was filled with the throbbing sound of approaching helicopters. 'Here come the fucking birds!' someone shouted, and then they were there. The four Sea Kings flared as they crossed the shoreline of Elephant Bay then hover-taxied over the dunes, one aircraft heading to each of the sticks of troops, doors open ready to receive us. We were already up. Moving towards them as soon as they landed, we scrambled on board. In thirty seconds we were loaded and ready to go.

Crewmen slid doors shut, and the aircraft lifted. Curled into a space near one of the port windows, with my back against the ribbed fuselage, I relaxed and exhaled hard as the adrenaline subsided and the balm of relief flushed through me. Pitching as the Sea King turned to make its flight out to sea, I caught a glimpse of aircraft burning brightly in the shadow of First Mount. Then the images were gone, as the nose of the helicopter dipped and it dropped down to wave-top height. We flew back out to HMS *Hermes* fast and low and in jubilant mood.

We were airborne for less than an hour. The pilots from 846 Squadron had been exceptional. They had flown throughout the night in difficult conditions at low level, using recently acquired, unfamiliar technology in the form of NVGs, but their navigation and timings had been spot on. They had certainly earned their flying pay that night.

Landing back on deck in daylight, we handed in our weapons to Wally in the armoury and went straight to breakfast. The whole ship's company seemed to be there when we entered the galley. A naval vessel is an all-informed unit, and the sailors knew something of what we had been about and that they had all been part of the risk in making Pebble Island possible. There were nods in our direction and a few handshakes.

The captain of *Hermes* came across the main broadcast as we joined the growing queue for the hotplate. When he announced the success of the raid in destroying the aircraft, the place erupted in cheering and clapping. To many of the matelots, it was one back for HMS *Sheffield*, and we were ushered to the front of the line to receive our food. Curiously, the captain made no mention of the radar. We hadn't seen anything resembling a radar the whole time that we had been on Pebble Island, which had been central to the Task Force commander's decision to take the risk of launching the raid. However, the Navy seemed more than happy with the destruction of eleven aircraft that had threatened the imminent amphibious operation and the morale-boosting impact of sticking it to the Argies by landing troops ashore.

The captain ended his announcement with a final 'well done' to D Squadron. 'Now,' he said, 'let's get the fuck out of here!'

With that he clicked off the microphone, and *Hermes* steamed at full speed back out to the open sea.

## 25

The raid on Pebble Island was a high point. It reset a sense of purpose within D Squadron, exorcizing the setbacks and mixed fortunes experienced on South Georgia. For the Task Force, it demonstrated that the force as a whole could reach out and strike the enemy on land as well as from the air and the sea. The destruction of eleven enemy aircraft had a material, as well as a moral, component to it; undoubtedly it saved lives by removing the Pucaras, but it was not the main event. The landings had been on everyone's lips for weeks, but when and where the amphibious operation to initiate the ground campaign that would recapture the Falklands would take place remained a closely guarded secret.

Based on intelligence and recce reports from G Squadron and the SBS, San Carlos Water on East Falkland had been confirmed by the Task Force as the preferred place to put British troops ashore on 10 May. Located close to the northern entrance of Falkland Sound, the enclosed inlet provided a deep-water anchorage with enough space for large amphibious assault ships and troop transports to offload men and equipment on to its beaches. Accessed by a narrow gap from the Sound and surrounded by rocky headlands on every side, it also offered shelter from the worst of the weather.

As the chosen landing site, San Carlos was a long way

from Port Stanley, the ultimate objective in the liberation of the islands. However, distance had its advantages. Landing 50 miles from the capital, where the Argies expected the Task Force to come ashore, made for an indirect approach. If the planners got it right, choosing San Carlos meant that the bulk of Argentine forces could be avoided, and the area would only be lightly defended. But, once again, time and the onset of winter remained the additional enemies to be considered.

Most of the warships in the fleet had already been working close to the limits of their endurance for weeks. Storm-lashed vessels, naval equipment and aircraft were feeling the effects of bad weather and the high tempo of conducting operations thousands of miles from their home bases. If the Task Force did not make the landings and recapture Stanley by the end of June, logistical difficulties, unserviceability and the harsh South Atlantic environment were likely to combine to defeat it. While landing at San Carlos made perfect tactical sense to the admiral and his planning staff, the landings would constitute a major escalation in the level of conflict and risk.

The decision needed approval from the politicians and military chain of command in London, which Admiral Sandy Woodward had been pushing for. On 18 May, he got it. Later the same day, the amphibious ships that would be needed to make the landing joined up with Woodward's carrier group, and the CO of the Regiment landed on board the admiral's flagship. Mike Rose had been party to the decision to select San Carlos Water from the beginning. During his passage south to join the Task Force aboard HMS *Fearless*, his regimental headquarters' planning cell had worked from the confines of a steel Portakabin lashed to the large flight deck of the amphibious assault ship to establish the role of the SAS in the forthcoming landings. The CO flew across to *Hermes* to tell Cedric what our part in the plan would be. He also came to tell us that we were now on the wrong ship.

The landings were scheduled to begin during the night on 20 May. The amphibious ships would detach from the carrier group of the Task Force in the late afternoon and would be escorted into San Carlos by HMS *Antrim* and six frigates using the cover of darkness. Logistics ships, landing craft and helicopters would then begin landing 3 Commando Brigade's five infantry units, of Paras and Marines, on to the beaches, along with their artillery and other supporting elements. Prior to the ships venturing into Falkland Sound, the SBS would attack and neutralize a company of enemy dug in on the high ground of Fanning Head. They were the only Argentine forces our SF patrols had observed in the vicinity of San Carlos. Although small in number, their position overlooked the narrow entrance of San Carlos Water to its north. It was an ideal location from which to report the approach of the amphibious group and engage it with their mortars and anti-tank recoilless rifles.

The only other enemy that might interfere with the landings was a force of 1,000-odd infantry, supported by artillery and Pucaras, located 20 miles to the south at the settlements of Darwin and Goose Green. Mike Rose briefed Cedric that his job was to use D Squadron to prevent that from happening and divert the enemy's attention away from San Carlos. Having given his intent, the CO left it to Cedric to decide the 'how' of implementing the task he had been set.

The imperative of operational security prevailed, and the rest of the Squadron had no inkling of any of this, other than the fact that we were about to move ships once again to relocate from *Hermes* to HMS *Intrepid*. We received the order to cross-desk to *Intrepid* just before midday.

D Squadron's move to the second of the Royal Navy's assault landing ships was part of a decision to redistribute units across the amphibious force to ensure it was properly combat loaded, so that the troops would be ready to fight straight off the ships before they dropped anchor in San Carlos. Risk was another reason to alter the tactical configuration of the embarked land forces. Three of the landing force's units, 40 and 42 Commando, plus 3 PARA, had steamed from the UK aboard the requisitioned cruise liner SS *Canberra*. The risk of having so many troops on one single ship entering the narrow waters of the landing area was considered too great by the chain of command in London. Consequently, the Task Force was ordered to cross-deck 40 Commando to *Fearless* and 3 PARA to *Intrepid*. It would be a huge undertaking, requiring the use of landing craft and helicopters from across the fleet to move 2,000 men and their equipment between ships and have them in place by the time the amphibious group started its journey towards the Falklands. It would also be a perilous undertaking if it had to be conducted across stormy seas.

The weather on 18 May had been bad. When dawn broke the next morning, the high seas and winds of the previous day had abated, to be replaced by a gentler rolling swell of foam-streaked waves and a slackening breeze.

Most of the Squadron's kit had been stored in a bay area on *Hermes'* hangar deck. It would be an all hands to the pump affair to cart it on to the aircraft elevator to lift it to the flight deck, Gemini engines and all, then load it on to Sea Kings to be flown across to the assault ship. The process started after lunch. Most of the blokes headed to the hangar, but Bilbo, Alex Brown, Jimmy Clyde and I were detailed to move the Squadron's ammunition, which was stored in a small arms locker area in *Hermes'* magazine, located in the very bowels of the ship. Before passing Selection and joining the Squadron, Jimmy had been in the RAF Regiment and hailed from Ulster.

We spent the rest of the afternoon humping heavy liners of 7.62 mm link, each containing 800 rounds of belted machine-gun ammunition and weighing over 30 lbs, as well as even heavier metal cases packed with grenades, bandoliers of 5.56 mm bullets, 66s and 81 mm mortar bombs. Each box had to be manhandled on to a small dumb-waiter-type lift, which then carried each batch several decks up to the flight deck, where more of the blokes stacked it ready to be loaded on to the helicopters with the rest of the stores, when an aircraft came in to collect it.

It was back-breaking work, which lasted for several hours. The only respite came in the form of an unwelcome air raid warning. The four of us were sweating in T-shirts under the harsh glare of the magazine's artificial lighting when the intercom piped the possible approach of enemy aircraft. We paused, looked at each other, grabbed our anti-flash and made to get to our action station position two decks up. The urgent clanging of metal clipping fast over metal on the decks above us stopped us in our tracks. Heavy, watertight Zulu hatches were being bolted home. The significance of being locked down well below the waterline at the bottom of the ship wasn't lost on any of us. Casting his eyes upwards, Alex summed it up succinctly: 'Oh fuck.'

'Do you think they have forgotten us?' I asked.

'Ah, we could just have a wee problem,' Jimmy said in his broad Belfast accent as he sat back down heavily on one of the ammunition containers. 'I doubt that they even know we are here. And even if they did and the ship gets blatted, we wouldn't stand a chance down here.'

'As I said,' interjected Alex, 'oh fuck.'

The air raid lasted for thirty minutes, which was plenty of time to reflect on our mortality. The 'all clear' and unclasping of the hatches above us provoked a collective sigh of relief before we went back to the task. It was getting towards dark by the time we had loaded the last container of ammunition and made our way up on to the flight deck, pausing only to grab our weapons and kit from the mess decks.

The breeze was slight, but it was bitterly cold, and my smock did little to keep out the biting edge of the wind, although, after several sweat-dripping hours of labour just above the ship's keel and the risk of entrapment below the waterline, it was good to breathe the sea air. A Sea King was turning and burning on the deck, some of the last loads of equipment, stores and ammunition were being passed hand-over-hand through the troop door on the aircraft's right-hand side. Ahead of me, Bilbo and Jimmy were called forward with a nod from the crewman, then the helicopter lifted. It didn't have far to go. I could see *Intrepid* clearly through the gathering gloom a half mile or so off from *Hermes* on the port beam, riding gently on the swell. I was keen to get across, find a bed space, get sorted and grab something to eat after hours of humping and dumping ammunition.

Another Sea King settled on the flight deck. I joined the chain to load the rest of the kit, then stood in line just behind Lawrence Gallagher and Sid Davidson, waiting my turn to climb in. Alex Brown and Chris Seakins were up ahead of me and piled into the cab. By the time I got to the door, the helicopter looked full. Too full. Every part of the interior was jam-packed with men and equipment, from the space behind the pilots to the tail-plane. So I stepped back and shouted to the crewman above the noise of the engine that I would wait for the next lift.

It was the same Royal Marine corporal who had crewed the back of the Sea King that took us in and out of Pebble Island. He shook his head, shouting to be heard above the noise of the engines, 'This is the last lift of the day, and we are not coming back. You need to get on this one.'

'OK,' I shouted back and began climbing on to the aircraft.

Clambering over ammunition carriers, boxes of rations and large silver steel Alcon containers, I wedged myself next to Lawrence and Sid near the back of the helicopter on its left-hand side. Sitting shoulder to shoulder, we shuffled up as best we could to make space for the Marine crewman to lever himself in behind the door-mounted

GPMG. He half closed the troop door as the helicopter cranked on the power and climbed into a vertical hover above *Hermes*, turned and then dipped towards the sea, as the curtain of nightfall drew itself across the ocean.

The inky blackness had closed in over the waves below us as we headed to *Intrepid*. It had been a long day. My thoughts were full of the comfort of a warm ship, and I was thinking, *There might be time to get on board, have a shower and find a beer in the NAAFI before getting my head down.* That prospect seemed tantalizingly closer as we came over the stern of the assault ship and flared to land from its port side.

The size of two tennis courts, the flight deck was illuminated dimly by light spilling out from the open hangar and the subdued glow of the deck lights. Through the half-open door of our helicopter, I could make out the silhouetted outline of another Sea King with rotors turning, which was already on the landing platform. Beyond it, towards the hangar, sat a high-stacked jumbled line of the Squadron's stores, equipment and ammunition, which crowded the flight deck further. A helmeted Flight Deck Officer emerged from the shadows, his yellow-coloured surcoat noticeable in the ambient light. He started to wave the pilot of our Sea King off. There was no space to land. I felt the attitude of the aircraft change as the pilot banked into a wide, low turn to burn time before coming back in again when the deck was clear. The shower and that beer would have to wait.

I shouted out to Sid, 'Fucking great. I bloody hate flying in these helicopters. I wish they would just put us the fuck down.'

I didn't have time to hear Sid's response. There was a distinct thump and an immediate winding-down of the engines. To me it felt like an express train suddenly pulling on its brakes. I was thrown forward, and the next thing I knew was that we were in the sea and under the water.

The Sea King was designed to float if it made a controlled emergency hover landing over water, but there was nothing controlled about the way we hit the surface of the sea. Striking the water in an involuntary dive, we didn't stand a chance.

The helicopter turned on to its side as it struck the surface. Its spinning rotor blades thrashed into the waves, biting deep into the water, as the weight of the roof-mounted engines rolled the airframe over and forced it beneath the rising swell. The troop door imploded in a wall of freezing white water, flooding the troop compartment from the floor to the ceiling. It all happened in an instant, but somehow I managed to snatch a lungful of air as we turned upside down and went under.

I struggled to hold my breath as the shock of the cold water hit me like a blow from a piledriver. Somehow I fought off the near-overpowering sensory overload as the world closed in to become a frantic, frenzied jumble of entwined kit, legs and arms thrashing around for survival like fish caught in a barrel.

When inverted and trapped in a flooded compartment, the body and mind need a visible or physical point of reference to indicate the way to an exit. On that night in the back of that helicopter there was none. Wearing heavy belt-kit, jammed tight together and trapped under the water in a confusion of weapons and boxes of stores, we could see no orientation and no obvious way out. Each one of us was fighting with primal urgency to live in a cauldron of freezing darkness and terror. As men exhaled, the desperate sound of their last breath was attenuated through the sea-filled interior. We clawed in the water for some means of impossible escape. I could feel Sid and Lawrence as their bodies twisted against mine in their struggle for life.

Time seemed to slow down, but the frantic convulsing of those around me began to subside. I could sense that Lawrence and Sid had stilled, their life breath gone. I felt my own body shutting down. My mind was a blur of panic and fear. *Fuck, fuck, I am losing the fight to stay alive and I am going to die.*

My chest burned with the pain of holding my breath. Struggling to keep my mouth clamped shut I knew that I was about to let the water flood into my lungs and surrender myself to the sea. Then the overturned aircraft shifted. Hit by a rolling wave, the airframe rode bodily upwards, causing the water inside to shift, somehow creating an air pocket. My head broke through the surface. I groaned as I exhaled and then snatched in another desperate gulp of air. Nothing else moved in the aircraft. I was alone and alive in the darkness, but I was facing backwards to the rear. I could make out the small, dark outline of a ship in the distance, caught against the ambient light of the horizon visible through a hole torn in the fuselage where the helicopter's tail-plane had been. I now had a point of reference to fix on. And a means of escape.

The weakest point of the structure of a helicopter is

where the tail joins the main body of the aircraft. Ours had sheared off from the impact. I saw my chance, and pure survival mode kicked back in with purpose. *I am not going to die*, I thought. Seizing another lungful of air, I ducked back under the surface and pushed through the water, pulling myself through kit and a wall of motionless bodies, as I half swam and half clawed my way towards the hole in the back of the aircraft in a frenzied bid for life.

I got to the ruptured tail-section and squeezed myself into its narrowing confines, making for the point where it had broken off, barely a shoulder width wide. I wriggled forwards and upwards, ignoring shards of twisted metal that cut into my head. Then my waist stuck, wedged fast by the stuffed pouches of my belt kit. I could progress no further. *Fuck, fuck, fuck, I can't move, I am stuck*, panic again confusing my thinking. I was wedged fast by the narrowing sides of what was left of the broken tail boom, unable to move as the aircraft shifted again and began to tip and slide backwards beneath the waves. Panic almost overtook me and threatened to defeat the will to live. Then a flash of clarity. I'd tailor-made my own belt kit for exactly a situation as urgent as this. Instinct honed by a thousand drilled movements took over.

Reaching down with my right hand, I grasped the quick-release strap that I had sewn into my belt order, as a customized replacement for the standard fastening clip. I yanked it open, pushing off my shoulder straps at the same time with my left hand. If I had been using the general-issue fastening on the belt, I would have been dead.

Free of the heavy, trapping kit that threatened to arrest

my escape, I pushed up through the remaining part of the tail section, contorting, ignoring more cuts, as it continued to tighten. Then my head and shoulders emerged through the jagged gap. The fuselage groaned and shifted again below me, threatening one last time to pull me back with it. In one huge, final effort I flopped out of the broken tail section of the helicopter and dropped a few feet into the open sea.

# 26

I surfaced again, and for a moment the cold of the water hardly mattered. I kicked my legs, my body moving upwards and downwards with the rising and falling swell, as I sucked in the spray-filled air and grabbed for a foam seat cover floating near where I came up for air. It would give me vital additional buoyancy as the deadly muscle-numbing chill of the freezing water began to sap my strength.

I thought that I must be the only survivor, until I bobbed up on the crest of a wave and saw the others. Forty or 50 metres off to my right through the darkness, I could make out a cluster of other bobbing heads. People in the water, lost to me in the crush as we crashed and turned over, but fortunate enough to have sat close to the emergency exits. The only thing that had given them a shot at survival. But if I was anything to go by, none of them would be wearing life-preservers.

Pushing my own makeshift buoyancy aid in front of me, I struck out towards them. The distance was less than two lengths of a standard swimming pool, but the effort of swimming through the freezing sea in soaking wet clothing and boots heavy with water was arduous in the extreme. My feet felt like they had weights attached to them, my clothes sucked at my limbs and I willed myself to keep going as I slowly made progress through a swell rising and falling 7 or 8 feet. Then they saw me. Voices called out to me through the darkness as I approached, offering encouragement and indicating their location.

'Oi, over here, mate, keep coming, keep coming.'

There were eight people in the water, including the two pilots clinging to the sides of a one-person aircrew survival dinghy. Each pilot was issued with one of the small inflatable craft as part of their survival packs. They clipped into them when strapping into their seats, so that the survival kit would leave with them when they exited the aircraft in an emergency, and the dinghy would automatically inflate when it came into contact with water.

James, Alex and Chris were there. Chris had somehow got hold of a life jacket. Hands reached out towards me and pulled me close into the inflatable. I grabbed the sides, letting go of my seat cushion and wrapping one of the straps hanging from the dinghy around my wrist. Besides the pilots, there were also two attached medics and a signaller holding on with us, but James, Alex, Chris and I were the only badged members of the Regiment present.

'Is this it?' I exclaimed.

'I think so,' said Alex, his teeth chattering with the cold, 'you must have been the last to get out.'

But the full-scale shock of the enormity of the loss we had just suffered would come later. The only imperative now was to survive. It was desperately cold. The pilots were the only people wearing goon suits – rubber immersion garments worn under their flying overalls that would hold off the worst effects of it for a time. But they were only issued to aircrew, and time was ticking faster for those of us without them.

'Fuck, it's cold. We need to get picked up soon or we are dead,' said James.

The average person can survive for between five to twenty minutes in a sea temperature of 5 degrees centigrade. The temperature of the sea we crashed into was just above freezing. We were exceeding expectations. However, the signs of advancing hypothermia were already upon us. Unable to generate heat to compensate for the loss of body warmth, all of us were shaking uncontrollably and hyperventilating involuntarily from cold stress and temperature shock. But our bodies were already slowing down. Our speech was becoming slurred and stuttering, our movements more confused, laboured and clumsy, as our core temperatures plummeted, and our heart rates reduced. With every passing minute we spent in the water we were losing the battle to retain heat, unable to check the blood that was retreating from the extremities, weakening muscles, draining strength and impeding coordination. We were freezing alive.

'Why don't we k-k-kick our l-l-legs to keep our c-circulation going?' Alex suggested, his words distorted.

'That's a b-b-bad idea,' said James in a cold-induced stutter, 'it will only dispel any warmer water trapped inside our clothes.'

'Yeah, James is r-r-right,' I said. 'Fuck off, Alex, and keep your b-b-barking ideas to yourself.'

'Fuck off, you h-h-hat,' gasped Alex, 'I was only trying t-t-to help.'

If the situation hadn't been so desperate, we might

have laughed. We had to keep our arms and legs pressed tight to the body, to minimize surface exposure and prevent the loss of any accumulation of mildly warmer water.

James came up with a better suggestion. 'Get a f-f-flare up,' he said to one of the pilots.

The aircrewman groped into a valise on the side of the raft and pulled out a small red plastic pistol. He fumbled as he tried to load it and dropped the pistol into the water.

'For fuck's sake, man,' Chris cursed.

The pilot fished the flare pistol out of the sea and loaded a cartridge with freezing fingers. Snapping it shut, he stretched it out over his head and pulled the trigger. Nothing happened. Another cartridge was loaded, and again nothing happened.

'Fucking hell!' More cursing, this time from more people and with more edge to it.

The pilot loaded a third time. There was a short, low pop and the Very flare arced out into the darkness in a climbing trail of red. We watched it as it seemed to hang for a moment and then burst brighter into a star of light, before fading as it began to burn out in the blackness of the sky.

There was no visible horizon, and we couldn't see any ships; the one that I had seen from the inside of the helicopter had disappeared. *Perhaps it's been obscured by the waves? Perhaps we have drifted? Maybe we are lost?* I began to wonder whether anyone was coming when I caught the unmistakeable sound of a Sea King helicopter beating low over the waves. Dark thoughts were dispelled by a surge of adrenaline.

The aircraft swept in low, passing right above us, but it

didn't stop. One of the non-badged survivors cried out, 'Come back, come back, don't leave us!'

But making a dead stop right over our position in the dark was never a likely option. With the pilots of the downed Sea King we offered reassurance to the stricken man. We told him that we had been seen and the search and rescue helicopter would be coming back to get us. A minute passed before it returned. Hovering above us, it lowered down a strop from a winch. One of the non-badged blokes was winched up first. The painter of the dinghy was still attached to one of his wrists, so the inflatable was lifted clear out of the water as he ascended towards the helicopter, provoking a moment of farce. The rest of us were pulled upwards as a wretched clinging mass of humanity, until the cord snapped and dumped us with an inelegant slap back down into the water.

'Fucking crap hats!' Alex shouted as he hit the water, and it would have made for an inauspicious start to our rescue, had it not been for the timely arrival of an inflatable RHIB from HMS *Brilliant*.

I was the first one that they pulled out of the water. Strong, steady hands lifted me up and over the side of the large twelve-man RHIB. I could hear the crew telling me, 'OK, mate, we have got you, you are going to be all right. Just hang on and we will get you back to the ship.'

Up until that point I had been totally lucid, but as I landed in the bottom of the boat in a tangle of frozen limbs, I immediately passed out. Of the seven of us recovered by the RHIB, every other man also lost consciousness at the moment they were rescued. It was a natural reaction to an extreme hypothermic condition, when the mind and body finally gives in to the cold. Another ten minutes in the sea and we'd have started dying. However, we were not yet out of the woods.

Ultimate survival from severe hypothermic exposure depends on how fast you can rewarm the casualty, and time matters. The sense of urgency to get us back to the ship and begin the warming process was not lost on the coxswain, who opened the throttle and roared back to *Brilliant*. It must have taken no more than a few minutes before we were under the stern of the frigate and being winched on to the quarter-deck by a boom hoist one at a time. I regained consciousness when I landed on the deck. I had been wrapped in a blanket and looked back over the side as two sailors picked me up. Out-to-sea searchlights criss-crossed the surface of the water in a desperate bid to find more survivors, but it turned out to be a forlorn hope. Most of the men had died inside the Sea King and were taken to the bottom of the South Atlantic when the helicopter sank beneath the waves. I didn't know it for sure at the time, but I sensed they were gone and then I blacked out again and was carried down into the sickbay.

Some of the blokes from the Squadron were on *Intrepid*'s flight deck and saw the Sea King go down. Billy Ratcliff had recently joined the Squadron by blagging his way down to the Falklands, having convinced the CO that he spoke Spanish, which was enough to persuade Mike Rose to allow him to return to the Regiment from a detached duty posting. Billy had just got off the chopper on the flight deck in front of us when he heard someone shout, 'My God. She's gone down.' At the same time the ship's klaxon sounded, and an urgent voice came through the pipes: 'Aircraft ditched. Crash teams, close up! Aircraft ditched. Crash teams, close up!'

Some of the blokes were inside the ship talking to the Toms from 3 PARA when they heard the alarm and raced up on to the deck. Cedric and Danny were in the wardroom when they heard the tannoy announcement. They didn't immediately make the connection that the helicopter might have some of our people on it. Ditching helicopters had become a near-routine occurrence since the Task Force had sailed, and he assumed that it must have been an ASW aircraft on one of the constant anti-submarine patrols. It was Roger Edwards, our naval liaison officer, who came and told them. Cedric headed up to the bridge with Roger. By the time he got there, rescue boats had been launched, and the Sea King that responded to the incident had arrived on the scene and was hovering above us. Danny was already preparing to begin the grim task of marrying up who might have been on board with the reports of survivors – to start the process of working out who had lived and who had died.

Some of the blokes leaned over handrails and strained their eyes out into the pitch darkness, vainly looking for a sign – anything that might indicate that their mates were alive. Apart from the searchlights, there was nothing to see. Some felt the rescue had taken too long, but in truth the Navy took great risks in doing all they could to get to the survivors, as the beams of light must have been visible for miles, and no effort was spared. The blokes' frustrations were understandable. Powerless to help, they could do nothing but wait, desperate for news, wondering about the fate of their friends. In the end only one body was recovered from the crash and brought on board *Intrepid*. Dave Love had been killed instantly, when he was hit by the heavy metal of the machine gun mounted in the doorway. He was the Royal Marine aircrewman that I had been speaking to just before I got on the helicopter. He was twenty-two years old.

I came to again on *Brilliant*, standing naked in a warm shower and held up by a matelot who was rubbing my thigh muscles. I don't imagine that he was enjoying the experience any more than me. I felt shit, which had nothing to do with the effort to restore the circulation in my limbs. I was washed out by what had happened, as if every ounce of energy and all my mental capacity had been sucked out of me by the struggle to survive. My main concern now was the caustic gagging taste of aviation fuel that seemed to slick the insides of my mouth and throat. I hadn't noticed it when in the sea, but now the heavy kerosene-based liquid seemed to have permeated the soft tissue of my palate. I was desperate to get rid of the taste of it.

'Mate,' I said in a groggy voice, 'I need some water.'

'It's all right, mate,' the matelot replied. 'I will get you a nice hot cup of tea.'

They fed me hot, sickly-sweet tea when I was moved back to the sickbay, but all I wanted was water to rid myself of the foulness that polluted my mouth. Still insisting on water, I was dressed in spare sailors' rig of dark cotton trousers, a blue shirt and a heavy navy-blue jumper, with a pair of white plimsoles for my feet. I didn't know what had happened to my own clothes, but I didn't care at that moment in time, as I was fixated by the need to drink water to flush away the biting tang of AVGAS.

The medics had stitched up several gashes on my head and wrapped me in blankets, as part of the vital reheating process along with the tea. But despite being dressed and swaddled I just couldn't get warm, and my body shivered uncontrollably. By the time I had come to, I also noticed that the base of my neck hurt like hell. The ship's surgeon checked me out.

'I think you might have broken your neck,' the doctor said. 'Can you move it?'

'Yes, but I just need some water to wash out my mouth.'

'OK, I will fix you up with a neck-brace and then will get one of the medics to make you some tea,' he said.

'Oh Christ,' I groaned, as a thick white supportive surgical collar was fastened round my neck.

I was not the only one injured in the crash. Chris had broken his arm, and one of the pilots had fractured his ankle when he kicked open his crew door. The only other injury from the crash was a broken collarbone sustained by Alex. Although uninjured in the helicopter, James was still suffering from the splinter in his leg that he had picked up during the raid on Pebble Island.

I continued to shake as we were bedded down in the petty officers' mess deck. The senior naval ratings had given up their beds for us, so that we could get an unbroken night's sleep. I lay in my bunk, still feeling numb and frozen to the core, when a couple of POs came into their vacated quarters. The two men didn't say much – there was probably nothing much they could have said anyway. They dragged a large plywood MFO box behind them. It was full of hardcore pornography. Given the state we were in, I am not sure quite what they expected us to do with it. They looked a little uncomfortable and then departed, leaving their treasured stash of grot on the middle of the deck. As well as surrendering their bunks, it was their way of acknowledging what we had been through and that we had taken losses.

After the lights on the mess deck were switched off, I lay in the darkness. Still shivering below a mass of blankets and nauseous from the lingering aftertaste of aviation fuel in my mouth, I struggled to process the magnitude of what had just befallen us. My head was still befuddled and I struggled to shift it out of its default setting of pure survival. For a flickering moment I thought there might be a chance that others had made it out of the helicopter and had been picked up by different ships. *Perhaps, like us, they were now tucked up in bunks somewhere else among the Task Force.* But deep down I knew that I must have been the last one out of the helicopter.

There would be no more survivors, and the Navy had done all it could do. I tried to form, and then tick off, a mental list of those that might have been on the helicopter from D Squadron. In my semi-confused state, it was too much for me. But I knew that too many good men had died that day. We had formed friendships that would have endured through the years into the future, but now they were gone. I thought of Sid and Lawrence and it dawned on me that the likes of Paddy Armstrong, Phil Currass and Lofty Arthy must also have been on board. Most had been from Mountain Troop, and no one who had been in both helicopter crashes on the Fortuna Glacier had survived this one. *Christ, it was all too much*, I thought, as I longed for the blanketing balm of sleep. From somewhere on the mess deck, one of the medics or the signaller wailed and moaned in the darkness. I closed my eyes; it was going to be a long night.

# 27

When the Sea King went down on 19 May, the Regiment suffered its biggest single loss of personnel since the Second World War. In total twenty-two men died in the helicopter crash. Between them, D and G Squadron lost twenty men, which was greater than the number of casualties incurred during the Borneo and Radfan campaigns put together.

As well as Corporal Dave Love, the only body recovered from the scene, Flight Lieutenant Garth Hawkins, who had been attached to D Squadron from the RAF as our forward air controller, was among the victims. Paddy O'Connor, who had parachuted into the sea and provided us with some instruction on how to use a Stinger, was one of the G Squadron blokes who died. He would now never get to say goodbye to his wife and kids. Wally Walpole, who worked with Graham in the stores, had also gone down in the helicopter. But of all the men killed, 19 Troop took the biggest hit. With the loss of Phil Currass, John Arthy and Sid Davidson, all the Mountain Troop senior NCOs had been killed in a stroke. When the death of Paddy Armstrong and the state Chris, Alex, James and I were in were taken into account, the Troop had lost just over fifty per cent of its strength.

I woke from a fitful night's sleep to the sound of the soft hum of the ship's ventilator and the rhythmic throb of the engines, as their screws made steady progress through the sea. For an instant everything seemed normal. My brain was still clouded, as if I had been having a dream. But then, as I began to slowly take in my surroundings, I remembered the enormity of what had happened to us.

Others around me stirred, stretching stiff limbs, yawning and wiping the night's sleep from their eyes. Initially, nobody spoke. It was as if we were suffering from some enormous collective hangover. The clothes we had been wearing when we went down had been laundered and were placed folded neatly at the end of our bunks. We got dressed, back into T-shirts, smocks, jungle trousers and boots, before making our way to the galley.

The four of us sat together, the food slowly revitalizing us, as our brains began to function more normally again. Over breakfast we began to talk, gradually piecing it all together and what it meant. There had been no news of other survivors being picked up and no expectation that there would be. Initially, the focus was on who had been in the helicopter with us, but our conversation soon turned to how each of us got out and what we thought might have happened to cause the helicopter to go down.

'I thought you were a goner, Splash. You must have been the last one out.'

'I thought I was too, James.' And I told them about the wave that hit the helicopter and how it had revealed an escape route via the broken tail.

'Jesus, man. You were lucky,' James said. 'Alex and I were sitting by the forward crew door behind the pilots, which must have been jettisoned almost as soon as we hit the water. We saw the opening and just went for it. But Chris, you were further back, so how the fuck did you get out?'

'I was sitting on some of the stores, and there was so little room that I was pressed up hard against the domed Perspex window on the port side. Just before we got on the heli, some matelot picked up a buckshee life preserver he found on the deck and gave it to me. When the heli hit and the water came in, I pulled the inflation tab. The next thing I knew, I was being sucked through the window and bobbed up on the surface. The Perspex must have popped out with the sudden pressure of the preserver inflating against it . . .' Chris paused. 'Shit, I nearly didn't put it on.'

'Why the hell did it go down?' Alex said.

'I haven't got a scoobies, mate,' I replied. 'Maybe it lost an engine? Maybe the crew lost the horizon? It was as black as a witch's tit out there. Fucking helicopters, they're dangerous bits of kit.'

In truth none of us had any idea why the helicopter went into the sea. It might have been the result of a bird strike. The carcass of an albatross was discovered floating near the scene of the crash. Subsequent investigation suggested that the large seabird had been sucked into one of the Sea King's engine air-intakes, causing it to shut down, which might have explained the mechanical clunk some survivors heard just before the aircraft went in. The crash might also have been the result of a simple accident or mechanical failure. In pitch darkness, without NVGs and with no discernible horizon, the pilots would have been flying on instruments. If they lost sight of the visual reference of *Intrepid*'s flight deck, going round again in complete blackness at low level would have been a flying manoeuvre that was fraught with risk, especially for an aircrew that had been flying all day and who were operating in a state of fatigue and at flying condition limits.

Whatever the cause, accidents are part of the bloody business of war. For all our speculation, as we sat together in *Brilliant*'s galley, it was a harsh reality that all four of us accepted as soldiers.

On *Intrepid* the Squadron had spent the night working out, with ever-growing certainty, who had lived and who had died. Once the rescue effort had been called off, Cedric and Danny were able to complete the grim process of compiling a list of the casualties and file a notification report for Regimental headquarters.

The sheet with the names of the Squadron's personnel had two columns. Everyone's name was entered into the column on the left of the page. Once they were accounted for as being on board *Intrepid* or picked up from the crash site, their names were moved to a column on the right. Those that remained on the left-hand side of Danny's list were dead. Cedric used the Tacsat to speak personally to Mike Rose, telling him the names of every man who had been lost. That information, along with the names of the men from G Squadron who had also been lost in the Sea King, was then beamed back to the UK by satellite link.

Eight thousand miles away, the casualty notification report was being acted upon in Hereford, as the solemn procedures for informing the next of kin were initiated.

Liz was one of many wives who received a telephone call from Stirling Lines, asking her to report to the gym in camp later that morning. When Liz got there, she found out that she was one of the lucky ones. The collective gathering of spouses was told that if they were present, then their husbands were OK. As they listened, shocked by what they were hearing, they went through their own grim process of deducing who had died from the wives who weren't there. It was a necessarily blunt, but effective, way of ensuring that those spouses who had lost husbands could be personally informed by the Regiment's casualty visiting officers, and that they were properly supported by the unit's welfare team and the padre.

After breakfast, we spent the morning passing on what we knew about who had been on the Sea King to a petty officer detailed to look after us. I doubt it did any more than confirm what the head shed on HMS *Intrepid* had already established. We spent the rest of the day returning to the galley for meals and leafing through the matelots' MFO treasure trove of explicit grot. Its loan had seemed a little incongruous, given the circumstances, but it helped to pass the time and distract us from darker thoughts. There had been no word from the Squadron, but that afternoon we were told that we were due to be moved from *Brilliant* to a hospital facility that had been set up on the SS *Canberra*.

The P&O cruise liner was one of the fifty-four civilian ships taken up from trade, or STUFT for short, which were requisitioned by the government to support the Task Force. As well as being converted to act as a casualty-receiving hospital, the ship had also been brought into service to act as a transport for the 2,000 troops of 3 Commando Brigade, who had been cross-decked to the Navy's assault landing ships the previous day.

It was dusk by the time that we were called up to *Brilliant*'s flight deck. In view of our own recent experience of cross-decking between ships, we were given bright-red immersion suits for the short flight to *Canberra*. We pulled them on over our clothes and fastened them by means of a large zip running diagonally across our backs, before making our way to the frigate's stern. The rotor blades of two Wasp helicopters were turning on the pad when we got there.

A crewman strapped us in. 'Sorry that we are asking you to make another flight,' he said, no doubt conscious that we had also been involved in the helicopter crashes on Fortuna.

'No worries – nine lives and all that,' I said weakly, suppressing my true feelings about climbing back into a helicopter.

He gave me a thumbs-up and slid the door shut, and we lifted from the deck. The sea state was relatively calm, the waves rising 5 to 6 feet in the swell beneath us, little different to the conditions the day before, when we had taken off from *Hermes*. As I looked down on the green-grey swelling mass of water, I thought of lost comrades lying somewhere beneath the depths, lost for ever in the wreckage of the Sea King.

We had only been in the air for a few minutes before we were coming in to land on one of *Canberra*'s new helicopter pads. Fashioned from steel deck plates welded on to the superstructure amidships, over what had once been a swimming pool, it was one of three platforms that had been added as part of a hasty conversion into a troop ship before sailing from Southampton. Nicknamed the 'Great White Whale' by the Task Force, even in the fading light she looked impressive. The distinctive white paint job, just the ticket for cruising the high seas and making an impression at overseas ports, was stained orange with rust.

Though battered by the sea, at 44,000 tonnes and 818 feet long, the liner retained a majesty not shared by the surrounding battleship-grey warships. Concentrated forward of the *Canberra*'s two iconic yellow funnels, the midship flight deck provided the closest entry point to the casualty receiving area, which was located on the games deck towards the ship's bow. We zipped out of our immersion suits and handed them back to the Wasp crews before being guided down a flight of metal steps to what our guide referred to as the 'Stadium'.

Originally a promenade deck for the exclusive use of first-class passengers in evening dress, it was now being used as a triage area, operating theatre and post-op recovery ward. Each of the functional areas of the Stadium had been screened with arctic camouflage netting and was absent of patients, save for an unfortunate naval rating who had fallen through a Zulu hatch. I suspected that the attendant medical staff of doctors and surgeons were anticipating being a lot busier once the landings commenced. We were examined by doctors, who didn't seem to have the faintest idea of what had happened to us. As

I sat naked on a medical couch, the white-coated medic examining me sucked his teeth.

'How did you come by such nasty cuts on your head?' he asked.

'In a helicopter crash.'

He said something like, 'Ooh, that sounds nasty,' but I didn't bother to enlighten him further.

The pain in my neck had eased, although the doctor didn't seem too bothered about it, telling me to keep the neck-brace on for the time being. Having had the wounds on my head tidied up, I was allowed to get dressed before being ushered over to another screened-off area to see a psychiatrist.

In a soothing Irish brogue, a silver-haired naval surgeon commander explained that it was standard procedure for all evacuees to undergo psychiatric screening, regardless of their injury or circumstances. I didn't like the sound of the word 'evacuee'. There was also nothing soothing in what he was about to tell me. When I had answered a couple of his questions about my mental well-being, he started talking about repatriation.

'What do you mean, sir?' I asked, still not entirely sure what he was driving at.

'You are going to be evacuated, corporal, via the Task Force hospital ship SS *Uganda* to Montevideo in Uruguay and then on to the UK by aircraft.' He sounded as if I ought to be pleased. I wasn't. He looked at me quizzically. 'But, corporal, you have suffered a great trauma, to be sure.' He knew about the Sea King.

'Sir, I am perfectly OK and I want to go back to my Squadron.' I cursed inwardly as I fingered the thick white surgical collar around my neck, regretting that I hadn't taken it off: it hardly engendered a picture of perfect health.

The soft-spoken Irishman gave me a beguiling smile and said, 'No, corporal, I think it is for the best that you go home.'

I half expected him to say, 'For you the war is over, my friend.' But he didn't. As far as he was concerned, I was going back, and that was the end of it.

As far as I was concerned, injured or not, I was buggered. The Geneva Convention prohibits the return of troops to a combat zone from a neutral country. Once I was transferred aboard the *Uganda*, I would be as good as home, despite the 8,000 miles still to travel to get back to the UK. I was feeling decidedly dispirited as I bedded down on a mattress on the floor of the Stadium that night. Of the four of us, I was the least badly injured. I surmised that my neck was probably just whiplash, and the cuts on my head, although 'nasty', weren't serious. Alex and Chris had broken bones, and James still had the piece of shrapnel stuck in his leg from Pebble Island. I alone was fit enough to return to the Squadron, but I was about to be sent home.

As I went to sleep in high dudgeon later that evening, the amphibious element of the Task Force had already detached from the carrier group and was beginning to make its final approach to the shores of the Falkland Islands. The ships of the amphibious group, with *Canberra* in their midst, steamed through the night at a steady speed of 12 knots to cover the 150 miles to their station in San Carlos Water, from where the landings would begin in the early hours of 21 May. The armada of escorting warships, transport ships and logistic landing vessels sailed under the cover of a blanket of fog and low cloud.

As they approached the northern entrance to Falkland Sound, the SBS attacked and neutralized the enemy company occupying Fanning Head. Around the same time as the SBS were dealing with the position that dominated San Carlos Water, D Squadron launched its diversionary attack on the Argentine garrison at Darwin, creating the impression that the Argies were under an assault from at least a battalion of British troops and drawing attention away from the amphibious operation 20 miles to the north.

While I was still asleep, Para and Marine units of 3 Commando Brigade began disembarking from the assault ships by landing craft. The LCUs then headed towards the beaches, where the troops began to wade ashore, unmolested by Argentine Pucaras. The ships had slipped into the anchorage undetected by the enemy, and, as I woke up on my mattress in the Stadium, D Squadron were already making their long tab back from the Darwin isthmus. The Paras and Bootnecks were already digging in on their objectives and preparing for the Argentine response, which was bound to come as daylight revealed the presence of the British landing force. Crammed into the inlet aboard ships, ferrying stores ashore or establishing defensive positions around the beachhead, it was only a matter of time before their presence attracted attention.

The day dawned bright and clear. There was only the slightest of breezes, and the sheltered waters were tranquil and calm as the sun rose, a fiery orange globe on the eastern horizon. A perfect day for flying, and the Argies weren't about to waste it.

Small cracks of light filtered through the gaps in the blocked-out windows of the Stadium, and I began wondering when we would be moved to *Uganda*. Unlike the smaller liner, *Canberra*, despite her casualty-receiving role, was never designated as a hospital ship or adorned with red crosses, as she also carried troops and warfighting material. As a result, the red paint she carried in her hold remained unused. But as a declared hospital ship, *Uganda* had a non-combatant status and was kept well out to sea in a designated 'Red Cross Box' area of the ocean. Consequently, I suspected that it would take some time for us to be flown out to her, especially as it was likely that most of the cabs were otherwise engaged supporting the landings. I was certainly in no rush to go anywhere, as I listened to the clatter of helicopters as they shuttled busily between ships and the shore, lifting equipment and stores inland.

*Canberra* was anchored in a wider stretch of water at the head of the inlet, close to where the narrow passage of San Carlos Water provides access into Falkland Sound from its northern end. Stretched ahead of us, running south along the length of the inlet, were the vessels of the rest of the amphibious group. The big assault ships *Fearless* and *Intrepid* were docked down off to our port quarter towards the shoreline on the eastern side of the inlet. Their sterns would have been partially flooded with water by blowing out vast air tanks, allowing each ship to act as a floating dock for landing craft to enter and leave. Running further down the water, five landing ships logistic, or LSLs as they were called, were anchored and off-loading stores much closer to the beaches. Beyond the headlands of San Carlos Water, the deeper expanse of Falkland Sound bristled with the radars and weaponry of the warships, which were stationed to protect the anchorage from attack.

All of this was going on around us, while we remained confined to the Stadium, taking in what little we could from the gaps in the windows. As well as being boarded up with plywood, they were covered by parts of the heavy wool carpet that had been ripped from the floor. The thick shag-pile in the Stadium had been removed to prevent it becoming a bio-hazard, as it was feared that it would become saturated with blood and body fluids spilling from the operating tables. Later that morning, the first casualties from the landings were brought aboard. Some of them were Argentine wounded from Fanning Head, and the medical staff in the Stadium started to get busy. They were treated no differently from our own wounded.

Four of the casualties were British. Three were dead, and one was alive. The one who lived was the sole surviving crew member from two light utility Gazelle helicopters which had been shot down near the settlement at San Carlos by some of the Arg troops who had managed to escape from the SBS's attack on Fanning Head. The aircrew sergeant was pretty shaken up by what he had been through. After being treated by the medics, he clearly needed to talk and told us his story, over a brew, as we sat about on mattresses on the Stadium floor.

'Our aircraft was hit in the engine by Arg ground fire

when we flew over San Carlos on a recce, forcing us to crash in the water near the beach,' he began. 'My pilot was wounded, but I managed to drag him out and started pulling him to the shoreline. That's when they opened up on us again with a machine gun.'

'Bastards,' said Alex, 'bloody bastards.'

'We got to the beach, but my pilot died in my arms. He got hit again when we were in the water.'

'Shit, mate, I am sorry, I truly am,' I said.

His account of what had happened made our blood boil with the collective desire to even the score. It was made all the worse by the fact that, as the land campaign to take back the Falklands was unfolding around us, none of us would be part of it. As awful as it was, it was remarkable that the downing of the two Gazelles was the only case of the enemy shooting back at us during the landings. Casualties had been light, and, except for the loss of the helicopters, the activities of the landing operation had gone unimpeded. But that was about to change, and two hours after sunrise it started.

The first air attack was a probing sortie by a lone Argentine Macchi. Coming in low at high speed from the north of the Sound, the little attack jet homed in on the first British ship it came across. Raking IIMS *Argonaut* with its 30 mm cannon and 5 inch rockets, the Italian-built aircraft then banked fast out of its attack run towards Fanning Head, which brought it face on to *Canberra*.

The first we knew of the attack was the metallic voice booming out of the ship's tannoy: 'Dye hear there. Dye hear there. This is the bridge. An air attack is developing from the north. Aircraft inbound. Take cover! Take cover! Take cover!'

We didn't need telling twice, let alone three times, and threw ourselves on to the deck, arms pressed tight over our heads, as the jackhammer sound of several machine guns reverberated overhead, followed by a large, explosive bang. Above us, the four GPMGs mounted on the guard rails of the forward wings of the bridge, crewed by Marines of 42 Commando, spat out thousands of one-in-one tracer rounds, filling the air around the jet with multiple hosing lines of red tracer, forcing the pilot to brake right for the cover of the high ground inland. A Bootneck also got off a shot with a Blowpipe missile. He missed the Argentine raider but put a healthy dent into the bulkhead of the chief officer's cabin with the back blast from his launcher.

The first attack caused only light damage to *Argonaut*, although three of her crew were injured. But the game was up. The Argies now knew that we had begun landing at San Carlos, and we were about to feel the weight of their air forces. Ten minutes later, the tannoy voice boomed out again, and once more we sprawled for deck space. Pucaras had been scrambled from the airstrip at Goose Green, although one was shot down before they could get close enough to launch an attack on the ships.

There was then a pause in the attacks, which allowed the ship's crew to take stock. Above the steel hull, the liner's superstructure was made of aluminium, which cannons and rockets would slice through like butter. Given the vulnerability of the Stadium's position, it was decided that when the next air raid warning came in, all patients and non-essential medical staff would leave the casualty treatment area and take shelter in the stairwells amidships on D Deck. Five levels down and inside the hull, it was the innermost part of the ship and was deemed the safest place to sit out an air attack.

Steel bulkhead or not, I was not sure that it would do much to stop high-velocity projectiles travelling at over 1,000 feet per second and would be no defence against a bomb. However, we took refuge there half an hour later, as the first concerted air attack swept in low over the hills of West Falkland in the form of three supersonic Dagger fighter jets, which had been launched from air bases on the Argentine mainland. One was blown up in mid-air by a Seacat missile fired from HMS *Plymouth*. The other two pressed home their attack, screaming across the Sound towards East Falkland at 50 feet. One shot up the frigate *Broadsword* with its cannons. The other released its payload on HMS *Antrim*. One of the Dagger's 1,000 lb bombs hit and smashed through the destroyer's Seaslug missile magazine doors before crashing through eight bulkheads and ending up in the after heads, having failed to explode. Minutes later, three more Daggers hurtled in at several hundred miles an hour at wave-top height. One strafed *Antrim* with cannon fire, adding to the fires that were already burning on the ship from the first attack.

The aircrewman of the Wessex called Humphrey, which had rescued us from Fortuna, was wounded by a shell splinter, and a flight crew petty officer who maintained the helicopter was blinded by cannon fire. One of the trio of jets lined up on *Canberra*. Flying through a wall of lead put up against it by the Marine GPMG gunners, it banked away at the last minute without firing its cannons.

There was a pause around lunchtime, then the attacks started coming in again, and we went back down to the stairwell on D Deck. The captain of the naval party on board *Canberra* kept up a running commentary over the tannoy on the ship-to-air battle raging around us, reporting numbers of aircraft, their direction of approach, when they were shot down and the damage they were causing.

'Incoming enemy aircraft from the west, heading for *Ardent*,' he said, as if he was giving a commentary at a rugby international.

'Skyhawks this time! One of them has been splashed, but *Ardent* has been hit by a number of bombs and looks like she is on fire.'

He also told us that there were casualties. Later, we were updated that the frigate had to be abandoned by her crew. The captain's words, calm and authoritative, chimed strangely with the cacophony of noise surrounding the ship, as the after-burners of Arg jets roared overhead, and their cannons made a ripping sound as they fired. Their bombs thudded or exploded, depending on whether they hit something solid or landed in the water. In reply, British machine guns thumped back like pneumatic drills, missiles blasted out of launchers and 4.5 inch guns barked back in rapid fire. The knowledge that ships were being hit and people were being killed was sobering, not least as we knew that at any minute it could be happening to us.

As the day wore on, the number of people in the stairwell seemed to increase. By the afternoon, there were a couple of hundred non-essential personnel sitting four or five to a step on the grand sweeping staircase below the long mirrors, which had been boarded up. Each time the air raid warning sounded, more showed up, as if each attack was narrowing the odds and forcing them to reassess their status of criticality to the operation of the ship.

There were quite a lot of 3 PARA there from the start. Forming the support echelon elements of the battalion, they were eager to get off and join the unit's rifle companies already ashore. They moved about with their heavy bergens and long SLR semi-automatic rifles, looking fit, determined and keen to get stuck in. As ex-Paras, Chris and Alex knew some of the troops, and we got talking. We told them about the Gazelle pilot, which made them even more impatient to get on dry land, where they would be in a position to start taking the war to the Argies.

'When you get ashore, give them shit, mate,' I said.

A Para NCO grinned back at me. 'We will, mate. We are 3 PARA. All the blokes in the battalion are scrappers anyway and can't wait to get stuck in.'

I said, 'I wish we were going with you. Good luck, mate.'

We envied them, but all we could do was wait out each attack, sitting there powerless and vulnerable on the Great White Whale, sticking out like a sore thumb in the midst of all the other smaller, better camouflaged and better armed ships jammed into the inlet. At the time *Canberra* was the tallest cruise liner in the world, and it seemed impossible that the Argies could miss her.

The last raid came in just before sunset. To my surprise, sitting next to me on the stairwell was a trim, attractive woman. Our conversation provided a welcome distraction to the sound of heavy naval fire directed against five incoming Skyhawks. Suzie West was one of fifteen women on board *Canberra*. At thirty-one years old, she was a qualified GP and the cruise liner's assistant surgeon, who, like most of the British members of the crew, had volunteered to stay with the ship when it was requisitioned to sail with the Task Force. Suzie was more used to looking after passengers in their mid to late sixties but was now having to help treat young men in the prime of their lives suffering from horrific combat injuries. She was also responsible for assessing whether patients were sufficiently well enough to be moved from the Stadium to the passenger cabins, which had been vacated by the Paras and Marines. We chatted, as gunfire echoed across the water beyond the bulkhead.

'When we volunteered to come south with the ship, I didn't think it would be necessary to make a will, but the company were encouraging us to lodge them with P&O Head Office,' she said.

There was another thud as a bomb splashed into the water not far away. She shuddered.

'I am glad that I did now.'

We both laughed at that, as another bomb thudded into the water somewhere across the anchorage, sending up a tall column of water that splashed down on the decks of a ship it had just missed. We got on to the subject of my evacuation.

'I reckon that I am fit enough and just want to get back to my Squadron.' I saw Suzie look at my neck-brace. 'But that Irish psychiatrist is having none of it,' I continued.

'It's probably for the best,' she said, no doubt thinking

that I was a complete nutter for wanting to stay around here.

From the look on my face, I can't imagine that Suzie felt that she had managed to make me feel any better about the situation, but it was good to have someone to sound off to. Especially someone as good-looking as her.

The captains of the warships and their crews out in the Sound might also have raised an eyebrow over my enthusiasm for joining the fight. As the day drew to a close and the arrival of darkness ended the attacks, they began to lick their wounds and assess the cost of defending the anchorage. One warship was abandoned and was sinking, two were severely wounded, both harbouring unexploded bombs aboard them, and two more were damaged. Twenty-seven men had been killed, and scores more badly injured.

In all, seven air attacks were reported as being made against *Canberra*. After the war several Argentine pilots stated that they deliberately avoided attacking the liner, as they were aware that she had medical facilities on board. Others regarded her as a legitimate target. It was impossible for us to know either way. But Argentine targeting intentions were also the subject of debate among British senior commanders. London was having kittens about the intensity of the air attacks, and there were real concerns about the psychological and propaganda impact if *Canberra* was hit and sunk in subsequent air raids. Therefore, orders were issued that the liner should be withdrawn from San Carlos Water under the cover of darkness and should then steam back out into the safety of the open sea beyond the range of enemy aircraft.

The decision was made and received late in the day, with no thought given to the fact that all the second-line medical capability for the landing force and a large component of their stores were still aboard the ship. There would be no time to offload the supplies for the fighting units, but a hasty call was made to try to get as much as two-thirds of the medical capability off the ship and establish a hospital ashore at a disused meatpacking factory at Ajax Bay. The problem was that there were only three and a half hours to do it before the ship sailed. It provoked a blizzard of activity among the medical staff on *Canberra* and their support teams as they hurried to get ready to disembark.

As a lowly full screw, I wasn't consulted on such decisions and was unaware of the race to get personnel, treatment facilities and operating theatres off the ship in the space of a few short hours. Had I still been in the Stadium, I could have hardly missed the flap that had been generated to get everything needed off the liner in time. But we had been deemed fit enough to move to passenger accommodation two levels down on B Deck. I had been allocated a two-bed cabin with James. It was an anomalous situation, to be ensconced in a level of luxury which neither James nor I could have hoped to have afforded on our meagre Army salaries, while at the same time being slap in the middle of a war zone with bombs raining down around us. I had resigned myself to my fate and was about to indulge in using the bidet before getting my head down on the freshly laundered avocado-coloured sheets when there was a knock on the door. It was the attractive blonde from the stairwell.

Responsible for the 'out patients', Suzie West was checking that James and I were OK having moved down to the cabins from the Stadium. She also told me about the flap.

'They are using a landing craft to take the medics and their kit ashore.' I nodded, not quite sure where she was going with this. Then she said, 'Apparently, it will be returning to *Intrepid*. Isn't that where you said your Squadron is?'

'Yes,' I said, as the penny suddenly dropped.

I realized that she had raised the possibility of me rejoining them, if I was quick and could get myself on to that landing craft. Suzie didn't need to spell it out and I seized the opportunity she presented.

'Thank you,' I said, 'and goodbye,' and hastily shut the door to the cabin.

I turned to James, who had overheard the conversation.

'I am off, mate,' I said.

'I know, mate,' he said, 'look after yourself and give Binsy and Bilbo a kiss from me.'

His leg wound prevented him from coming with me, and I knew it sounded cheesy at the time, but I followed up with 'See you in Blighty, mate. Get home safe, and it's your round when I get back.'

I set off in search of what Suzie had referred to as the 'gunport doors' somewhere on E Deck. There was no time to seek out Chris and Alex to say goodbye, and I didn't need to stop to pack, as my only possessions were the clothes that I was standing up in and my newly acquired neck-brace. I thought that I might get lost in the maze of corridors and stairs as I rushed down through the decks.

But as I descended further into the bowels of the ship, I picked up a stream of medical staff, troops and sailors hurrying through the lower passages, carrying an assortment of boxes and clinical apparatus. They were heading towards what one helpful rating pointed out as being the 'gunport doors'. I mingled in with the hectic throng, hoping that what appeared to be organized chaos might prove to be my salvation.

# 28

The landing craft that bobbed up and down in the swell was bigger than I expected. At 120 tonnes, it was large enough to carry a main battle tank or 120 fully laden troops in its wide-open cargo hold. It was already almost full with medical personnel and piles of stores and equipment. It rode ominously in the swell as the Royal Marine crew worked hard to stop its heavy metal sides crashing against *Canberra*'s hull. In flat water, the sides of the LCU would have been level with the lip of the gunport doors, but the rhythmic heaving of the waves caused the craft to rise and fall dramatically above and below the lip of the door. The motion of the sea also created an opening and closing gap between the two vessels, as their hulls heaved unequally in the shifting mass of water. Combined with the 8 foot drop into the deck of the cargo hold, it spelt leg-breaking and pelvis-crushing potential.

I spared a thought for the Paras and Marines, who would have had to make the jump carrying heavy packs, weighed down with ammunition and weapons. I helped pass down a few surgical stores, gas canisters and cardboard fluid-replacement boxes, then timed my move. Pitching my feet on to the side of the landing craft, I made it just before it dropped down and away from the gunport door, opening up a gap between the two hulls wide enough to consume a man. Amidst a bustle of stores and personnel, no one gave me a second thought as I climbed further down on to the landing craft tank deck and perched on a metal container under a starlit night.

The crew slipped the securing lines, and the LCU pulled away from the towering sides of P&O's flagship with a throaty growl from its powerful twin Paxman diesels. Behind us, as we made the trip from San Carlos Water to Ajax Bay, the Great White Whale was already getting under way, her great pale bulk steaming in the direction of Fanning Head. I spared a thought for the crew. Most were civilians who answered the call when they had no obligation to do so and had braved a frightening day of air attacks without complaint. Though not technically combatants, they had thrown themselves into the unique set of circumstances in which they found themselves. In between running the ship, some of the bridge crew had even taken turns at firing the GPMGs at incoming aircraft. But among them all, Suzie West stood out for me. Without her, I'd now be on my way home.

An hour or so later, the landing craft drove itself on to the shingle beach at Ajax Bay, then dropped its 10 ton ramp. Somewhere, beyond the rocky shoreline, I could make out the long, dark shadow of what must have been the disused meatpacking plant. There were a few shouts and commands from an RAMC senior NCO, and I joined a human chain that formed to unload all the kit and pass it up to the factory sheds beyond the top of the beach. Troops already ashore emerged out of the darkness to help us.

I made sure that I kept my place at the start of the chain near the ramp of the landing craft. It was bitterly cold, but unloading most of a field surgical facility by hand built up a sweat, and we laboured for an hour or more. It was another hour before the last item was handed to me. I passed it on and then deftly stepped back on to the landing craft. No drama. There was a groan of hydraulics as the ramp came up smartly behind me and another roar as the engines were pushed into reverse to pull us off the shingle and back out into the water and blackness.

I didn't bother to try to ask the crew where we were headed; I had faith in Suzie, and the Bootnecks were shut up in the wheel house and didn't look like they were in the mood to talk. The enclosed bridge area looked warm and cosy. Lit by the faint glow of the binnacle lights from the control panel, I could see the coxswain looking down at me in the hold as he sipped at a steaming-hot brew. I must have struck an odd figure with no belt kit, headgear or weapon and wearing a thick white foam collar brace around my neck. It was freezing cold, and the T-shirt and smock I had on did little to keep out the biting wind and stinging spray as we lumped through the waves. There was easily room enough for three people in the wheel house, with a small galley and bunk area behind it, but the buggers didn't invite me in. I was almost hypothermic again by the time we approached the stern of an assault ship.

The landing craft slowed and began to drop its ramp as it glided into the flooded dock in the ship's stern, home to *Intrepid*'s four LCUs. The cavernous space was half covered by the flight deck, with the other half open to the sky and the stars. It felt like we were entering a huge, open-ended swimming pool, lit only by the soft glow of night-vision-friendly red lights.

The coxswain juggled the throttles, easing the LCU forward towards a sloping ramp running out of the water to a vehicle deck known as the 'beach'. The LCU's forward ramp dropped on to the beach with a resounding metal clang, signalling our arrival.

I didn't wait to say thanks for the lift before stepping off the ramp and on to the vehicle deck. It was noisy, thick with engine fumes and busy with sailors and Marines as they prepared vehicles and equipment to go ashore. I spotted a metal door to the side of the deck, which looked like the sort of exit you would expect to find on a cross-Channel ferry. I opened it and disappeared inside. I didn't know how to get there, but I knew where I was trying to go.

Although not as big as the *Canberra*, HMS *Intrepid* was still a large ship. I had no idea where D Squadron might be accommodated and I had no intention of asking. In leaving *Canberra* with no official sanction and in direct contravention of medical orders, I was, at best, technically AWOL. On its own, this was a serious military discipline offence. In my defence, though, I was running towards the fight rather than away from it, but I wasn't convinced that the silver-haired Irishman and the medical chain of command would see it that way. Having disobeyed a direct order from a superior officer, I reckoned that I could be in serious trouble. Even worse, I could end up being put on the first available helicopter and flown out to *Uganda* – unless I got to the Squadron first.

My plan was to find the galley and wait for the blokes to turn up for breakfast, as scoff would never be far from their minds. I suspected that I might have a better chance of getting there if I looked less conspicuous and ditched my neck-brace. Avoiding anyone who looked like they might have rank, I sounded out a young junior naval rating, who directed me to the galley on Deck 3 in the heart of the ship.

Designed to accommodate a sizeable body of troops, the galley area ran across the width of the ship. It was still early, but the chefs were labouring in their anti-flash on the other side of a long stainless-steel hotplate. I grabbed some food that was probably left out for the night watch and helped myself to a brew from a large tea urn before sitting at a Formica-topped table in a cheap plastic chair facing the main entrance, at the other end of the dining facility. I ate and then waited, as troops started to file into the galley for breakfast.

About an hour later, a group entered, sporting longer-than-regulation hair, sideburns and a few days' worth of stubble on their faces, which still bore the traces of camouflage paint. It was unmistakeably D Squadron, just back from the diversionary raid at Darwin. Bilbo and Binsy spotted me first and came over, ahead of the rest of the blokes. There was a look of surprise on their dirty features, and I sensed that they were about to ask me how I got there and what had happened. Then they both paused, and a look passed between them. Binsy smiled and then just said, 'Where the fuck have you been, Splash? We were about to start auctioning your kit.'

And Bilbo asked, 'And where are the rest of the South Atlantic synchronized swimming team?'

I smiled. It looked like it was business as usual. And I was back where I belonged.

# 29

If an outsider thought that the men of D Squadron were unmoved by the loss of so many of our comrades, they would have been mistaken. There was no visible expression of grief, no outward evidence of shock, or even a sense of anger about what had happened when the Sea King went down. It might have seemed like callous indifference, but make no mistake, the deaths of our mates had hit us hard. We were a tight-knit squadron, and we all felt the loss. It was hard to believe that men who we had been laughing and joking with only the day before were suddenly gone. We had not only served with them but also socialized with them back in the UK and we knew their families and kids.

When Danny West had finished compiling the list of casualties after the helicopter went down, he was asked by one of the officers in the Squadron, 'How bad is it?'

Danny handed over the list of names that he had compiled, then slipped into an empty cabin, shut the door behind him and wept.

That night, John Hamilton also found a quiet place on *Intrepid* and, alone with a bottle of whisky, drank himself into oblivion. But these were private acts of grief, kept hidden and behind closed doors. Dwelling on what had happened or talking about it would not have made it any easier to bear. Black humour did.

The same evening that the Sea King went down, Mike Rose had flown to *Intrepid* from *Fearless* as soon as he heard the news. He spoke to the Squadron and some of the members of G Squadron, who had gathered on a darkened hangar deck.

The CO started by saying, 'We can't expect to get through this war without taking some losses, but to lose so many people is a very difficult thing to accept.' He went on to say, 'Our mission is only half done, so we have to put this terrible loss behind us and crack on.'

He assured those present that the families were being informed and looked after in Hereford, and went on to start telling D Squadron about its next task and the diversionary attack on Darwin, when the air raid warnings went off.

The CO had to raise his voice to be heard over the noise of anti-aircraft fire and the blast of exploding bombs, which made the superstructure shudder with the concussion. He paused while people pulled on their anti-flash hoods. Before he started speaking again, from behind one of the masks an affected Monty Python-style, high-pitched, shrill voice remarked, 'I've never been so frightened in all my life!'

Everybody burst out laughing, and the tension broke.

The blokes who were there appreciated what the boss had to say about the hit we had taken as a regiment and the importance of pressing on, but it was the first and last time the incident was spoken about during the rest of the time that we spent in the South Atlantic. There was still a job to be done, and the battle to retake the Falklands continued without a pause. Memorials and grieving would have to wait. The Squadron had to crack on.

Everyone knew it was what they would have wanted, and it would also be the best way of honouring them. The raid on Darwin and Goose Green to divert attention from the main landings at San Carlos provided just that opportunity. And something of an unexpected bonus too.

As I was making good my escape from *Canberra*, D Squadron were tabbing hard through the darkness. Having engaged the enemy garrison positioned around the two settlements, Cedric was under strict instructions to cover the 20 miles back to San Carlos and be within the air defence cover of the bridgehead established by the Marines and Paras by dawn. If the Squadron was caught out in the open in daylight, they would be exposed to the risk of Argentine attack from the air. They were behind schedule.

Encumbered by the heavy weight of their kit, they were finding the going difficult, and the sun was already rising above the eastern horizon as they contoured round the slopes of Mount Usborne. San Carlos still lay off in the distance at the end of a ridgeline of hills, and an enemy air patrol was prowling the skies. Bilbo told me that they heard the Pucara before they saw it. As they were strung out along the side of the mountain, the valley behind them was suddenly filled with the droning sound of approaching turboprop engines. The snaking line of troops instantly went to ground, but it was too late.

The pilot in the first Pucara spotted movement half a mile down to his left, as the blokes broke formation and sank into the scant cover among the clumps of scrub

A Sea King lands on SS *Canberra*. The large, converted passenger liner was where I ended up after becoming a casualty.

SS *Canberra* streaked with rust in San Carlos Water. Her large 'gunport doors', where I made my escape from being evacuated as a casualty, are open and being accessed by launches on her port side.

HMS *Intrepid* in San Carlos Water. A Lynx helicopter sits on her large open flight deck, which provided the ideal vantage point for the assembled members of D Squadron when they participated in the shooting down of an attacking Argentine Skyhawk jet.

This Argentine Skyhawk attacking the Navy's ships in San Carlos Water is similar to the one we shot down with small arms fire, which earned us a rollocking.

The bow and stern sections of HMS *Antelope* in San Carlos Water after the ship was sunk by an Argentine air attack on 24 May 1982. It was a sombre moment as we watched her slip beneath the waves.

Some of the blokes from 16 Troop, taken around the time of the diversionary raid on Darwin. The trooper at the rear of the photo has a Stinger anti-aircraft launcher protruding from his bergen, which was used to bring down a Pucara during the operation. The two men in the front carry GMPGs.

An SAS trooper with a Stinger missile. Dropped to us by parachute before the landings, D Squadron secured a first when they used one to shoot down an Argentine Puacra ground-attack aircraft.

After a cherished night in the warmth and dry of the ship, members of D Squadron are in buoyant mood as they wait for a heli lift by the hanger doors of HMS *Intrepid*.

D Squadron's headquarters position on Mount Kent. Known as the 'head shed', Cedric Delves used the Tacsat radio in the foreground, which was state of the art technology at the time, to keep in touch with the CO of the Regiment and our base back in Hereford.

Looking from Mount Kent on to the ridge the Squadron held until relieved by the Commandos on 3 June. BP marks the location of the mortar baseplate, where I was positioned. From 16 Troop's position it was possible to see the outskirts of Stanley.

Major Cedric Delves, the officer commanding D Squadron, standing with the Regiment's operations officer by a destroyed Pucara on the airstrip at Pebble Island at the end of the war.

Inside the helicopter Humphrey at the Royal Navy's Fleet Air Arm Museum. The back of the Wessex Mk III was designed to carry four people at the most. Seventeen of us were crammed into its cramped interior during the rescue from Fortuna.

The memorial wall in the cemetery of St Martin's Church in Hereford. Starting fifth from the right, the twenty-one plaques commemorating those that we lost in the Falklands.

Posing on Pebble Island by the remains of the Argentine Skyvan we destroyed on 15 May. Elephant Bay can be seen in the background.

Handling an Argentine 7.62 mm assault rifle of the captured type that I used in the later stages of the campaign. I preferred it to the smaller calibre Armalite, as it had better stopping power.

The inside of the shearing shed at Port Howard where Roy Fonseca was held captive by the Argentine garrison after the firefight in which John Hamilton was killed. The old wool press has long since been removed, but was located beneath the feed of the farm manager I am in conversation with.

Captain John Hamilton, MC and his grave at Port Howard on West Falkland. John was the newly joined troop commander of Mountain Troop who lost his life trying to fight his way out of his OP position on 10 June.

and meagre scatterings of grey rock. The pilot climbed for altitude and then pulled his aircraft into a turn, before lining up to begin a strafing run along the length of the ridge. Throttling back for the attack, he thumbed off the safety covers on his fire control button and lined up his reflector sight, capturing the dark shapes of men in his gunsight.

'He's lining up to attack!' someone shouted, anticipating the rain of cannon and rocket fire to follow.

'Get him with a Stinger!' another voice cried out.

16 Troop had no intention of taking it lying down. Two blokes stood up from behind a rocky outcrop, one with a missile launcher on his shoulder. Still several hundred metres away, the Pucara had settled into its attack run. The Stinger operator tracked the incoming aircraft against the cold, clear, blue sky.

The distance between the Pucara and the missile operator closed. The Stinger's seeker-head scanned the sky, searching urgently for a hostile heat source. Precious seconds ticked by. Then the growl of the missile suddenly pitched up in frequency, indicating lock-on. There was no need to give the enemy aircraft any lead, as it was coming straight at them. With a pull of the trigger there was a flash and a split-second pause, as the missile left the launcher and seemed to hang for a moment suspended in the air. Then there was a *whoosh* as the flight motor kicked in.

The warhead streaked skywards, trailing dirty grey smoke in its wake. The missile powered upwards for several seconds, twitching as it made tiny adjustments to its targeting. It looked as if it was going to go too high and miss. Then suddenly the missile exploded in a flash, the *crump* of its detonation rolling back down the valley. The blokes lying in the grass looked up in awe. The Pucara's turboprop engines roared in angry protest as the pilot struggled to maintain height. But his aircraft was hit. Realizing that he was about to lose his fight with gravity, the Argentine flyer ejected. A canopy of white silk popped open against the blue as the Pucara nose-dived into the ground.

A stunned silence followed, as the Squadron sat in the grass and watched the single parachute drift slowly earthwards on to the valley floor beneath them.

Binsy broke it when he exclaimed, 'Fucking hell! Did you see that?'

They watched the pilot land and get up. The airman cut a lonely figure as he started his long walk back to the airstrip at Goose Green.

Taking out the Pucara was the first operational downing of an aircraft by a Stinger missile, and was a remarkable success, given the limited training on the brand-new weapon system that Paddy O'Connor had managed to pass on to us as we sat on the bunks of *Hermes*' mess deck.

Not to be outdone, another one of the blokes in 16 Troop decided to have a go with a Stinger when a second Pucara appeared to investigate what had happened to his wingman. This time the excitement of the moment was too much. The missile was fired in haste before it achieved lock-on. It launched, hung momentarily in the air and then piled into the ground 20 metres away in the middle of 18 Troop. A second attempt was made, and the same thing happened, provoking the fury of Mobility

Troop as they scurried for cover amidst shouts of 'Read the fucking manual!' Bilbo wasn't sure what the second Pucara made of the farce unfolding on the ground below it, but, having seen what had happened to his buddy, the pilot thought better of sticking around and flew off to the east.

The downing of the first Pucara was witnessed by the men of 2 PARA, who had been hacking out defensive positions from the boggy peat on the slopes of Sussex Mountain. They cheered as they saw the enemy aircraft get hit by the missile and crash. By the time the Squadron patrolled back through the Paras' lines, enemy air attacks were about to start becoming routine, as the first multiple sorties of Argentine jets came in thick and fast against the warships stationed out in Falkland Sound.

Some swept in from the east low over the heads of the blokes as they made their way back into the San Carlos bridgehead. Everyone, including the Toms in 2 PARA, had a go at them with rifles and GPMGs as the jets screamed over the shoreline and headed out to sea in search of the ships.

'We didn't hit anything,' Bilbo said, 'but it felt fucking good.' He paused and then added: 'It was just what the doctor ordered.'

The attack on Darwin and the bringing-down of the Pucara provided everyone with a focus after the loss of the Sea King. Apart from the Irish shrink on *Canberra*, the only person who spoke to me about the accident in any sort of official capacity was Cedric after he got back in from the raid on Darwin. He wanted to know if I was

OK and whether I would prefer to stay on board *Intrepid* and help Graham out in the stores, rather than deploy on further operations with the Squadron. The boss mentioned that, with the loss of Wally Walpole, Graham could do with the help.

Cedric would have felt every loss, but I knew that Lawrence's death would have hit him hardest. The two men had been close. In any sub-unit, the dynamic between the OC and the sergeant major is critical, and the bond between Cedric and Lawrence had been strong. The big man had been popular and respected by all of us; he would have undoubtedly gone on to have become the RSM of the Regiment, and his loss was felt widely. For Cedric the relationship had gone beyond the professional though, and the two men were firm friends.

But Cedric showed no hint of his personal grief when he asked me how I was.

'I'm OK, boss,' I replied. 'Thanks for the offer of a job with Graham, but I am fine, and my place is with 19 Troop.'

Cedric smiled and nodded, as if the answer I had given him was precisely what he would have expected. 'No problem,' he said.

I thanked him and turned to leave his cabin.

'Oh, Splash?'

'Yes, boss?'

Cedric paused. 'Nothing, it's just good to have you back, that's all.'

'Thanks, boss. I'm glad to be back too.'

Others had a different view of my return to the Squadron. When my silver-haired Irish friend discovered that I was no longer on *Canberra*, repeated calls were made to D

Squadron, demanding to know if I was with them and that I should be immediately returned. The signallers denied any knowledge of my presence. Eventually, the medical authorities gave up in their quest to find me, and as well as being AWOL, I was now also technically missing in action.

If Binsy had been serious about auctioning off my military kit he would have been a disappointed man. My belt order, as well as my weapon, had been lost in the helicopter. Ironically, some of the bergens which we thought we had been forced to abandon on Fortuna had been recovered from the glacier and had found their way back to us at the same time as we arrived on *Intrepid*. However, they had been well rifled by some bastard before they were returned to us. Opening my rucksack, I discovered that little of worth was left, and my sleeping bag had also been nicked.

'Wankers,' I said to myself, as I searched out Graham in the Squadron stores for replacement items of kit. He issued me with spare webbing, which allowed me to make up a new set of belt kit, with the odd item being thrown in by some of the blokes. Graham also gave me his own personal civilian Gore-Tex bivy bag, which was at the leading edge of hi-tech outdoor living in those days. There were no spare sleeping bags to keep me warm, but at least it would keep me dry when sleeping out in the open.

There were additional Armalites in the armoury, but I drew an FN rifle, which had been taken from the Argentine garrison at Grytviken. Similar in design to the standard-issue British SLR, it was longer and heavier than the M16 and fired 7.62 mm, rather than 5.56 mm ammunition. Though the weight and feel of the two weapons

273

was different, I preferred the benefit of the greater punch the larger-calibre FN offered. Unlike the SLR, it could also be fired on fully automatic and had a folding frame stock, which made it wieldier than the British equivalent.

There was no replacement for my large black K Bar knife. I had bought the Bowie-bladed weapon in the PX store in Fort Bragg during a trip to work with the US Special Forces. The blue-black blade and leather handle had a lovely feel to it and would have made Rambo proud, but unfortunately it wasn't a loss that Graham could make up from the stores. However, less the K Bar and the sleeping bag, I was pretty much good to go again.

While I had been sorting myself out, Mountain Troop had also undergone a degree of reorganization. With the loss of half of 19 Troop's strength, Cedric had been faced with a choice. He could either break up what was left of Mountain Troop and redistribute the remaining manpower across the other troops in the Squadron or he could do what he could to reinforce 19 Troop and make up some of its shortfall. He chose the latter option, although the Troop would now be reorganized into two, rather than the normal four, patrols.

Ade Robertson was drafted in from one of the other troops. As a sergeant, he would command one of the two remaining patrols; John Hamilton would continue to command the other patrol. It was a decision that met with the approval of the rest of 19 Troop, and we were glad that we would be staying under John's immediate command. He had proven his worth as the new troop officer in South Georgia and during the raid on Pebble

Island and had cemented his position as the boss of Mountain Troop.

Roy Fonseca would also be rejoining the Troop. Having been left behind, stuck on his mountain course in Germany, he managed to get back to the UK and then blagged and hitched his way down south on a series of ships. No one knew quite how he achieved it – like me, he was only a Tom – but there was no way he was going to be left out. He was sore that he had missed the raid on Pebble Island. However, it was good to see the smiling Seychellois, and he would help make up the numbers.

The other piece of welcome news came in the form of the issue of Gore-Tex waterproofs. The plain olive-green Berghaus jackets had been purchased from Cotswold Camping. The Regiment's quartermaster bought out the civilian outdoor store's entire stock and then had them airdropped to us in the middle of the South Atlantic. They were a brilliant bit of kit. Unlike the Army-issue waterproof, they kept you dry, but the material also allowed sweat to evaporate through it, which helped retain body heat. They were to prove their worth during our next mission.

It was good to be back with the Squadron, although, like the rest of the blokes, I soon became restless as we waited for the new tasking, with little else to do but sit through the air raids and hope that we didn't get hit. After the first day of air attacks, immediately following the landing, San Carlos Water was nicknamed 'Bomb Alley' and was becoming an increasingly dangerous place.

Living aboard *Intrepid* as the attacks came in also made for a curious way of life. Compared to the Marines and

Paras digging in ashore, sea basing provided an opportunity to shelter from the elements, eat regular hot meals in the galley, take a shower, dry your kit out and sleep in the warmth of a bunk on a mess deck. The troops on the island were living in bloody awful conditions of cold and incessant biting winds. Once they got wet – from the rain, flurrying snow showers and the water that oozed through the peat and filled their trenches – they stayed wet. But they could at least put up a fight against the enemy aircraft. Even if armed only with a rifle, they could hit back. A few feet of sodden earth was also a better place to take cover from the cannon shells and bombs compared with the claustrophobic confines of a ship, where only darkness and bad weather provided a measure of respite.

The attacks on the first day were just a taster of what was to come in the following days. Having failed to achieve air superiority before the landings, the British now faced a sustained onslaught from the mainstay of the enemy aircraft in the form of their supersonic Dagger and Mirage fighters and the slower, but no less deadly, Skyhawk jets. Intelligence reports at the time suggested that the Argentine air forces started the conflict with over 100 serviceable fixed-wing combat aircraft of all types, including their nasty little Pucaras. If the losses already inflicted on them were taken into account, it was estimated that they still had seventy to eighty aircraft left to throw at us. Against them, the Task Force had just twenty-five Sea Harriers operating from *Hermes* and *Invincible*.

The Harriers proved to be the more capable aircraft.

But the carriers remained far out to sea, which reduced the jets' flying time over the Falklands to twenty minutes or less. The Sea Wolf and Sea Dart missiles on the Navy's frigates and destroyers would do something to fill the gap in fighter cover, as would the Army's trailer-launched Rapier missiles, which were being positioned on the high ground around the anchorage. However, both the Sea Dart and Rapier systems had serviceability issues.

The paucity of our own aircraft and the technical fragility of the missile systems had become apparent on the first day of air attacks. There was plenty of chat among the crew on the lower decks of *Intrepid* about the limitations and problems of the air defences of the ship. Although we were never conversant with the technical details, what we did know was that there were holes in our defences. It sounded like the Args had plenty of aircraft left, and quite a few of them were going to make it through to where we were anchored. They also received a degree of inadvertent help from an unexpected quarter, in the form of the BBC. Many of the Argentine bombs had failed to detonate when they struck the sides of a ship as they had been incorrectly fused for low-level attack. When the World Service reported the error, the enemy took note and made the necessary adjustments to their bombs, which pissed us off beyond belief when we heard about it.

The Squadron took refuge on *Intrepid*'s tank deck during the air raids, where we mustered with the rest of the crew who were not needed to operate the ship during an attack. Some of the younger sailors were visibly frightened, but then they were just boys and they knew the consequences of being hit better than we did, from their training and what had happened to their mates on other ships, like HMS *Sheffield* and *Ardent*. I think if we had been better informed, we would have been shitting ourselves too. The reality of our predicament hit home on the morning of 24 May, when we watched HMS *Antelope* break up and sink.

The Type 21 frigate had been hit the previous day by two bombs, which had failed to detonate on impact, and she had been withdrawn into San Carlos Water and anchored a few hundred metres off our stern. Later that day one of the Argentine 1,000 pounders stuck in her hull exploded during attempts to defuse it, which set off the munitions in her magazine. Explosions aboard the ship continued throughout the night and by morning her superstructure had been reduced to a twisted, smoking mass of melted steel. Binsy and I sat and watched the stricken ship through the large open ramp door of *Intrepid*'s dock, as the frigate's bow and stern lifted clear of the water as if in a sad final farewell salute, before slipping out of sight beneath the waves in a plume of hissing steam and smoke.

'Hell, look at that,' Binsy said quietly.

'It could have been us,' I replied, shocked at the sight of the sinking ship's broken back.

We were vulnerable: just waiting for it and taking it. Watching *Antelope*'s last moments made us even more desperate to get ashore. I thought of the poor souls who had died with her. For a moment I wondered how they met their fate. It made me think of the Sea King. I tried to cast the thought from my mind.

*

When the orders actually came through for our next mission, I wasn't entirely sure that I liked the sound of what we had been told. At 1,500 feet in height, Mount Kent is one of the Falklands' higher peaks. Sitting just 10 miles to the west of Stanley it is also the dominant feature among a ridge of smaller hills that ring the island's capital. Its position and topography made it what the military refer to as 'vital terrain', as whichever side held it would have a marked advantage in the coming battles for Port Stanley. When recce patrols from G Squadron reported that Mount Kent was not being defended by the Argies, Mike Rose saw it as an opportunity.

As the CO of the Regiment, Rose had some input in the strategic planning of the land campaign to recapture the islands. He was also close to Brigadier Julian Thompson, who, as the commander of 3 Commando Brigade, was the senior land-based officer on the ground at the time. The two men had served together in Northern Ireland and respected and liked each other. Mike Rose advocated that forces should be sent forwards to seize Mount Kent while it was still unoccupied by the enemy, arguing that it offered the key to unlocking the Argies' ability to defend Stanley, especially as it would provide an ideal artillery position from which the enemy garrison and airfield around Stanley could be brought within the range of British 105 mm field guns. Thompson supported the idea, but had more immediate priorities in building up his logistics in the bridgehead at San Carlos before he could start pushing forward his infantry units and artillery. The compromise the two men agreed on was that D Squadron should be flown in to dominate the feature and hold it until a larger force could be sent forward.

The strategic imperatives of Mount Kent were not readily apparent to me when Cedric gave the Squadron a set of orders in one of the bays off the hangar tank deck on *Intrepid* on the afternoon of 24 May.

'The CO has told us that we need to get forward to Mount Kent.' The boss pointed out the location of the feature on a map. 'We are to conduct guerrilla operations against the Arg garrison in the Port Stanley area. The CO also hopes that it will suck 3 Commando Brigade forward into the area and get the land campaign going.'

I had some doubts about it. It sounded as if we were doing no more than flying forward 40 miles from our own front lines to picket the heights around Stanley. There was also mention of setting up a base on the high ground from which to conduct raids against Argentine locations in the surrounding area.

'What do you think the real purpose is of going up to Mount Kent?' I asked Alex after the orders had broken up and we sat on the blue plastic mattresses of our bunks.

'Not sure, but it sounds like some sort of Dhofar gig, picketing the heights and all that. I suppose those tactics would have worked in the Jebel against Adoo tribesmen, but I am not sure that it is going to work here.'

Our conversation was overheard by the troop staff sergeant from 16 Troop, who stopped and gripped both of us.

'Listen, you two,' he said. 'You get paid to do whatever the boss has directed, so stop moaning and get on with it.'

That pissed us off: we felt that we didn't need to be

told. There was never even the slightest hint that we wouldn't do precisely what the boss wanted from us. We were merely doing what all soldiers do and exercising our right to carp about those above us.

We didn't appreciate the significance of what Cedric had in mind for Mount Kent, although we knew that the boss didn't expect us to do something that he wasn't prepared to do himself. Later that evening, Cedric took a four-man patrol and flew forward to Mount Kent to conduct his own reconnaissance of the ground, with the intention that the rest of the Squadron would follow him the next night.

# 30

Everyone was relieved to lift off from *Intrepid* after another day of air attacks spent sitting impotent on the ship's tank deck. The Argentine air force had changed its tactics. Switching focus away from the warships in Falkland Sound, the enemy pilots had begun to concentrate their attacks on the logistics ships anchored in San Carlos Water, which meant that the stretch of water where we were anchored was getting more attention.

The attacking aircraft missed *Intrepid* but they managed to hit and damage three of the LSLs with their bombs. The coming of darkness had brought a halt to the day's air raids, but the weather had begun to close in by the time the Sea Kings got airborne. We crossed the shoreline and headed inland through thickening fog. Even with NVGs, the crews would have been struggling for visibility, as the helicopters flew east beyond the bridgehead towards Mount Kent. We were in the air for over an hour, far longer than was needed to make a transit of 40 miles. John Hamilton eventually shouted back that the pilots were unable to find the landing site where Cedric's recce patrol was waiting to meet us.

The message was passed back through the cab man to man, but what wasn't mentioned was that the Sea Kings were running short of fuel and wouldn't make it back to *Intrepid* with us on board. We found that out when we were put down on the side of a ridge in the middle of God knows where. There were lights off in the distance, just visible through the murk in the lower ground to the south. We suspected that they must be coming from the settlement at Bluff Cove but we couldn't be sure. We also weren't sure about the presence of the enemy.

The Squadron had deployed with a thermal imaging camera. It was a new piece of kit and came with a specialist operator to use it. As the senior man present, Danny West told him to switch it on and check out the surrounding area for heat sources, which would give an indication of whether there were any enemy about. The operator switched the kit on and scanned the ground around us.

'Shit, shit,' he hissed in a low voice. 'We are fucking surrounded!'

Danny moved over to him and looked at the flickering black and red screen. Sure enough, numerous dark shapes moved slowly out in the blackness.

'You eejit,' Danny responded, 'they're bloody sheep!'

Sheep or not, it was freezing, and there was no other option but to mount sentry stags, wait for the coming of dawn and trust that the helicopters would pick us up at first light. Absent a sleeping bag, Graham's bivy bag and a poncho liner did little to keep out the cold as the temperature dropped dramatically, and it turned out to be a long, miserable night.

Fog still clung heavy and thick to the hillside the next morning. The engine clatter of Sea Kings, invisible through the mist, indicated that the aircrew were as good as their word. They picked us up and flew back to San Carlos on instruments, then dropped down to sea level to get under the clag and make the last leg of the journey back to *Intrepid* at wave-top height. Above us, the sun was already burning through the mist. Assisted by a stiffening breeze, it began to lift rapidly as we approached the ship. By the time we landed on the flight deck, the warmth of the sun's rays and the wind had dissipated the fog to reveal a beautifully clear morning and perfect fast-jet flying conditions. It was Argentina's National Day, 25 May. If the enemy were going to strike back hard, we anticipated that today was the day they would do it. An all-out air attack had been expected. As it happened, they had decided to make an early start.

The air raid warning was already sounding as we scrambled off the helicopters and gathered on the flight deck. Klaxons and alarm whistles of other vessels were sounding across the water, as ships began to close up their crews to action stations and brace themselves against the report of inbound aircraft. The air raid alert was piped out on *Intrepid*'s broadcast system; there was a brief high-pitched squeal of feedback from a speaker positioned at the stern of the ship, and then a blaring metallic voice rang out: 'Incoming air raid. Take cover! Take cover! You men on the flight deck, get inside the hangar!'

The approaching roar of jet engines stopped us in our tracks. Instinctively, we turned. Two small delta shapes appeared black against the blue of the sky as they flipped over the headland to our north and screamed into San Carlos Water just 50 feet above the surface of the sea. They grew in size as they streaked towards us, and the voice from the tannoy became a little more frantic in its demands. Almost pleading:

284

'I repeat, take cover! Get inside the hangar! Now!'

*No chance*, I thought. We knew instantly what was heading our way. There were more than fifty of us, armed and dangerous on an open deck, and we weren't about to waste an opportunity to try to mallet a couple of Argie jets. The Skyhawks were almost upon us, coming line astern through the anchorage with ships to their left and their right. There was an enthusiastic fumbling and a frantic cocking of small arms, as rifles and machine guns were brought to bear. Then everyone who could get a shot in opened up, in a riot of deafening noise and fire. As the enemy aircraft swept past, we hammered away at them with everything we had.

Firing their cannons as they went, the Skyhawks were almost level with us and only 30-odd metres off *Intrepid*'s port beam. They were close enough for us to glimpse their pilots' white helmets. What looked like a distinct plume of white vapour hazed briefly from the second aircraft before they both roared out of sight behind the ship's superstructure. Binsy managed to get off a belt of fifty rounds from the hip with his GPMG, and the appearance of smoke brought out a burst of raucous cheering as we all leaped to the same conclusion that he had hit the trailing Skyhawk.

The fire ceased as the aircraft passed from view, the last empty cases tinkling on to a deck already awash with the brass of spent cartridges. There was a pause, as quiet returned to the stern of the ship. Then there was a crackle of static from the speaker above the hangar doors, and the disembodied voice made another announcement.

'Ah, hmm, well done, you men there on the flight deck.

You have just splashed a Skyhawk, which has crashed into a hillside.'

There was a break in the tannoy transition as another round of cheering and jubilant shouting broke out. The voice cut back in as the euphoria subsided.

'However, please be aware that we are not the only ship in the anchorage, and the captain of the ship opposite has just made a complaint that you managed to hose down his bridge and quarter-deck with several hundred rounds of small arms ammunition.'

The mild rebuke did little to dampen our elation at knocking one of the raiders out of the sky. However, we were almost immediately ordered to load back into the helicopters and were then flown ashore and dropped off near the 3 Commando Brigade logistics area. We never discovered whether we were deposited on land for our own safety or for the safety of the other ships in San Carlos Water.

Whatever the reason for putting us ashore, the Squadron spent the rest of the day holed up in a narrow re-entrant running inland from the shoreline. The brigade area was a hive of activity. Landing craft delivered stores to the beaches, helicopters shuttled to and from the ships with underslung loads, and forklift trucks deposited ammunition and kit from one pile to another around the beachhead. The brigade personnel showed no interest in us, and we were happy to keep out of their way while we waited for the return of the Sea Kings, which would lift us to Mount Kent later that night.

Secure in the bridgehead, there was little to do except enjoy the rare warmth of the sun, lie on our backs and take pot shots at the occasional Argentine jets that screamed overhead as more air attacks came in against the ships in San Carlos Water. Sheltered from the wind, the re-entrant soon filled with the prickly tang of hex-amine cookers and boyish shouts of 'Your bird, vicar' every time an enemy aircraft appeared within range.

There was almost a holiday picnic atmosphere in that small fold of ground that day. Listening to the laughter and banter between the blokes as we shared brews and enjoyed basking in the sun on dry land, free from the agony of helplessness and confinement afloat, I had a profound sense that we had healed. Through the raid on Darwin, shooting down the Pucara with the Stinger and Binsy's Skyhawk, we had put the tragic events of 19 May behind us and had bounced back as a Squadron. But while we made the most of our day of freedom and good weather, unknown to us, the Argentine air force had made the most of their National Day.

By evening, they had hit and sunk the destroyer HMS *Coventry* with their bombs and taken out the *Atlantic Conveyor* with two Exocets. The loss of this large cargo ship taken up from trade was to have profound consequences for the Task Force, and it would also impact on us and our next mission.

## 31

The fire came from the vicinity of Teal Inlet. A single looping line of tracer arced into the night sky in a vain attempt to find the Sea Kings as they flew us east. The rounds fell short, burning out some distance from the helicopters off to our right, but close enough to signal that we had advanced well forward of our own lines and were heading deeper into enemy territory.

Minutes later, the aircraft flared as they came in to land on a reverse slope on the southeast side of Mount Kent. We scrambled out, weighed down by heavy kit, and went to ground. Almost immediately, the helicopters lifted and were gone, leaving us alone once more. Nige Smith moved off and closed in on the boss. I could hear muted voices from the huddle of men unseen in the darkness, as Cedric briefed Nige and the rest of the command team. Jake Dutton and I waited for him to return, as the warmth of our bodies was stolen away by the icy chill of the wind.

'Fuck, Jake, it's brass monkeys out here in the ulu,' I whispered, as we huddled in the damp clumps of grass and waited for Nige.

'Aye, Splash, it is, mate, but you will be feeling it more than me because you are a fooking hat.'

Jake was a 5-foot-nothing ginger-haired jock from 18 Troop who had started his career in the mortar platoon of

3 PARA, and in the eyes of all Paras I was a crap hat and he was not.

'Fuck off, you ginger twat,' I hissed back, not wasting breath on wit when abuse would do. Jake just chuckled, and we traded insults in hushed tones to keep our minds off the cold.

We were glad to get moving when Nige came back. The going was difficult as we trudged upwards and stumbled over clumps of grass and scrub, labouring hard, with each of us carrying one of the three heavy parts of the 81 mm mortar. It weighed a total of nearly 80 lbs on top of our personal kit and weapons, and we were soon sweating with the effort. Even with our body heat restored, it was a relief to drop the burden of the barrel tube from my shoulders when Nige indicated that we had reached the baseplate location that Cedric had selected in the lee of a craggy line of rocks.

The blokes in the other troops had further to tab, having first dropped off a greenie bomb container before moving on past our position. The depleted members of 19 Troop also filed back into the blackness once they had added to the growing stack of 81 mm ammunition. I would not be going with them, as I had been detached to form part of the three-man crew for the mortar, along with Nige and Jake, from 16 and 18 Troops. The solid, round baseplate, bipod and barrel of the indirect fire support weapon were cached along with the greenies in the lee of a large slab of rock, and then we started to dig.

Even on elevated ground, the peat oozed water with each cut of our entrenching tools, and soon we were hacking through inches of liquid. Then we hit quartzite.

Unable to go deeper we had to use the surrounding loose rocks to build up the sides of the shell scrape. The shallow dugout continued to ooze moisture from its peaty sides, which added to the pool of wetness already forming in its bottom, and the wind whistled through the rocky out-crop as we dug, occasionally carrying with it the sound of muffled digging and the odd click of a spade against stone coming from the rest of the position invisible in the black-ness around us.

Dawn was not far off by the time we had finished, and we donned belt kit, picked up our rifles and stood to. Stand-ing to was the SOP for manning our battle positions in the hour before first and the hour before last light, when an enemy assault on a held position is considered most likely. I looked at my watch – the hour around first light always seems to be the longest – as we waited for the landscape to gradually take shape in the slate-grey half-light of dawn.

I shivered. Although I was glad of my new Igloo Gore-Tex jacket, it was still bitterly cold. As the hands of my watch ticked round, thin slivers of light began to encroach from the eastern horizon. As the shadows retreated, our surroundings were revealed. We were dug in halfway along the spine of a craggy ridgeline, cutting through a saddle lying like a web between two fingers of a hand, with Mount Kent extending as an extremity to our north-east and Mount Challenger curling out in the form of a spur-like digit to our southeast.

Around us lay a rumpled landscape of jagged peaks and wind-eroded peat fissures. The slopes and depres-sions between the higher ground were covered in thick yellow tufts of grass, spreading patches of low-lying diddle-dee and large swathes of jumbled rivers of rock known as 'stone runs'. Cascading down the sides of the hills and across valley floors, the accumulations of shattered rock debris extended for hundreds of metres and were often 50 to 100 metres wide. Caused by thousands of years of freezing and thaw, they were impassable to vehicles, and each held limb-breaking potential for a heavily laden soldier.

Cedric had arranged the Squadron in a rough, rectangular-shaped position. 16 Troop were positioned to our front further along the ridgeline at the forward left-hand edge of the box overlooking the southern slopes of Mount Kent. From their location, the outskirts of Stanley were just visible 10 miles to their east. 17 Troop conformed to their south on the right-hand forward edge, as the saddle sloped up towards Mount Challenger at the eastern corner of the position. 18 Troop were behind them at the right-hand rear edge, with 19 Troop located at the rear left-hand edge of the formation. Squadron HQ was situated behind us further up the ridge, roughly offset from the centre of the oblong disposition of the four troops. Our own mortar position was sheltered by angular slabs of pale-grey quartzite rock, which sprang up along the ridgeline like spiked vertebrae rupturing the back of some prehistoric monster.

Standing up and looking through the gaps in the crags, I could make out some of the blokes in the other positions. Each troop was separated by at least 1,000 metres across the width of the box and by nearly 2 kilometres along its length. In daylight it became clear why the boss had decided on the formation and its location. Though dispersed, each troop could be supported by fire from another troop's location, and each position could dominate the ground in front out to the 1,800 metre effective range of a GPMG and to over 5 kilometres with the mortar. The dispositions made the best use of our limited numbers to provide all-round defence. We could cover an approach from any direction. More importantly, we dominated Mount Kent from its southern and eastern sides. From the mortar baseplate location we had a good view of the steep, dome-shaped mountain 2.5 kilometres away, looming a good 150 metres higher than the neighbouring peaks and ridges and dominating the landscape.

Stand-to ended with the completion of local clearance patrols, which confirmed the absence of any enemy in the immediate proximity of our box-shaped position. Later that morning, a patrol from 16 Troop also confirmed that there were no enemy on Mount Kent. They stopped to chat as they came in through our location.

'What's it like up there?' I asked.

'It's right in the middle of the ulu, and you can see into Stanley. If it's vital ground, there are no Argies up there, and it's there for the taking,' one of the blokes said, before adding, 'I reckon that the boss will be keen that it stays that way.'

'Let's just hope that 42 Commando get up here in enough force to hold it.'

'Yeah. With a full unit and some guns, they won't be able to dislodge us, and we could start pasting all their positions in and around the town. But let's hope they get here before the Argies start taking an interest in what we are doing.'

The idea of conducting guerrilla raids evaporated with

the realization that the key was ensuring that Mount Kent remained unoccupied by the enemy. If Mount Kent and the surrounding high ground could be reinforced without delay, not only could the Argentine defences around Stanley be brought under British artillery fire, they would also be rendered untenable by the presence of a large force which could be used as a springboard for any final assault on the town.

Until reinforcements could be flown forward, it would be up to us to ensure that the mountain remained clear of the enemy. Lacking the numbers to hold the peak ourselves, we would have to do what we could to keep it out of Arg hands from our neighbouring ridgeline position. That also involved lying low and trying not to attract too much attention to ourselves.

With Mount Kent lying uncontested and under observation, we went into a routine of patrolling, staying vigilant and fighting the cold. All we had to do was hang on and wait for the arrival of the Bootnecks and hope that the enemy didn't turn up in the meantime.

Hunkering down among the cracks in the rocks, we did our best to stay out of the incessant wind and keep warm. My Igloo jacket remained a godsend. Most of us wore the olive-green garment inside our camouflage smocks to avoid being misidentified. They were a civilian purchase, no other British troops were wearing them, and from a distance they had an uncanny resemblance to an Argentine army field jacket. I also wore a polypropylene thermal top, jungle shirt and fleece-lined Buffalo for additional insulation under the layer of Gore-Tex. But even with all of this, I remained bitterly cold.

Our feet were constantly wet and felt like blocks of ice. Before leaving *Intrepid*, I had smeared my boots with graphite grease, but that did little to keep out the water, which leached from the ground with every step to penetrate the cheap leather and stitching. After the first day I took off my sodden footwear.

'Ah, Christ, look at that,' I said, proffering one of my puffy white feet towards Jake. They looked like they had been left in a hot bath for far too long and were numb to the touch, the skin wrinkled and saggy.

'Aye, they look minging, mate. Mine are the same. Best we can do is wet and dry to try and stop foot rot from taking hold.'

It was the first sign of the potential onset of trench foot. I massaged some feeling back into them and put on my spare set of dry socks. Wringing out my wet pair, I then tucked them under my armpits, where my body heat would go some way to drying them out before swapping them over with the socks on my feet the next day. The semi-dry/wet sock routine was the only means we had of warding off what had once been the scourge of soldiers on the Western Front in the First World War and which became the common blight of the infantry soldier in the Falklands.

I envied those who smoked. Watching Jake as he pulled on a bine and inhaled smoke deep into his lungs, it seemed as if for a moment he had been transported away from the wet and the cold. But Jake couldn't smoke during darkness, and the nights were the worst.

Fourteen hours of darkness were punctuated by two hours on stag, when I took my turn on sentry duty and manning the radio watch, which I shared with Nige and Jake. The time stretched like an eternity, as you willed the minutes to pass, cold, hungry and sick with fatigue. Each stag was followed by four hours of sleep. The bivy bag helped to keep me dry, but without a sleeping bag, my core body temperature dropped as I slept. I woke up shivering; the frost cracked off my Gore-Tex shell as I got up to stamp and flap some warmth back into my arms and legs, before once again taking my turn on stag.

Food provided a brief respite from our privations. We lived off individual dehydrated arctic rations, which we pooled together in a single mess tin.

I cooked for the others before last light on the first day. But culinary variety in the field was never a great strength of the British army. There was only ever one menu available.

'Bloody Chicken Supreme and rice again,' I announced, to no one's great surprise. 'What a joy. What do you fancy, fellas? I can chuck in some AB bickies and some apple flakes if you like.'

'All right, Splash,' said Jake, throwing over a small green packet of the hardtack biscuits that wouldn't have looked out of place on one of Nelson's ships.

'Here, you can have my flakes too.'

'Thanks, Nige,' I said, breaking up the ABs and stirring them and the dried flakes into the mix of powdered chicken, rice and boiling water heating over the naked flames of a hexamine stove. I allowed it to thicken, before sharing the warm yellow sludge with the others. Meanwhile, Jake got a brew on of instant tea made from small white sachets of dust-thin tea leaves and powdered milk, which had been ground together. At night we were deprived even of these small luxuries.

After dark we lived by hard routine, so as to avoid giving away our position. No smoking, no cooking, no light of any kind. It was tactically sound but added to a state of permanent hunger and did little to help us combat the cold, which was compounded by the first fall of snow.

The flurries blew in on the wind, reducing visibility and adding to the general misery of conditions, as we sought what little shelter we could find among the wet, flapping ponchos and the shell scrapes hacked into the sodden earth, each one of us yearning for the commandos to hurry up and get forward. The Squadron had been sent to Mount Kent on the premise that 42 Commando would be flown in to relieve us within a day or two of our arrival. But there was a problem with that assumption.

# 32

The plan to airlift a half-battery of three 105 mm guns and all their artillery ammunition, not to mention a complete commando unit of 600-plus men with all their equipment and stores, forward to Mount Kent had been built around the arrival of the RAF's four heavy-lift CH-47 Chinooks embarked on the *Atlantic Conveyor*. However, when she was struck and sunk by the Exocet missiles on 25 May, only one of the large double-rotor-bladed helicopters had been flown off the container ship. It would need scores of individual Sea King lifts to do the job of the four Chinooks.

The problem was further compounded by political pressure coming from London for 3 Commando Brigade to break out of the San Carlos bridgehead and demonstrate early success against the occupying Argentine forces. Mike Rose maintained that the pressing political demands of the campaign could best be realized by bouncing enough forces forward and properly securing Mount Kent. However, others thought differently, and their opinions held sway.

As we froze our backsides off, watching and waiting from our positions among the rocks, 40 miles behind us and 13 miles south of the beachhead, 690 men of 2 PARA battle group began to advance on the settlements of Darwin and Goose Green. By morning on 29 May, after nearly thirty-six hours of hard gutter fighting, the Paras had taken their objectives and captured over 1,000 Argentine prisoners. Eighteen British soldiers were killed, and three times that number were wounded. The dead included 2 PARA's CO, Lieutenant Colonel 'H' Jones, who was later awarded a posthumous Victoria Cross. It was rightly heralded as an impressive feat of arms, but, with limited resources, 3 Commando Brigade could only support one major unit-level operation. 2 PARA's victory, while satisfying the politicians' demand for a demonstrable quick win over the enemy, meant that the movement of 42 Commando forward to Mount Kent had been delayed.

For us, 29 May dawned bright and clear, proving that the eco-climate of the Falklands can yield four seasons in any given twenty-four-hour period. The temperature was still freezing, and the wind never ceased, but for most of that day the sun triumphed over the wintry squalls. Unaware of what had occurred at Goose Green, our preoccupation remained with the weather, Mount Kent and the absence of the Marines.

I was grateful for any respite from the rain and the snow, as I was on sentry duty, tucked among the rocks and observing my arcs looking down towards Estancia House, which nestled in a valley several miles to the northwest. The slopes of the mountain to my front remained undisturbed, when I heard the slow, steady thump of helicopter blades. Carried on the wind from the other side of Mount Kent, it was neither the clattering noise of a Wessex nor the higher-pitched tone of a Sea King, but something less familiar.

The sound grew steadily louder, and then I saw them.

With an hour of daylight left and the sun already dipping below the hills in the west, a pair of Bell UH-1 helicopters emerged from behind the high ground. The Hueys turned as they came round the side of the mountain and beat their way along the valley, heading in our direction. The iconic utility helicopter had been made famous through its ubiquitous use in Vietnam. It was also an item of kit that the Americans had sold to Argentina.

The two Hueys landed in the lower ground, perhaps a kilometre away. I counted the number of troops as they climbed out of the cabs and watched them go to cover among the grass and the rocks, while the aircraft lifted and flew back down the valley. There were twelve of them. Even at 1,000 metres, I could see that each man was weighed down by their weapons and rucksacks. They got up, shook out into a loose patrol formation and started to move up from the lower ground towards us.

I pressed the 350 tactical radio headset to my ear and spoke into the mike, keeping my eyes fixed on the steadily advancing patrol. I kept my voice even but wanted to convey a sense of urgency without sounding overly alarmed.

'Hello, Zero Alpha, this is Zero Delta, sighting, over.'

'Zero Alpha, send, over,' came the reply at the other end of the net.

'Two times enemy helis have just dropped off twelve, repeat twelve, enemy pax, 1,000 metres to my north. I am observing. Over.'

Cedric acknowledged my sighting report and then signed off with the words, 'OK, Splash. Get down there and ambush them.'

'Roger. Out,' I replied. It had not been what I was expecting.

I looked at my fellow members of the ambush party – all two of them. *What the fuck?* I thought, but kept it to myself. Instead, Nige and I began to work out how our tiny force of three was going to deal with a party of Argies that out-numbered us four to one. As we prepared to leave the rock cover of our position, we made sure we were tooled up, checking that grenades were in pouches and spare mag-azines were readily to hand. We were about to start creeping down from the ridge to put in a snap ambush and take them from their flank, when the OC of 16 Troop came up on the radio.

'Hang on, Zero Delta, we are on our way down.'

He had been listening to the net, and moments later he and his blokes bounded down to us from their position further up on the ridgeline. He dropped on to one knee, ten of his men clustering behind him. Substantially re-inforced to something approaching even odds, we hastily rescoped a new plan.

'Nige, Jake and Splash, you stay put and provide fire support in conjunction with two GPMGs we have left further up the crag at our position. The remainder of 16 Troop will fan out down the slope and take the Argies and put a snap ambush in on them. OK?'

'Yep, got it,' we replied to Air Troop's boss.

It was a bit rough and ready, but it would have to do. Glancing back into the valley, I could see that the lead man of the enemy patrol was now only 400 metres away.

I squeezed myself into a narrow cleft between the slabs of rock, which formed a natural parapet, and took up a fire position. The light was fading fast. 16 Troop were moving down the slope, spreading out as they went, their outline becoming more blurred with the onset of darkness and increasing distance as they closed in on their prey. They had not been seen by the enemy, who were still coming on and about to reach the edge of a large stone run. The distance between the two advancing bodies of men was closing to 100 metres or so. I held my breath.

16 Troop held the advantage of surprise if they could get to their flanking ambush position before being spotted by the Argies. Soon they were lost in the gathering gloom.

Then all hell let loose.

The area around the stone run exploded into a chaotic two-way exchange of fire. It had become too dark to distinguish friend from foe, so I engaged the enemy muzzle flashes that stabbed out of the darkness in our direction.

The valley filled with the rapid crackle of trading rounds. The heavy automatic rattle of 16 Troop's Gimpies to our right, each killing burst full of fatal menace and power, was audible over the thinner percussion of semi-automatic rifle fire. Tracer shot through the darkness and bounced off the rocks. Shouts urgent and frantic mixed in with the tumult of noise, some in English and some in Spanish.

Someone on our side was yelling out for someone to put up light. The shout was repeated, more urgent and full of imperative: 'Get some fucking light up!'

I glanced in the direction of the mortar, still cached under the rocks, split up in its three component parts. *No time for that*, I thought. So I grabbed a Schermuly, knocked the cap ends off the handheld tube and fired the 1.5 inch illuminating rocket into the air. It shot up into the night sky with a loud, drawn-out *whoosh*, as the small rocket sailed vertically upwards, its point of light piercing the darkness to pop high above me in a sudden burst of brightness. It burned brilliantly under a small parachute, which cast flickering shadows of light across the ground as it drifted overhead. It was a big mistake. Illuminated behind it was a hanging trail of smoke, leading directly back to me. Shit.

# 33

For a moment, everything seemed to go into slow motion. Then the air about me was rent with fast-moving metal as the Argentines appeared to switch their aim and concentrate the bulk of their fire on to the bottom of the smoke trail. Rods of red tracer slashed their way towards me through the night. The rocks around me suddenly began to fizz with incoming rounds and splintering chips of quartzite as I ducked down below my makeshift parapet.

The noise was terrific, and my world closed in around me. I was digging in with my eyeballs in a frenzied attempt to make myself as small as possible. An endless stream of rounds buzzed above and about me like a swarm of angry bees as bullets smashed into the rock and ricocheted to my right and to my left. I couldn't be sure, but the Argies were probably firing with just their assault rifles. If they had a machine gun, the weight of the fire could have been heavier and more deadly. But even a splintered shard of rock would cause horrific damage if it found soft flesh. I prayed, my predicament exposing my mortality, and wondered how much longer it could go on for.

Then it was suddenly over. The fire in the valley began to slacken. More shouts from down below me, mainly in Spanish. The enemy were disengaging, using the cover of darkness to break contact and make their escape. I chanced a look over the edge of the rocks. The flare was dying out, and darkness was returning to the stone run. The odd shot rang out, and there was the last, brief chatter of a machine gun, as the Argies retreated into the night. The contact had probably lasted only ten to fifteen minutes, although it seemed like it had gone on for hours. Drills had kicked in on both sides, but surprise combined with speed and aggression had counted in winning the firefight.

Silence descended across the valley. It was broken by movement among the rocks and by shouts in English, as Air Troop reorganized, the OC calling out to check whether there were any casualties and giving instructions. The blokes responded to the command to pull back to the ridge and reported back that they were OK. Although two were not.

'Bash, you OK?'

'Yep, OK, boss.'

'Dinger, you OK?'

'Yeah, all right, boss.'

'Dickie, you all right?'

No response.

'Shit, Bash, get over to Dickie and check he is OK. Everybody, wait for Bash and then prepare to pull back up on to the ridge.'

The casualties from the firefight were brought back up to our location, as the mortar baseplate was also designated as the first aid post for the Squadron. A bloke called Al Rogers arrived first, limping heavily, assisted by another trooper. The back of one of his legs had been lacerated by rock splinters. We got him down, and I reached for the patrol medic pack. We started to tend to his wounds when

Dickie Palmer came in, half carried between two of the blokes. He was in pain and looked in a bad way. Skills honed in an NHS A and E department kicked in, and we immediately focused our attention on him.

Tearing open the med kit of IV bags, dressing and tape, I reached for the essentials that would keep a wounded man alive. Lying on his front, Dickie groaned as we pulled down his trousers, which at least confirmed that there was no need to check his breathing. The priority was on finding the bleed and stopping it. High-velocity bullets tear through flesh and bone, causing catastrophic damage when they hit major blood vessels and organs. But Dickie had been lucky. With the use of a shielded torch we could make out the deep gouge where a bullet had tracked through the muscle of his left buttock and cleaved an ugly wound 15 cm long and almost 5 cm deep. The round had gone in and out, missing his femoral artery and tibia, although it would have smacked home like the blow of a sledgehammer.

The blood was still oozing from the wound but, warm and sticky to the touch, it had already started to clot. Fingers probed to confirm that there was no deeper and more serious bleed. Dickie winced with pain. I tried to reassure him.

'Dickie,' I said soothingly, 'you are the only Royal Marine I know who has got two holes in his arse.'

'It's an upper thigh wound, you bastard, Splash.'

'OK, Dickie, whatever you say, mate, but it definitely hit you right in the arse.'

He managed a laugh and, among other things, told me to 'Fuck off.' He winced again with the effort of telling me that I needed to work on my bedside manner. More helpfully, someone gave him a shot of morphine, before cleaning the laceration and packing it tight with a first-aid field dressing to stem the last of the bleeding.

Between us, we managed to stabilize Dickie and Al, but they would both need surgical attention, and I put out a casualty evacuation request to Squadron HQ. Every medic and commander wants to get their casualties off the ground quickly. The time taken to move an injured person from their point of wounding to proper medical care in a hospital makes a difference to both their survival and the extent of recovery. However, despite the best efforts of the head shed, they informed me that a CASEVAC helicopter wasn't going to arrive any time soon to pick up our wounded. They didn't need to tell me why.

I suspected that the helicopters were being diverted to other tasks. The build-up of the land force was still consuming precious helicopter hours. The airframes were getting thrashed, not least because of the need to collect the casualties in the aftermath of 2 PARA's attack on Goose Green. Dickie and Al would have to wait patiently until serviceable aircraft could be made available. Word came back from the head shed that Cedric was hoping a heli insert scheduled for later that night would be able to lift them out.

We got them into sleeping bags and did what we could to make them as comfortable as possible. I checked on Dickie during the night. He was groggy with pain. Administering additional morphine took some of the edge off it, but as the shock of being hit wore off and his nerves adjusted to the impact of the wound, the opiate only had limited effect, and the cold and damp weren't doing much to help him. Looking after Dickie made me think about the weird geometry of chance in battle. He had been lucky, although luck is a relative term here. A fraction of an inch to the right, and the round would have sliced through his artery and shattered his thigh bone. If that had happened, he would have bled out in minutes, and I doubt that we could have saved him. If the bullet had been a mere shade off to the left, it would have missed him altogether.

The ambush site was cleared at first light the next morning. There was no sign of any Argentine dead, but 16 Troop found and recovered their rucksacks, which had been dumped in haste and left among the rocks. The blokes brought their captured booty back up to our position. The bergens were full of kit, and some of it was better than ours. We were like a bunch of kids at Christmas as they pulled out the contents of the rucksacks.

'Hey, look at this, a brand spanker set of NVGs still wrapped in its packaging and unopened,' one of them said. 'These look like the dog's bollocks.'

There were more of the night vision goggles, which would be pressed into service by the Squadron to supplement our own paucity of night vision equipment.

'How about these tinned rations? Not sure what vicuna is, but it has got to be better than Chicken Supreme. Hey, they have also got whisky miniatures.'

'White Heather? Never heard of it,' I said, taking a sip from a bottle before passing it to Nige and Jake. 'Not bad either.'

The Argentine rations were a culinary delight compared

to the freeze-dried arctic fare we had become used to. The small cans of vicuna meat, a South American relative of the llama, were delicious compared to our familiar mush. We shared the food, and there was an impromptu auction of other items of kit. No money passed hands, but a bid was decided on need. When a brand-new sleeping bag emerged, there was only going to be one winner. It was tossed over to me, 'Here you go, Splash, doss bag for you, complete with a few bullet holes.'

'Thanks, mate, chuffed to NAAFI break with this, and nothing a bit of black nasty can't sort.'

'Pleasure, mate. It doesn't look like its previous owner will be needing it again.'

It was stuffed with down, of four seasons quality, and without the long central zip stitched into a British-issue bag, which let the cold in and allowed you to star gaze through the gaps in its teeth when you lay in it at night. Someone also tossed me an Argie equivalent of a K Bar knife. Sheathed in leather and made of untempered steel, it was a cheap copy of my American original, but it had a serrated edge and would make for a handy utility tool in the absence of anything else.

The owners of some of the discarded rucksacks made a brief reappearance about an hour later, although they were too far away to make any attempt to reclaim their property. I spotted the remnants of the patrol as they skylined a distant ridge, heading towards their own lines in the direction of Stanley. They were 5 kilometres or so to our east. After the contact, we had set up the mortar, and the scattered figures made for a tempting target.

'Nige, I reckon we can just about reach them from

a map prediction shoot if we fired the mortar using maximum charge 8,' I said, referring to the propellant augmentation charge rings, which could be fitted around the tail end of an 81 mm bomb to give it extra range.

'Yep, we should be able to mallet them with that. Get on the net and ask the OC if he is happy for us to try a fire mission.'

I got on the radio and asked Cedric for permission to have a go at engaging the Argies, stressing that they were out in the open and we had a good chance of nailing them.

'Negative, Zero Delta,' Cedric's voice crackled back through the static, 'let them go.'

Cedric probably felt that we had drawn enough attention to ourselves already. We had given them a bloody nose, and killing the withdrawing patrol wouldn't have made any material difference to our ability to hold on to Mount Kent until 42 Commando arrived. He was probably right, although the Argies weren't done with us yet.

It was Bilbo who spotted them first. He was manning a GPMG in 19 Troop's position with Roy Fonseca, when he caught sight of a figure out of the corner of his eye. He looked again and saw two of them, moving cautiously out in the open near the rocks where 17 Troop were located on the southwestern corner of the Squadron position. He couldn't be sure, but they looked like enemy.

John Hamilton got on the radio and alerted Boat Troop's staff sergeant.

'Hello, One Zero Bravo, this is Four Zero Alpha. We think we have picked up movement around your position. Not sure if they are enemy or some of your own blokes. Can you reveal yourself to confirm? Over.'

'Four Zero, this is One Zero. You have got to be fucking kidding,' came back the response.

Suddenly there was a burst of firing, and the distinct crack of at least one grenade going off. We jumped into action as we heard the start of the engagement, receiving a call to provide support from the mortar over the net at the same time. The first round sent the baseplate hard back into the peat, digging itself into the boggy ground. I groaned inwardly, *Pebble Island all over again*. But the ground was firmer than the marsh by the Big Pond.

'Check fire, check fire, let me get something to stop the baseplate bedding in.'

I scouted around quickly and found what I was looking for: a thick slab of rectangular rock, about the size of a doorstep and big enough to wedge in at an angle behind the baseplate to stop it digging in and sliding back when it fired.

'OK, that will do.'

'Good,' said Nige. 'Fire another adjustment.'

After we loosed off another quick-adjusting round, Boat Troop reported that our next round landed close enough to the target. The quartzite backstop was working.

The radio from Boat Troop's location crackled back into life, 'Right 100, add 50.'

'Right 100, add 50,' Nige repeated back on the radio, loud enough for Jake to pick up the correction, and finished off with: 'Five rounds fire for effect!'

Jake altered the C2 sights on the mortar bipod, shouted 'On!' and then I set about dropping the mortar bombs as fast as I could down the barrel one after the other.

Seconds later, we heard the satisfying *crump-crump* as

the 81 mm rounds landed. But it was 17 Troop's GPMGs that did the damage, cutting down two Argentine soldiers, but not before they had crept close enough to Boat Troop to lob a grenade into the middle of their position.

One of the blokes took splinter wounds from the grenade in his back and was brought up to our position to be looked after. We now had three casualties to get out. The CASEVAC helicopter we had been hoping for later that evening failed to materialize, as the visibility closed in, and squalls of rain mixed with flurries of snow shut down the possibility of launching helicopters. It also meant that 42 Commando's move forward would also be delayed again.

The other casualty's shrapnel wounds were unpleasant but not serious. However, I was beginning to worry about Dickie. We tried to keep him warm by plying him with hot brews until last light. But he was suffering in the cold. The temperature might have reduced the risk of his wound beginning to bleed again, as well as warding off some of the risk of infection, but we needed to get him out soon.

17 Troop buried the two Argentine dead as best they could. Interning the bodies in the shallow peat, they topped the soil with quartzite stone before marking each of the graves. Both soldiers carried double identity discs. One was left with the deceased, the other was taken to be handed in with the coordinates of the burial location for subsequent reporting and recovery, if the Argentines cared to collect their dead.

It has never been established exactly what the enemy were trying to achieve by their activities around the area of Mount Kent. It had been reported that the feature was occasionally patrolled before our arrival, and the group ambushed on 29 May might have been sent with the intention of establishing some sort of a presence. Additionally, they might even have been dispatched with the purpose of trying to lay an ambush against us. The subsequent actions may have been deliberate attempts to recce and probe our positions. They could have been isolated groups of the enemy attempting to make their mark, or simply soldiers separated from their units and desperate to get home.

There may have been a more concerted Argentine attempt later that day, but it was stopped in its tracks by a pair of RAF GR3 Harriers. I saw the first jet scream in low between our position and Mount Challenger, filling the valley with the roar of its Pegasus Rolls-Royce engine. It swooped out of sight into the lower ground towards Stanley. The distant explosion of ordnance rolled back towards us, indicating that it had found its target, which had been called in by an unseen G Squadron patrol. The Harrier malleted an Argentine Marine company group with its cluster bombs and rockets, as the hundred-odd enemy soldiers moved into position in lower ground. It was also a remarkable piece of flying.

The RAF's GR3 version of the aircraft had originally been sent south to supplement the Sea Harriers in the fighter air defence role. However, with the Navy's aircraft holding their own against Argentine air attack, the RAF pilots from HMS *Hermes* were able to focus on their primary ground attack role. Designed to work from land-based strips, the GR3's navigational system was incapable of initializing data uploads while on a moving and pitching deck. Consequently, the pilots were forced to operate without heads-up displays and GPS guidance for their navigation aids and weapons fit. Instead they had to do everything using a map, compass and stopwatch, while flying less than 100 feet above the earth and moving at up to 600 mph. It was technology no better than had been available to ground attack pilots in the 1940s, but they had not been facing modern radar-guided anti-aircraft weapons, as the first Harrier's wingman found out when he followed up the attack.

We watched the second GR3 sweep past us, roll over and drop below the crest to our front. This was shortly followed by a similar concussion of explosions, but this time a heavy crackling of automatic ground fire was added to the mix as the Argies bounced by the first strike shook off their surprise and put up everything they had as the second Harrier came in on the same angle of attack.

I didn't see it, but some of the blokes further forward watched the stricken GR3 as it pulled up, having sustained obvious damage. It was clearly in trouble, as the pilot attempted to nurse his aircraft back to *Hermes* stationed somewhere far out to sea. They mentally wished him luck, although they were uncertain of the aircraft's chances of making it. It didn't. With his fuel tanks holed by cannon fire, the pilot ejected over the sea and was rescued by a Sea King.

Whether or not the Arg Marine company were intending to come at us was unknown. But their hasty retreat didn't mean that the enemy were giving up. Indeed, there would be further contacts before the Royal Marines battle group finally started to arrive.

# 34

The five-man Argentine patrol was landed by helicopter in the low ground to the west near a place on the map called Estancia House, some distance beyond where 16 Troop had put in their ambush. They were spotted some way out, again heading in our direction, and were likely to arrive by last light, when the first elements of 42 Commando were expected. Cedric was notified and ordered John Hamilton to deal with them. Mountain Troop took the enemy on at range at dusk.

A crashing weight of machine-gun and rifle fire drove the Arg patrol into a stone run. Binsy was in his element as he engaged them with an L42 sniper rifle. He may have been one of the best sharpshooters in the Squadron, but the converted Lee Enfield bolt action weapon had a limited range out to 800 metres. Low light conditions would have reduced the effectiveness of the telescopic sight to make for even more difficult shooting. However, with two GPMGs and a sniper on their case, the enemy went to ground among the rocks and stayed there. That's when we got the call to provide mortar support.

John sent Nige the target indication over the radio, as Jake and I took post on the mortar. Nige marked the data John had sent him on to a plotting board and began working out the coordinates. He was an expert, and within seconds he was shouting out the bearing and elevation of the fire mission.

'Fire mission, charge 3, bearing 5400, elevation 1211.'

Jake set the coordinates into the C2 sight, spinning the adjustment handles on the bipod to achieve the right alignment and repeating the information back to Nige, before shouting a repeat of the data he had been given back to Nige and bellowing 'On!' when he was done.

With Nige's near-instant order to fire, I slipped a bomb down the tube, instinctively crouching and shielding my ears from the blast as the round fired and shot back out of the barrel with a weighty crack.

The next round was already in my hands as Nige reported 'Shot, 12' over the radio as the time of flight so that John would know when it was about to arrive.

There was a *crump* as the round landed, and a brief pause as Nige pressed his ear to the headset and listened for John's corrections.

'Right to 200, add 50,' Nige called out, repeating John's corrections.

'Right 200, add 50,' Jake bellowed back.

'Five rounds fire for effect!'

I fed the bombs down the barrel. Ducking between each round, grasping another and feeding it a split-second after the preceding round had left the mortar. Our drills were slick and fast; we had spent our time working with the weapon system in Kenya well. The rounds landed among the rocks where the Argentine patrol had taken cover with five distinct *crump*s, each a split-second apart. It was dangerous close fire, and the blokes in 19 Troop knew what they were asking for: rounds that would be landing in near proximity to their own positions. However, one slight error on our part and we could be killing or maiming our own people in a blue on blue. I scrubbed the barrel hard, with a mini chimneysweep-type of brush to clear the inside of the tube from built-up carbon residue, keeping it ready and accurate for the call for the next salvo. It came quickly.

The rounds were clearly having an effect. I could make out the excitement in John's voice coming over the radio as he shouted, 'On, on! It's hitting them! Keep it coming, keep it coming!'

'Bloody hell,' Nige muttered. 'All right, Four Zero Alpha, keep your hair on.'

The next round was already in the barrel. Jake checked the sight every couple of retorts to ensure that we were still on. I kept an eye on the makeshift baseplate backstop. The slab of quartzite was still holding and preventing the mortar from digging itself down into the peat. I yelled, 'Rounds complete!' as the final bomb was sent on its way.

Seconds later, the last sounds of rounds detonating as they impacted sang out across the valley and echoed off the sides of the higher ground. The rattle of small-arms fire also died away. Nige kept Jake and me informed of what was going on at the other end of the contact from reports that John was sending back over the radio.

'John says that the Argies are flying a white flag from the rocks; they have taken casualties and have had enough. John is sending some blokes down to them to take prisoners and treat their wounded.'

Nige beamed at me and Jake, 'Bloody good job. Well

done, and quite right too. Given the quals we have we are probably the best-paid mortar crew in the British Army.'

The helicopters coming in that night with the commandos would finally allow us to get our own wounded out, along with the injured Argies. We were warned off to get our three casualties ready; the extraction couldn't come soon enough. The two blokes with shrapnel wounds would be able to make it down to the helicopter landing site with a bit of assistance, but Dickie was in a bad way and would need to be portered down to the HLS in a poncho.

It took four of us to carry him down into the depression of ground lying towards the southern edge of the Squadron's box position, which meant carrying him and his kit across 300 metres of uneven broken ground in the dark. We started moving just after 19 Troop's contact and we were still sweating and grunting from the effort when we heard the approach of helicopters from the west. The throbbing noise of multiple rotors beating through the darkness towards us grew louder as they got closer, and then another firefight broke out to the south of 18 and 19 Troops' positions.

The head shed had told the pilots that the HLS was clear, so God knows what they thought as red lines of tracer slashed through the blackness beneath them. There must have been a whole squadron of Sea Kings, and with them the sole surviving Chinook. To speed up the lift, Mike Rose had persuaded the pilot to fly in and support the Sea Kings. It was a big ask.

Call sign Bravo November had been completing a routine flight when the Exocets struck the *Atlantic Conveyor.*

Flying to *Hermes*, the big helicopter had been threatened with getting pushed overboard, as it was obstructing critical Harrier operations. Eventually finding a home in San Carlos, but without any maintenance support, the RAF pilot was flying his first combat mission with the aid of NVGs, which he had never used before. The Chinook came thumping in, carrying an underslung 105 mm gun, with two more inside with their crews. Having dropped off the artillery pieces, it lifted fast. Constrained by the tunnel vision of the NVGs and, no doubt, distracted by the lines of tracer fire, the pilot clipped the surface of a pond, damaging one of the wheels, and only just managed to nurse the pranged airframe safely back to San Carlos.

The battle-experienced crews of the Sea Kings made for a less eventful insertion, bringing in the rest of the battery and the lead company elements of 42 Commando. We got ready with the casualties as they landed, moving straight up to the side of the troop doors as the Marines piled out. The faces of the young Bootnecks were a picture of startled awe as they were greeted by the sight of wounded men waiting to be loaded on to the helicopters while the night sky around them was being criss-crossed with the trace of bullets.

'What kept you, Royal?' someone shouted, as the Marines filed off into the darkness heading towards Mount Kent.

We loaded Dickie and the two shrapnel cases on to the helicopters. I shouted to make myself heard above the roar of the engines and the blades beating above my head, 'You'll be all right now, Dickie. Try and stay off your arse, and look out for those pretty nurses when you get to a ship.'

'Thanks, Splash, good plan.' With that he gave us a thumbs-up and disappeared further inside the confines of the cab with the aid of a crewman.

We turned to tab back to our positions as the Sea King took off. The retreating sound of aircraft was replaced by the noise of a half-battery of guns coming into action in a commotion of shouts, grunts and metallic clangs, as artillery trails were lifted, ammunition was broken open and metal aiming posts were hammered home.

The skirmishes going on around the position to the south kept us busy for most of the rest of the night. I was concerned that we would run out of mortar rounds keeping up with the demand, but we were able to blag some extra bombs from the Marines' mortar platoon, which had started to set up their six tubes next to ours. Mike Rose turned up at our position, as he had come in with the Marines.

Along with him was a tall man dressed in an old camouflage Para smock, wearing a pair of thick glasses and smoking a cigar: the journalist Max Hastings. The CO turned to me.

'Hello, Splash, can you brief us on your situation up here?'

I looked round for Nige, wanting to pass the buck up the chain of command, as no soldier relishes briefing his commanding officer. Then a fire mission came in and saved my bacon.

'Sorry, boss, I'm a bit busy,' I mumbled, and then bent to the task of servicing the mortar.

During another lull in the firing, Max Hastings returned on his own to our location. I was about to admire the

319

towering newspaper man's pluck and thirst for information, but instead of asking us for an interview to add to one of his dispatches, he had a more pressing concern.

'Forgive me for troubling you, chaps, but you haven't happened to see a respirator case lying around here, have you, as it contains my two cameras, which are quite expensive?'

'Not seen it, I'm afraid. Are you sure you had them with you when you came up here with the CO?'

We hadn't seen them, although I am not entirely convinced that he believed us, as he wandered off in search of Mike Rose.

The Marines' mortars weren't in action that night, and the Bootnecks had used the opportunity to get their heads down. The mortar platoon commander and his senior NCO crawled into a two-man tent and promptly fell asleep. When the next call came in, I hesitated for a moment before posting the first mortar bomb and looked at Nige.

'Should we wake up the sleeping beauties before firing?'

Nige wrinkled his nose, as if thinking about it, and then just said, 'Nah.'

As the round crashed out of the barrel, the two Marines shot out of their cosy little basha and threw themselves to the ground. It was all we could do to keep the fire going and not piss ourselves with laughter. I suppose it was Nige's way of saying welcome to Mount Kent.

While the Marines didn't fire their own mortars that night, the gunners from 29 Commando Royal Artillery did just after first light. Soon after stand-to, the ground in the depression behind us cracked open in a tremendous cacophony of sound as 105 mm shells were fired on maximum charge. The muzzles of the artillery belched stabbing flashes of flame, which lit up the dull morning sky, as gun trails thumped backwards into the peat. Breeches snapped open with an audible clang as empty brass cases were ejected and fresh rounds were rammed home.

It was an impressive sight, punctuated with the shouted commands of fire control orders, as the half-battery worked a methodical rhythm, unleashing high-explosive shells on distant Argentine targets in the east around Stanley. 29 Commando gave the honour of firing the first round to the CO, which was a fitting tribute to the man who had pushed so hard to get Mount Kent occupied.

Max Hastings never recovered his cameras, but he got his wish of seeing the lights of Stanley before any other reporter. The CO also allowed him to use one of the SAS Tacsats to file his story straight back to his editors in London, which gave him a scoop, as he was the only journalist on the ground and could also bypass the cumbersome MOD official channels for filing copy. He then flew back to San Carlos on a helicopter with Rose. As they lifted off, leaving Mount Kent behind them with the light guns plugging away at enemy positions around Stanley, the CO turned to the journalist and said, 'Who dares wins, Max.'

The Argies put a few 155 mm rounds back our way, which meant that we had to move around with one ear cocked for the whistle of an incoming projectile. Although of a much bigger calibre than our own guns, the enemy shells were infrequent and exploded in a shower of sodden muck, as the peat absorbed most of the shrapnel. Had they landed in greater volume, with greater accuracy, and fallen among the rocks where we were located, it would have been a different matter. But the Args never got their eye in. For the next three days D Squadron remained in the lee of Mount Kent, doing little more than listening out for the odd shell and our best to keep warm.

With several hundred Marines occupying the higher ground and a battery of guns behind us, we no longer felt lonely. The Argies made no more attempts to probe into the area, and what opportunity they might have had to seize the vital ground had been lost. On 3 June, 3 PARA were spotted tabbing in towards us from the area of Estancia House; 45 Commando were reported as being hard on their heels.

They had tabbed, or yomped, the 40-odd miles from San Carlos, and if our feet were anything to go by, theirs must have been in a shocking state. They still had another 10 miles to go to reach Stanley, but the ultimate prize of the campaign to free the Falklands appeared to be within their grasp. There would be some hard fighting ahead, but the Argentine defences around the capital were now under the guns of our artillery, and the battle for its possession was about to begin.

However, as the rest of the British land forces prepared to continue to advance east, 19 Troop were about to be tasked on a job much further to the west.

# 35

I looked at the faces of the blokes sitting opposite me in the helicopter. Each one a mask of fatigue from the privations of Mount Kent. Each one a mirror image of my own, shaggy with a week's worth of beard and etched with tiredness. Exposed skin was burned ruddy by prolonged exposure to the wind, lips chapped, blistered and dried by the cold, and eyes blurred and gritty from days without proper sleep. Heads nodded and drooped on to the chests of sodden smocks, stained black and caked stiff with dirt and sweat.

We were nearly sick with exhaustion and hunger, and the prospect of a shower, a proper meal and a decent night's sleep in the warmth and the dry of a ship was the uppermost thought in everybody's mind. The expectation seemed tantalizingly close as the Sea King crested the higher ground around San Carlos Water. But it was to be delayed by a busy flight deck, which waved us off and sent us round into a holding pattern somewhere off the stern of HMS *Fearless*.

*Oh Christ, not again. Just set this damn helicopter down.* I forced myself to look out of the window and focus on the world below me. It was late afternoon. The anchorage seemed more crowded, as small craft shuttled urgently between vessels and the shore to keep feeding the burgeoning logistics dumps that had sprung up along the edges of the beach. Off to my right, I caught site of the main medical dressing station that had been set up in the disused meatpacking plant at Ajax Bay on the western edge of the shallow inlet on the night that I had escaped from *Canberra*.

It was where our wounded would have been taken. I thought of Dickie, and wondered if the surgical equipment unloaded from the landing craft that night I escaped from *Canberra* had been used to save his life. They came to call it the 'Red and Green Life Machine', as most of its customers were Paras and Marines. Working in primitive conditions, on operating tables set up among the ruined debris of the old slaughterhouse and its dust-strewn floor, the medics conducted essential surgery and treatment to stabilize casualties, before evacuating them for further hospital care on the SS *Uganda*.

The surgeons would have been busy after Goose Green, with 2 PARA's wounded brought in on stretchers, shocked and shivering after spending a night out on the battle-field. They would be even busier in the coming days, once the fighting for Stanley started. But through to the end of the war, every British casualty who made it to Ajax Bay left the place alive.

The helicopter began its approach to *Fearless*'s flight deck. Thoughts about the wounded were displaced by the anticipation of creature comforts aboard the ship. But our hopes were quickly dashed.

Almost as soon as we touched down on the deck, we were told that we were going straight back out again. Ade Robertson broke the news to us as we collected our kit in the hangar deck.

'Fast-ball warning order, guys. Two patrols are going out tonight to conduct OP ops on West Falkland. The boss and I have got a briefing with the head shed. We'll let you know the details and then come up with a plan.'

Shit. If we were lucky, we might just get some scoff and clean our gats, but then we would be straight into battle prep before the off, without any time to dry our kit or get our heads down.

'Looks like we will be going out wet and in clip,' I said.

'If you can't take a joke . . .' Binsy's voice trailed off behind me, but we were too tired to laugh.

'Get your weapons cleaned and get some scoff. John and I will be back from the briefing in an hour,' said Ade.

With the unstoppable build-up of British forces ashore and the seizure of Mount Kent by 3 Commando Brigade, the Argies knew that it was now only a matter of time before their defences around Stanley were overwhelmed and their brief tenure of East Falkland came to an end. The ferocity of enemy air attacks against the ships in the anchorage had also dropped off, and, as they were unable to provide close air support to their own forces around Stanley, there was little more the Argentine Air Force could do to influence the outcome of the war. The Task Force had won the air battle. And with the bulk of the enemy's forces dug in around the capital, the main focus of the British campaign turned to defeating them there.

However, the Argentines still had over 2,000 troops garrisoning the two main settlements on West Falkland, and they had the potential to cause us problems.

Largely unmolested, save for the occasional naval

bombardment and Harrier attack, and the destruction of some of their supply ships, their presence caused concern. If left unchecked, the Arg forces on West Falkland had the potential to launch raids across the short distance of Falkland Sound against the logistics area at San Carlos. They could also be reinforced, either to strengthen the Argentine position in any subsequent negotiations following the fall of Stanley, or with the intent of prolonging the war and making the need to retake West Falkland more costly.

As we were landing on *Fearless*, intelligence assessments were already suggesting that Buenos Aires was planning to drop a battalion of paratroopers on to the island. As a result, our senior commanders wanted to deploy some element of the British land force on to West Falkland to keep an eye on the Argies already stationed there and defeat any additional troops if they were dispatched from mainland Argentina. With all the British units committed to East Falkland, the task fell to D Squadron. It was exactly the kind of covert role that the Regiment had trained for in any European war.

Lying 12 miles from East Falkland across the water, West Falkland has a similar landscape of rugged hills, grasslands and peat heaths to that of its larger neighbour. Some of its population of just under 300 people were dispersed between isolated farming settlements, but most were concentrated around its two largest communities at Fox Bay in the south and Port Howard in the north, which were at each end of a 20-mile-long steep coastal ridge of hills running along the eastern side of the island. G Squadron's recce patrols on West Falkland had been withdrawn by the beginning of June, but they had reported the stationing of Argentine battalion-sized units of roughly a thousand men supported by artillery and helicopters at each of the settlements.

'OK, guys, I hope you had a chance to get some scoff down your necks. This is the score,' John said, having gathered the Troop together on the hangar following his and Ade's briefing from Cedric.

'The OC's intent is to prevent the enemy on West Falkland receiving reinforcements. His Conops is to insert recce and OP patrols and be ready to trigger the use of the Squadron to thwart their efforts if they try and bring in more troops or make a move with what they have already got on the island.'

John paused to let what he had said sink in, and then outlined the Troops' missions.

'16 Troop will stake out a possible Argentine drop zone which has been identified in open ground astride the main track running between the two main settlements. Equipped with Stinger missiles, Air Troop will shoot down any enemy aircraft and defeat any surviving Arg paratroopers on the ground. 18 Troop will move in and observe a possible Arg observation post on the top of Mount Rosalie. Situated 10 miles to the north of Port Howard, it is believed to be reporting on British ship movements in Falkland Sound. If the right situation arises, Mobility Troop will be cued in to take it out.'

We nodded, as John pointed out various locations on his map.

'Our mission is to conduct OP patrols on the settlements of Port Howard and Fox Bay, here and here.' He used the nib of his pencil to indicate the two settlements on the map.

He looked up at the seven faces in front of him. 'We only need two four-man patrols. I will take Port Howard, and Ade's patrol will set up an OP to cover Fox Bay.' We knew what was coming next. 'That means one of you will have to stay behind and will be detached to 17 Troop, who the boss is keeping back as a reserve, and will base with Squadron HQ on *Sir Lancelot*. They'll be on fifteen minutes' notice to move as the QRF, if we need more muscle or need to be dug out of the shit. The ship's been bomb damaged, but Cedric says the LSL is in good enough shape to accommodate the Squadron, so it will be the new base location once we leave. Any questions?'

There was an obvious one, but no one asked it.

'Good, we'll plan the task by individual patrols. The heli is scheduled to take us in just after last light. No move before then. So let's get cracking.'

As we broke up, I saw Roy go up to John and say, 'Hey, boss, can I have a word?' I didn't pay much attention to it at the time, as there was much to do.

Last light was only a few hours away. If we were lucky, by the time we had planned each of our patrols and prepped our kit, we might get a hot shower and grab another meal in the galley before we lifted. The luxury of drying our clothes and getting a decent night's sleep disappeared with the operational imperative of time. The Squadron's stores had already been cross-decked from HMS *Intrepid*, and my grip yielded some dry socks, a T-shirt and one pair of underpants, but everything I had worn on Mount Kent – boots, gloves, smock and socks – was wet and would stay wet. We were also exhausted from a week spent living in sodden peat shell scrapes exposed to the elements.

We drew maps, observation scopes, digging tools, radio batteries, and restocked our ammunition, as well as splitting down enough arctic ration packs to last the six days we were due to be on West Falkland. Again, there was only one menu, and we would face another week of eating freeze-dried Chicken Supreme. Bergens were packed on the hangar deck, the placement of every item debated, as everything we needed would have to be carried on our backs. What dry kit I had was placed in a US-issued rubberized canvas rucksack liner, and individual items were wrapped in plastic bags for additional waterproofing. We would be out for less than a week, so the one spare pair of underpants I had would do for the duration of the op.

For 19 Troop, the task was to observe and report rather than fight, so we restricted our weaponry to rifles and a few grenades; the GPMGs and 66s would be left behind. Stealth and concealment would be our main weapons, and any information we had about Fox Bay would be key. G Squadron's reports were made available for us to study the detail of the target locations, so Ade and I sat down with a brew to read through the information and did a map recce of the route in and likely OP locations.

As ever, battle prep passed in a blur, as the daylight beyond the tank deck was beginning to fade. I was just about packed, with my bergen sitting ready to go on the steel deck by my camp bed. I did a quick time estimation in my head. *Maybe I can grab a shower and get a few minutes on my scratcher before the off?* Then the word came to stand down. 'Bad Met, no fly-in tonight, op delayed by twenty-four hours.'

Bloody marvellous. Time for that shower and then some head-down. There is a God up there somewhere.

John was on the hangar deck by the time I got back from the heads. I saw him say something to Roy. Then he took Bilbo aside and spent a few minutes talking to him before coming in my direction.

'All right, Splash?'

'All right, boss.'

'Ah, Thomas Hardy's *Far from the Madding Crowd*. Enjoying it?' He had spotted the dog-eared novel lying on the top of my doss bag.

'Yes, boss. I like losing myself in the Dorset country-side, which is a long way from here, so good escapism.'

'I need to catch up on my reading when I get back,' he said. I knew that he was fairly recently married, and the mention of home made him pause, before thoughts returned to the South Atlantic.

'Anyway, good news about the delay, I think we could all use a decent kip before we go back out.' He stifled a yawn. 'Right, I am off for my bed. See you tomorrow, Splash.'

'See you tomorrow, boss.'

John turned to head to his quarters with the other officers.

'Hey, boss, I've almost finished with the book. Take it for the journey home if you like.'

'I might just do that. Cheers, Splash. Sleep well,' John said, as he disappeared through a steel door in the bulkhead.

'He's a good one,' Binsy said after him, as Bilbo walked over to join us. He was looking glum. 'What's occurring, mate?' Binsy said.

'I'm not going on the op. John just told me. Roy asked him if he could go, as he didn't get to do Pebble and he is keen that he doesn't miss out on the chance of more action before all this ends.'

'Fat chance, mate, it's just about done, and we are going to sit in holes for a week freezing our arses off. If there's any malleting to be done, likely as not it will be the QRF, which is where you will be, mucker,' Binsy said with a grin. 'Anyone got a buckshee bine?'

Binsy and I would be going to Fox Bay in the second patrol, commanded by Ade, and Roy would join John's patrol going to Port Howard. But that was a whole twenty-four glorious hours away, due to the fact that the weather had closed in with heavy squalls and thick, low-lying cloud; conditions too poor to fly in. It was as if we had just been given a temporary reprieve from the hangman's noose.

There was no accommodation available on the mess decks for other ranks, so we bedded down the tank deck. And when sleep first came, it was fitful and dirty, as overly tired bodies readjusted to the unaccustomed opportunity for unbroken slumber.

# 36

The Met the next evening was good for flying. Cedric came up to the flight deck to see us off. As the Sea King that would fly us into West Falkland began to crank its engine in the background, he gathered us together in the fast-fading light. Looking at John, he said, 'Guys, this will only last another week, then the Argies will have thrown in the towel. So stay safe, don't do anything stupid and come back alive. See you in five days.'

John's patrol was dropped off first, somewhere to the north of Port Howard. We flew on, heading south and putting down behind a 2,000-foot-high feature marked on the map as 'the Bosoms'. The double-coned hill screened the landing site and the noise of the helicopter from the settlement at Fox Bay lying more than 7 miles further to the south. It was a moonless night, with a cold wind blowing towards us from the southwest. Both would help conceal our approach to the OP area we had selected from the map, a mile or so short of the settlement.

We patrolled forward, each one of us weighed down with nearly 100 pounds of kit. Despite the weight, the going was easy compared to the terrain we had traversed on Pebble Island and Mount Kent, so we made good progress. Too good.

It was the fence line that threw us, appearing suddenly to our front and obstructing our path as we crested a small rise in the ground. Constructed to control dispersed flocks of sheep, the wire fences on the Falklands extended for several miles and were marked on maps, which made them good reference points. But this one shouldn't have been there.

The patrol stopped and went down on one knee. I moved up to Ade, who was checking the map coordinates. 'Shit,' he whispered, 'this fence line should be another two clicks to our front.' Then we both froze. Spanish voices carried on the wind towards us through the blackness from somewhere up ahead – maybe a half-dozen soldiers in a trench position, a commander doing his rounds.

It was then that we realized: the map wasn't wrong, we were. The fence line was the one marked and noted in G Squadron's report, which meant that we were almost inside the Argentine position. We had patrolled too far and were about to stumble into the enemy's forward trenches. The ground we had crossed sloped gently downhill; it had also been trodden and nibbled flat by generations of free-grazing sheep. It meant that we had covered it more quickly than we thought. *Shit!*

There were more voices, several of them. It didn't sound like they had detected us, but it was getting close to first light. The patchy lines of dawn were already smudging the sky. As well as being compromised when darkness lifted, there was a further danger at hand. HMS *Glamorgan* was due to bombard the settlement at daybreak. If we stayed where we were, even if the Argies didn't see us, there was a good chance that we could get killed by our own 4.5 inch high-explosive shells. We needed to move, to escape from the danger of our guns

333

and get into cover before we were seen. And we needed to do it quickly.

'Move back,' hissed Ade.

We retraced our steps, slinking backwards into the darkness, not daring to make a sound. After withdrawing a couple of hundred metres, we quickened the pace. Only distance and cover would save us. We were once more racing the daylight, which would spell our doom if we were caught out in the open. We had to move faster.

We hit a cart track leading down out of the settlement. Good and not so good. It meant we could move more quickly and it would aid us in getting further away from the shells of the Navy's guns. But it was an obvious feature, which would be registered by the Argies' own guns; if they caught us here, they would have us cold.

We tabbed harder, legs and lungs protesting with the effort and the weight on our backs as we laboured for the safety of distance and the need to find cover. I wasn't sure that we were going to make it. The light was already filtering through the blackness and painting our surroundings in a monochrome tone. The outline of shapes was becoming more perceptible. I could make out individual rocks on the ground, the silhouettes of the blokes around me were becoming more defined, and it confirmed the surrounding terrain was bare arse. There was nowhere to hide, and we were losing the race against time, distance and speed.

I was expecting to hear shouts of alarm and then the crackle of automatic fire, when Ade spotted it. A deep-sided re-entrant by a bend in the dirt road. 'In here, fucking jildi.'

The depression in the ground contoured north, the direction of safety.

It also offered a modicum of cover from hostile eyes and lethal shrapnel, but it was still too open, and it was getting lighter. Absent of any other choice, Ade decided that it would have to do. We moved into the defile, its sides obscuring our flanks, but our backs would still be visible to the enemy once daylight came. We pushed on over stone and bog, the going becoming more difficult, slowing us. The peaty mire sucked at our boots, filling them with water and adding to the friction of movement, our thigh muscles aching with exertion. I slipped on a rock, the weight of my bergen pitching me over, and I went waist-deep into a patch of bog.

'Get me out of this, Binsy, I'm stuck.'

Binsy helped pull me out of the quagmire, just managing to suppress a laugh at my misfortune. The hopelessness of the situation was becoming readily apparent, when Ade disappeared round a kink in the re-entrant, which dog-legged to the left. He reappeared, vigorously pumping his arm with a clenched fist upwards and downwards to indicate haste. The bend in the re-entrant would obscure us from the settlement and it also yielded a clump of high-growing vegetation – enough to provide temporary concealment to a patrol of four men about to get caught out in the open.

'Get in, get in,' urged Ade.

We took off our bergens before pushing and cutting our way in, snipping out space and folding the unbroken stems behind us. We pulled in our rucksacks and caught our breath as the light of morning spotted bright between

335

the small gaps in the foliage above our heads and the first shell of the bombardment began to land in the settlement. Each round landed with a mighty crack, the noise pushing up the re-entrant towards us. But we were far enough away, the immediate danger had been abated and for the time being, we were safe.

'Fuck, that was close,' I whispered.

The immediate risk of being caught by *Glamorgan*'s shells or being spotted by the Argies had passed. However, we were still too close to the enemy, and any diligent clearance patrol would have a good chance of finding us if they decided to sweep through the re-entrant. The vegetation offered cover from view, but it was not a good place to fight or escape from. The odds of surviving a shootout against an enemy patrol while trapped in the gully would be slim. But moving in daylight would be madness. Our only option was to sit tight, hope the Argies didn't come looking for us and wait for the cover of darkness. If we needed a piss, we would just have to roll over and hope that the steam rising from our urine as it condensed in the freezing air didn't give our position away; otherwise we just lay there and shivered in the biting-cold temperature.

A couple of hours passed. Ade nudged me. 'Splash, get on the radio and report in to the Squadron.'

'Roger.' I switched on the 320 high-frequency radio and heard the slight hiss of static crackle in the headset.

To get comms from the dead ground of the defile I would need to set up an aerial. I parted the bushes and peered out cautiously, before crawling from the foliage and up the side of the re-entrant, trailing a wire behind me. Using my cheap K Bar as a picket peg, I fastened the wire to the knife to create a sloping antenna. Keeping the wire low to the ground would make it harder to spot, although the earth was likely to absorb some of the signal. However, it was our only means of radiating an HF transmission without putting up a long tell-tale whip aerial.

I slithered back down the slope and into the vegetation. I started to transmit, using hand-keyed telegraph procedures, shorthand Morse.

'Zero Alpha this is Four Two, over,' which transmitted as: dah dah dah, di dah, dah, di, di di, di dah dah dah dah, dah dah dah dah di.

There was no reply from the Squadron ops room on *Sir Lancelot*. I adjusted the gain on the set and tried again but all I could hear was the faint hiss of static in the earpiece. I keyed out the message again, a sequenced tapping of dots and dashes, but again nothing. I kept trying until Ade told me to stop.

'SOP. They won't start to flap if we don't report in and miss a sched for the next forty-eight hours, so we can try again once we move.'

'Roger. We must be in a dead spot here, and the sides of the gully are screening the signal.'

So we settled down, each pair taking it in turns to mount a guard from our leafy confines, and waited until it got dark.

'Anything from the Fox Bay patrol?' Danny West asked later that morning back in the Squadron operations room, which had been set up in a disused cabin space near the bridge on *Sir Lancelot*.

'No, boss,' the signaller manning the bank of radios replied.

'Hmm, still within the standard operating procedure grace period, so no need to worry yet. Let's wait out and see if they make the next sched.'

'Yes, boss, but call sign Four One at Port Howard have followed up on their initial report and also met their first sched earlier this morning. They said that they still have to establish their OP, although they have eyes on the settlement.'

'OK, thank you, good man. Let me know when you hear anything from Fox Bay.'

Danny wasn't overly concerned. *If I haven't heard anything by the end of two days, then I will start to get worried*, he told himself as he left the ops room to let Cedric know that John Hamilton had reached Port Howard safely.

The location John and Roy had eventually chosen to establish their OP, nestled among tumbled rock and spikes of quartzite on the spine of the high ridgeline overlooking the settlement of Port Howard, was far from ideal. The position was close to the skyline and lacked the space for the supporting LUP, which had to be located several hundred metres away at the bottom of the other side of the ridge. It meant that the patrol would be separated over a wide distance and unable to support each other in the event of trouble. First light revealed a clear view of the settlement stretched out before them on the far side of a sea loch half a mile away. The coming of morning provoked movement between the score or more of tin-roofed dwellings and outbuildings, as Argentine troops began to emerge around their positions and members of the small civilian community started going about their day.

'Large white house in the centre with the green corrugated roof, must be the farm manager's house,' John said, with his eye screwed into the Swift scope, which was mounted in a gap of rock.

Roy sat next to him, close enough for them to talk in quiet voices as they exchanged information about what they could see. 'Roger,' Roy acknowledged.

'Looks like it's being used as a headquarters. There are Arg troops dug into the high ground above the settlement directly behind it; could be at least a company in strength.'

'Seen,' Roy acknowledged. 'Possibly more troops up there too and on the flanks of the village.'

'The dark buildings on the left-hand edge of the settlement on the water's edge look like the sheep sheds mentioned in the G Squadron report. It looks like the Argies are using it as a logistics area, and the small quay is where they probably receive supplies.'

'Check,' Roy said, adding it to the mental inventory of enemy dispositions he was making in his head.

'Ah, look at that. Artillery piece, between the two red-roofed houses below the company position. Probably 105 mm pack-how. Yep, there is another one, over to the right, just beyond the schoolhouse behind the manager's pad. Send all that down to the others so they can get what we have seen so far back to the Squadron.'

'Roger, boss.' Roy brought out the small, waterproofed code book and began sending what he had seen over the radio to the other two members of the patrol in the LUP.

The laying-up point was located not much short of a mile away from John and Roy's position, in a small cave at the bottom of the eastern side of the ridge. The nature of the terrain precluded siting the administrative area anywhere closer to the forward OP. It was not standard procedure, and John didn't like separating the two elements of the patrol over such a large distance. Nobody did; they were too far away to support each other with mutual fire, but it was a decision that was dictated by geography. There was not enough room up on the ridge without risking being spotted. Everything John and Roy observed in the settlement would have to be relayed back to the two men in the cave by tactical short-range radio and then relayed on to the ops room on the LSL from the LUP in Morse using the 320 set at the predetermined sched times.

The bush concealing us may have been a lucky find, but we still didn't have eyes on Fox Bay. The rest of the bleak, open moorland around the settlement was devoid of cover, and it took all the next night to move to a new location and establish the OP. We found a small, raised knoll 4 kilometres north of the settlement. With no trees or hedgerows, we would have to dig for concealment.

Our spades cut easily through the soft, peaty topsoil, and we took care to stack the sods of tufty grass to one side. Then we hit rock. Heaving a pickaxe, one of us broke up the hard ground and another then dug out the broken stone, placing the spoil on to a poncho. Once it was full, the other pair in the team then carried the nylon sheet, heavy with rock and soil, and dumped its contents in a tarn 200 metres away. The small pond would hide the debris, but it was slow, back-breaking work. The digging pair made only a few inches' impression in the hard ground before another poncho load needed to be lifted and dumped. It went on for hours, until the OP was deep enough to accommodate two men in a sitting position, their eyeline just level with the lip of the surface of the ground.

The sods were then laid across a stretched poncho sheet to provide overhead cover, to shelter the occupants from the weather and to ensure the OP blended in against the background of pale-yellow tufts of grass. A slight gap was left between the roof of the dugout and the ground running across the front of the hide, just wide enough to create an observation slit. The final work that night was to enhance a low-lying depression and turn it into a shallow trench 50 metres to the rear of the OP. Camouflaged with ponchos and individual camouflage nets, the LUP could conceal two men lying down and facing in to each other. It would also serve as an administrative area and provide protection to the rear. First light was not far off by the time we had finished. The arrival of morning confirmed that we had selected a good position. The OP blended into its surrounds, invisible to anyone, unless they walked right on top of it. It also afforded an excellent view of Fox Bay.

I stayed back in the LUP with Binsy, while Ade and his oppo sat forward in the OP. The settlement lay out in the distance before them, as the terrain sloped down to the sea. Even at 4 kilometres, the cluster of farm sheds and white houses with their green corrugated-iron roofs were discernible to the naked eye. The buildings stretched out towards the shoreline and a single jetty running out into the bay.

With a Swift scope we could make out the detail of individuals moving about the settlement. 'God, they are a sorry-looking lot,' Ade remarked under his breath. Through the ×60 magnification of the optical scope he could see the details of a queue of Argentine soldiers lined up for breakfast at a field kitchen near the largest dwelling, its size marking it out as the farm manager's house. Almost shapeless in their ponchos and US-style helmets, they shuffled about in the line, stamping the early-morning cold out of frozen limbs while clutching their mess tins, with their rifles slung carelessly on their shoulders.

The location of the feeding station suggested that the Argies were using the house as their headquarters. Most of the Arg trenches were dug in along the shore, facing out to sea. Others were scattered about the settlement under gorse bushes, which had been imported on to the islands and cultured over the decades to act as wind breaks for the buildings. A group of dugouts had been positioned on either side of the track leading into the settlement. Facing in our direction, they were the positions which we had almost patrolled into the previous night. Every dugout seemed to have a machine gun manned by a least one soldier. Cold and miserable as they looked, they also gave the impression of being alert.

Further back, Ade counted four Argentine 105 mm pack howitzers, small and stubby in appearance. The presence of a battery of artillery confirmed that Fox Bay was likely to be occupied by at least a battalion of infantry. It was a formidable force, which would have been capable of holding out against a complete brigade. They might have been suffering in the elements, but there were lots of them, and with their machine guns and artillery they would make short work of a four-man patrol armed only with rifles if they discovered that we were watching them.

While our new location was good, the comms were not. I had been trying to reach the Squadron since first light. I risked using a longer sloping wire antenna and making it higher to reduce ground interference, but it yielded nothing. What we were transmitting wasn't being picked up 50 miles to our east in San Carlos. If the signallers in D Squadron were sending to us, we weren't picking it up either. Even at the pre-arranged scheduled timings, when both the Squadron ops room and deployed patrols would be on the net, there was nothing other than the squelching mush of electronic interference when I transmitted the sched.

'Still no comms, Ade.'

'Shit. Is the set working properly?'

'The set's good, Ade,' I assured him.

'What about the other end?'

'I don't see a problem there. The scaley-backs in the ops room are good. They will know we have missed our sched and will be trying to reach us.'

The fact that we weren't picking anything up during the scheds was beginning to concern me. If we couldn't get comms, we would have to move again.

However, the Argies soon took the decision out of our hands.

# 37

I was trying again to raise D Squadron on the radio around midday when the two high-velocity rounds cracked over our heads. I froze. The sharp reports woke Binsy. He shimmied out of his sleeping bag and instinctively reached for his rifle and belt kit. I pressed a finger to my lips and indicated the presence of enemy using a thumbs-down hand signal and picked up the small tactical VHF radio set, which linked us to the forward OP.

'Contact. Enemy patrol, eight men. Less than 800 metres away. I am observing. Wait out.'

I passed on what Ade had reported to Binsy in a hushed tone, as we fingered the safety catches on our weapons, poised and ready to react if the shooting started. It seemed like an age, the tension like a compressed spring. In seconds we could be fighting it out, or making a break for the emergency RV. *Shit, no comms.* Whatever happened, we would be on our own and unable to call for help. Even if we did raise someone back at Squadron, it was unlikely that they would get to us in time.

The minutes continued to tick by in agonizing slowness. Then Ade came back on the radio. 'Stand down. Looks like a foraging party out shooting sheep. They are heading back to the settlement, and I don't think they have seen us.' I acknowledged with a simple 'Roger out.' Binsy and I both sighed with relief.

'Fuck, that was a close call.'

'You're not fucking kidding,' Binsy replied. 'I wonder why they're shooting sheep.'

There was clearer evidence of what was going on with the sheep at Port Howard. Through the scope, in their OP position on the ridgeline, John observed a tractor towing a long, flat farm trailer, as it left the sheep sheds and drove up towards the Arg company position they had spotted on the higher ground. The tractor stopped at each trench when it got there. 'What are they doing?' Roy asked.

'It's two civvies, and I think they are throwing offal to the Argies.'

'Offal?'

'Yes, fuck me, it looks heaving. I think the locals are feeding the Arg troops with what's left of the sheep they're slaughtering in the sheds.'

'Probably beats Chicken Supreme.'

'I'm not sure about that, but the Argies must be short of food if they are resorting to eating mutton.'

The Arg patrol we'd seen near Fox Bay confirmed that we were still too close to the settlement. If the Argies were coming out to shoot the sheep that wandered freely across the moorland, to supply their garrison, they were likely to be back when they needed more food. Binsy and I looked at each other, both knowing that we'd have to move again as soon as it got dark.

Rising proud from the flatness of the surrounding moorland, the Bosoms looked like the best option for a new OP. We filled in the old position to cover our tracks as soon as it got dark, carefully replacing each of the heavy sods of earth. Then we tabbed back 6 kilometres, climbed up the feature and began to dig a new position just below its crest on the forward slope. We finished it just before first light. The coming of morning revealed that the OP had good arcs of observation down to Fox Bay.

Although we were now 10 kilometres away, the clear Falklands air meant that, using the scope, it was still possible to make out the outline of the papers the Argies were reading in their trenches. As a bonus, the higher ground yielded comms with Squadron HQ for the first time in three days. We had got through to them while we were digging in the OP.

But there was also a problem with the new location. Daybreak revealed the presence of a low white shepherd's croft lying in a valley a mile away to the west at the foot of a peak. It was marked on the map as Mount Sulivan, but what the map couldn't tell us was that it was occupied by the Argies.

'What do you reckon, Ade?' I said, lying flat in the clumps of grass just behind the new OP.

'At least a platoon. Thirty troops, maybe more, dug in round the building with machine guns.'

'So we are well within range?'

'Yep, they could easily reach us up here. They could pin us down with their machine guns and then call in artillery from the settlement. In short, they could slaughter us if they spot us.'

'Do we move again tonight?'

The ground between the Bosoms was flat and unbroken,

and we risked being seen up on the higher ground if we stayed where we were, but the map suggested few alternatives to place another OP which would have both comms to the Squadron and good visibility to the settlement.

'No, let's stay put and avoid any movement during daylight,' Ade said. 'You and Binsy man the radio in the LUP, and we will stag on here in the OP.'

'OK. I'll wait for the next sched and send a SITREP back to the Squadron.'

I wriggled back slowly from the OP to the admin hide and filled Binsy in about the enemy platoon as I prepared the radio.

After our silence following the insertion, the Squadron was relieved to be receiving regular SITREPs from both OPs. It seemed as if everything was on track.

# 38

It was raining. The weather rolled across us in bands from the west, sometimes laden with rain, sometimes carrying flurries of snow, and occasionally breaking to reveal the sun.

For the next three days we kept the settlement under observation, logging details to build up a pattern of life to confirm the enemy's number and likely intentions and identify any high-value targets. We clocked the odd vehicle moving in and out of Fox Bay, recorded their facilities and noted how the Argies regularly repositioned their artillery pieces in an attempt to protect them from naval bombardments. We watched the queue for the field kitchen form up each morning in a long, snaking line, and then tracked individual groups of soldiers as they dispersed back to their trenches, which allowed us to verify their strength and the precise locations of their defensive positions.

But the bitter cold and the bone-chilling wind remained unceasing. We worked in shifts, two forward in the OP, the other pair in the admin position, taking it in turns to man the radio, cover the approaches to the rear, get some sleep and eat. Lying motionless in the frozen ground became an agony of endurance, as the damp seeped into clothes and sleeping bags. Brews of hot, sweet tea were a godsend. During the daylight hours, out of sight and below ground, we heated our rations and ate our Chicken Supreme before it got dark.

At night the temperature dropped several degrees below freezing, but darkness also provided the one opportunity to take some exercise and stretch stiff, tired, aching limbs. On the second night in the new OP, I headed out to collect water for the rest of the patrol. In pitch darkness, I made my way down the rear slopes of the Bosoms to a pond located 400 metres down in the lower ground. It was out of view of the enemy, so I was not overly concerned about being on my own.

I was approaching the tarn and enjoying the return of warmth to my core when I heard movement ahead of me. I stopped and went down on one knee, at the same time easing the safety catch to the 'off' position on my FN. Still festooned with water bottles, I paused, scanning the darkness ahead of me and listening intently for any sound. Nothing. I moved cautiously forward, still trying to scan the blackness around me: still nothing. Suddenly there was a flurry of movement and noise to my front. The butt of my rifle was already in my shoulder, the barrel instinctively coming up into a fire position, my finger curled around the trigger, as sight and sound computed in my brain. Registering the flapping feathers, my thumb automatically depressed the safety as a pair of startled upland geese rose up in a discord of honking from the darkness and beat their way into the air over my head.

My heartbeat had returned to normal by the time I got back to the hide. 'Fuck me, Binsy,' I whispered, 'almost just got compromised by a couple of geese.'

Binsy nearly pissed himself as he sought to stifle an

outburst of hysterical laughter. 'Bloody hell, Splash, you should have clubbed one of the fuckers. It would have made for a welcome relief from chicken nasty.'

Apart from the risk of being given away by a pair of frightened geese, or spotted by the enemy platoon at Suli- van House, the other threat of discovery came from the air. Each day an Argentine Agusta 109 thumped over- head, as it transited between Fox Bay and Port Howard. As the Bosoms was an obvious navigation feature between the two settlements, the helicopter flew over the top of it low enough for us to make out the pilot's moustache and mirrored aviator shades through the gaps in the netting of the hide.

Each time the Agusta flew over, I prayed that he wouldn't look down. He never did. I suspect he was pre- occupied by the demands of low flying and the need to be on the lookout for prowling Harrier jets. We sent back the helicopter's movements during the routine sched transmissions, along with all the other information we had logged. What we sent back was met with a simple acknowledgement from Squadron HQ. There was never any suggestion that our reports were going to provoke any response, but it didn't stop me asking. I ended each trans- mission with 'Have you anything for us?'

The reply came back in the cadence of Morse dots and dashes: 'dah dah di dah, di dah di, di di dah (noth- ing for you – out)'.

Beyond our world, the Task Force was otherwise occu- pied in preparing to take Stanley and, unless we reported something significant, such as a major reinforcement or movement of troops, they were content to leave Fox Bay to be dealt with once the capital fell. We had no knowledge of events unfolding 50 miles away on East Falkland, such as the tragic loss of over fifty British lives in an air attack on the Welsh Guard aboard *Sir Galahad*. HMS *Glamorgan* was hit by an Exocet launched from the shore. Ignorant of the wider war, we remained cocooned in our own quiet little backwater world of West Falkland. But that was about to change – with dreadful results.

Smoke from peat fires drifted from chimneys and was carried away over the corrugated tin rooftops by the early-morning breeze. Working dogs barked in their pens, and cocks started to crow, as the daylight filled the eastern horizon behind Roy, and the settlement at Port Howard began to stir. It might have made for a tranquil, bucolic scene of rural idyll had it not been for the fierce cold and the presence of the Argies. They were already beginning to form up in a line for a meagre breakfast from the field kitchen located near the schoolhouse of the settlement, which stretched out along the opposite shoreline in the valley below him in a small cluster of houses.

Roy had moved back into the forward position with John just before last light to relieve Jimmy and his oppo when he spotted a discarded sweet wrapper. Roy hadn't noticed it before and he was sure that it hadn't been there the previous day, when they had moved the location of the OP further along the ridgeline. But its presence lying there among the rocks spelt trouble. Roy tried to process what he had found. He discounted the possibility of the kids from the settlement, as the Argies kept all the civilians confined to Port Howard.

*Shit, this is bad*, he thought. *It must have been discarded by a soldier in an Argie patrol. We need to get the hell out of here.* The trouble was that the boss had gone for a piss. What neither man knew was that the other half of their patrol was already on the radio, trying to tell them just how bad things were about to get.

It was with the emergence of first light, when he looked out from the cave at the bottom of the ridge, that Jimmy saw the dark shapes that seemed to be all around them. They hadn't spotted the LUP, but a dozen or so Argentine soldiers were moving up the ridgeline in front of them, heading in the direction of the OP.

This was no chance clearance patrol: the enemy appeared to be moving with purpose, as they gained height and climbed steadily up the steep sides of the ridge. They had several hundred feet to climb, and there was still time to alert John and Roy to the approaching danger. Jimmy got on the 320 HF set and transmitted a warning.

'Four Zero Alpha, this is Four One Bravo, over.'

Nothing.

'Four Zero Alpha, be aware we've got company, twelve times enemy pax advancing up the ridgeline behind your position. Over!'

Still no response from John and Roy.

Jimmy kept trying. In desperation he switched to the small two-way tactical radio set and ventured out of the cave to adjust his position in an attempt to get better comms. His voice was becoming more imploring, his mind pleading: *Pick up the damn message!* But the atmospherics

352

were against him; the signal was too weak to bounce up over the ridge.

Still nothing, as he watched the enemy patrol climbing further up the ridgeline. They were out of range from effective small-arms fire, and then they disappeared as they crested the ridge.

Twenty miles away, and unscreened by mountains, across the open reaches of the Sound in San Carlos, Jimmy's frantic broadcasts had been picked up by the more power-ful radios in D Squadron's HQ. The signals team called Cedric and Danny into the ops room.

'Boss, listen to this. OP at Port Howard looks like it's just about to get compromised.'

'Are you sure it's John's patrol?'

'Yes, boss, it's his call sign, and I could recognize Jimmy Clyde's Morse style anywhere. It's definitely them. Boss, Jimmy is now coming through on the VHF.'

Cedric felt physically sick. It was a nightmare coming true: one of his patrols about to be compromised behind enemy lines, and the odds of numbers were stacked heav-ily against them.

'Danny, crash out 17 Troop as the QRF. Get hold of a helicopter. There is a chance, albeit a slim one, that we might get there in time.'

Boat Troop were on standby for such an emergency. They tumbled off bunks, grabbed their kit and weapons and charged down companionways to gather on the LSL's flight deck. With the urgency of the situation upon them, they were ready to go in minutes to try to dig their mates out of the shit.

But the initial request for a helicopter was turned down. The desperate urgency of the situation wasn't shared by everyone in the higher command chain, and Cedric was informed that no helicopters could be made available.

The Argentine patrol crested the feature high up above John and Roy's position. That was when John saw them. He dived back into the OP, shouting to Roy, 'Bloody hell, Fonze, we're surrounded!'

Roy hardly had time to register what he had heard when a metallic object bounced down the rocks among them. Both men threw themselves to the ground as the grenade exploded in a blinding flash of black smoke, ear-splitting sound and hot fragments of metal.

Miraculously, they were unhurt, and immediate action drills triumphed over the shock of the blast. Roy made an urgent call on the radio for help, but there was no response. Communications failure again. John was already shooting as Roy broke from the limited cover afforded by the rocks. Moving fast, using the covering fire of his boss to make the first bound up the slope, he then dropped to one knee and began firing, instinctively knowing that John would be starting to move behind him, as the repeat sequence of fire and manoeuvre drill, practised a thousand times on live fire ranges, kicked in.

John started shooting again, which was Roy's next cue to move another bound. Firing an underslung M203 as he went, he charged up towards the enemy like a man possessed. The initial response of taking the enemy head-on was working, the fury of John and Roy's assault forcing them to take cover. But the Arg patrol's superior numbers began to count as they recovered from the initial shock of John and Roy's violent offensive reaction and started shooting back at the two desperate SAS men skirmishing towards them out in the open.

Roy was moving once more, John firing behind him, as he made his next bound forward. He dropped back to one knee and started firing again to cover John's next move.

But John didn't move; instead he shouted out, 'Fonze, I'm hit. Make a break for it.' With that he started firing again in an attempt to cover Roy's desperate bid for freedom.

Roy went to make a move, when a grazing round took him in the arm, sending his rifle spinning, its force knocking him to the ground. Other incoming Argentine rounds kept him there. With his Armalite beyond his grasp, he was pinned down. As bullets plucked at the earth around him, he looked for John and spotted him lying motionless further down the slope behind him. His mind raced. He bellowed at the top of his voice at his assailants: 'Sto-o-o-p!' and 'Check Fire!'

The bark of sudden command, loud, clear and full of authority, caused the Argies to cease fire. Roy lay desperately still as two enemy soldiers emerged from cover to strip him of his belt kit and take him prisoner. Others moved towards John and immediately started administering first aid, although it was too late. He had already bled out by the time they got there.

# 39

When the coded signal came in, I knew it was bad. By the time the message reached us, the Squadron head shed had worked out that John had been killed and Roy was a prisoner. It was shocking news, but we still had a job to do, and the events at Port Howard carried implications for us. As the other patrol's signaller, Roy would have held all the one-time pad codes for encrypting our signals, and it had to be assumed that they were now in the possession of the enemy and had been compromised.

The one-time-use pad system is based on a long sequence of random letters or numbers, which produce a meaningless cypher message. This can only be unencrypted by a receiving radio operator if the recipient holds an identical pad of codes to the one used by the sender. It was an unbreakable code, but a cumbersome system, especially when sent and received in Morse. I readied myself to receive a weighty transmission, as the new codes were issued over the radio. It began with the first of a series of dots and dashes, which started to arrive later that night.

The comms dropped out intermittently and I had to keep asking the scaley-back at Squadron HQ to repeat what they had sent.

'Hello, Zero Alpha, this is Four Two, say all again after . . .'

Then it would start again. I couldn't code in gloves, so the mind-numbing work had to be completed with freezing fingers under the cover of a poncho with the aid of a handheld red torch. It took three and a half hours to decode and construct the new one-time pad. But my discomfort paled in comparison to what Roy was going through at Port Howard.

After he had been captured, Roy was taken down to the settlement, where he was blindfolded and had his hands tied behind his back. Initially thinking that he might be shot, he was instead incarcerated in the 6 foot by 3 foot hole of a wool press, in the large shearing sheds near the settlement's jetty. Stinking of sheep dung and mutton fat, and without any light, it became a makeshift dungeon into which Roy was cast to await his fate.

As Roy was being dragged off as a prisoner, a struggle for the release of a Sea King to fly in the QRF was taking place in the operations room aboard HMS *Fearless*. Cedric's request for a helicopter was turned down on the basis that all airframes were needed to sustain preparations for the final push on Stanley, and the plight of our comrades fell on deaf ears. The pilots of 846 Squadron wanted to fly the mission, but the amphibious group commander was unrelenting; all the helicopters were needed to support the battles unfolding around Stanley in the east. It took Mike Rose's personal appearance and collar-gripping intervention to make the senior naval officer see sense, and it was agreed to launch a helicopter to make a desperate bid to try to save the patrol at Port Howard.

The Sea King flew fast and low as it carried the blokes of 17 Troop across Falkland Sound. Cedric and Danny West went with them, but it was already too late for John and Roy. The response force managed to pick up Jimmy and his oppo, after they had first swum across a few hundred metres of freezing inland water in order to make good their escape and evasion and reach the emergency helicopter landing site. But with the contact over, there was little more that Cedric could do, other than to return to San Carlos with a heavy heart in the knowledge that he had lost two of his Squadron.

The bad-luck compromise at Port Howard also meant that we had to consider the viability of our own position. If the Argies had found one OP behind their lines, they would be on the lookout for more. We detected an increase in the frequency and size of the patrols sent out from Fox Bay, which added to the risk of being discovered. We began to see groups of twelve soldiers leave the settlement at regular intervals, sometimes on foot, sometimes being pushed out and dropped off further by vehicle. They would fan out in an extended line, advancing cautiously and scanning the ground for any sign of an observation position. But moving the OP once night fell entailed as many risks as staying put. So we bit our nails and held our breath each time a patrol came out.

As the days progressed, hunger became as much of an enemy as the Argies. John's death and Roy's capture occurred on 10 June. The day before that, we had eaten our last meal of Chicken Supreme. Sent into the field on

4 June for an anticipated duration of less than a week, we had taken six days' worth of food, including one emergency ration pack we carried in our belt order. After the sixth day, we searched desperately through our kit for the odd stray teabag in the bottom of a bergen, or a piece of chocolate lying forgotten and mouldy in a pouch on our belts. Each find was celebrated with undisguised glee, but we had soon stripped every item clean of anything edible. Hunger gnawed at our bellies, and our heads ached with the lack of sustenance. The biting cold made it doubly worse. The wind chill was murder, and although the position provided a degree of shelter, our feet and hands suffered dreadfully from hours of inactivity.

The one consolation of the shortage of food was that it reduced the need to defecate. If we needed a piss, we could roll to the side of the hide and relieve ourselves while remaining hidden. If we wanted to take a dump, we waited until darkness, climbed out of the hide and crapped in a plastic bag before burying the waste. But on one occasion I needed to go and couldn't wait until last light. I was on stag when I felt my bowels weaken. Binsy lay facing me, his face a few inches from mine as he dozed.

'Hey, Binsy,' I whispered, 'wake up, I need a favour.'

Binsy woke from his slumber. 'Yes, Splash, what is it?' the trace of sleep still thick in his voice.

'I need to take a shit.'

'Yeah? So what?'

'I need to do it now.'

'Yeah? So?'

'Well, I was wondering, mate, whether you could hold the bag.'

Binsy didn't even pause to think about it. 'You've got to be fucking joking!' he hissed back. 'If you think I am going to hold a bag between your minging arse cheeks while you lay a Richard the Third in it, you can think again, mate.'

'But mate, I'm desperate.'

'Then, mate, you are going to either have to crap your pants or wriggle outside and test whether a man can take a shit in the prone position.'

I went with the second option and can vouch that human beings are not designed to take a dump while lying flat on the ground and trying to remain concealed in a few inches of grass clumps.

At least that briefly took my mind off how hungry I was. But the pangs soon returned. I banned myself from fixating on my watch and willing the hands to move faster. It became a challenge to stay awake, even in the cold. During the night I strained my eyes, which felt like they were thick with grit, as I scanned the darkness to detect any sign of movement and the approach of the enemy. Fatigue played tricks on my mind, and strange shapes suddenly loomed out of the night as I hallucinated and fought off the seduction of sleep.

We were getting wearier by the day. The only solace was that the Argies in Fox Bay were suffering too. Most of them were living in trenches: through the Swift scope we could see them bailing out their waterlogged holes. Using their ponchos to muffle themselves against the cold, they shuffled about the settlement as misshapen figures of misery. We had seen nothing that we could identify as a resupply since we had got eyes on the settlement. Instead we watched other patrols go out and kill more sheep each day, which were then boiled up and served to them from their field kitchen.

It was no better at Port Howard. Out of rations and fed offal by the locals, the Argies were near starving. Roy languished in his hole in the ground. Periodically, his guards reached down to grab him and haul him out of the sheep press, before dragging him across wooden floorboards strewn with dirt and wool clippings and out into an adjacent Nissen hut for interrogation. His captors suspected that he was Special Forces and they wanted to know what unit he was from and what he was doing up on the ridge.

Roy's training had prepared him well for the initial phase of the interrogation the Argies put him through, and he stuck doggedly to the 'Big Four'.

The first officer who questioned Roy repeatedly asked him, 'Who are you and what were you doing with the *capitano* we killed? You are Special Forces, aren't you? SAS, yes?'

'Sir, I cannot answer that question.'

'What is your mission?'

'Sir, I cannot answer that question,' Roy repeated. And so it went on.

Although roughly handled, especially by the private soldiers when the Argentine officers were not around, Roy was not beaten. Then the tenor of the interrogations changed, when Roy's captors discovered that he and John had been carrying Argentine military equipment, which they had picked up in South Georgia.

Dragged back out of his hole once more, Roy was stripped semi-naked and tied to a chair in the Nissen hut. Another officer showed him an Arg 9 mm Browning pistol that they had found on John. They had confirmed the handgun's origins from the weapon's registered serial number.

'What was your *capitano* doing with this pistol? Where did he get it from? You are Special Forces.'

Each time the reply was the same: 'Sir, I cannot answer that question.'

Each time, the Arg captain became angrier and began to scream at Roy, as he repeatedly cocked and recocked the firearm, fingering its trigger and demanding to know where it had come from. Roy was in dangerous territory, unsure whether his captor was just trying to fuck with him or if there was a more sinister intent. Roy counted the rounds as they were ejected from the weapon and tumbled to the dirt floor. His interrogator became more agitated each time the pistol slide slipped forward and chambered another bullet from the magazine.

Roy knew that it could hold up to twelve 9 mm rounds and wondered whether the deranged officer was going to shoot him with the last bullet. He counted to nine, watching the ninth shiny-capped brass case as it spun through the air. Just before it landed in the dust, there was a mighty crash, and a blast wave rocked the metal sides of the hut, rattling its structure with concussive force and cracking the windows.

The Royal Navy shell had dropped short of its intended target of the Argie trenches on a hill above the settlement. It landed in the middle of Port Howard, where it obliterated the local food store, and brought an abrupt end to Roy's interrogation as his inquisitor ran for cover. The slight error in naval gunnery might have averted an untimely demise, as Roy was bundled unceremoniously back into the hole in the shearing shed by his guards, while better-aimed shells thumped in from the sea and burst on the higher ground above the settlement.

Apart from the first night, when we had patrolled too close to the settlement, the Navy didn't shell Fox Bay. We also saw nothing of the locals who lived in the settlement. They were fewer in number compared with Port Howard, and they had taken to living under the floorboards of the manager's house, which provided a degree of safety from Harrier strikes and naval bombardments. From what we could make out, there was little interaction between the so-called liberators and the liberated. Our observation of the former suggested that even the Argies might not have regarded themselves as such. After months of exposure to the weather and deprivations, their dejection made me wonder just how hard they would be willing to fight to defend Stanley. But we didn't know for sure.

During the radio scheds, we continued to ask for SITREPs, but the answer was the same: 'Nothing for you.' Consequently, we didn't know anything of the battles that were progressing on East Falkland until we received an indication on our eleventh day in the field.

A lone red-backed hawk flew high above me against a dark morning sky, which threatened snow. I was about to close my eyes, but it caught my attention through the gaps in the camouflage as I lay on my back in my sleeping bag, which was drawn up tight against my neck in a vain attempt to ward off the cold. The only thing I could hear was the faint chirping of the radio set as Binsy took a turn to tune into the latest sched and take the next guard watch. As I watched the hawk soar and hover, I felt strangely connected to it. Like us, it was alone, cut off from events, although while we willed away each interminable hour of hunger, cold and boredom, the bird of prey could at least move and hunt for food.

'Fuck me!' Binsy's exclamation broke my aerial reverie. He looked at me, eyes wide. 'I think the fuckers have fucking surrendered!' There was an unmistakeable edge of jubilation in his voice, which was probably less to do with victory and more to do with the prospect that the end of hostilities might bring food and warmth.

The Argentine military commander on the Falklands signed the surrender agreement at 2359 hours Zulu time on 14 June, and the news was passed on to us at first light the next day. In the six days that we had been without food, the Paras and Marines, along with a battalion of the Scots Guards, had attacked and captured the peaks around Stanley. They had taken casualties in some bitter uphill fighting, but their victories had brought about a collapse of the entire Argentine defensive position. Enemy troops had fled back to the capital in a disorderly rabble, and their senior commanders had no appetite to continue the fight for its tenure.

D Squadron, along with other attached SF elements, had played its part in launching another diversionary raid, although less successful than the previous operations at Darwin, on Pebble Island and on Mount Kent. The detail of events was not included in the transmission about the capitulation. However, it related to all Argentine forces, including those on outlying islands. There was a concern that the Arg troops on West Falkland might not know of the surrender or might not accept it. As a result, we were instructed to stay hidden and in place for another thirty-six hours before withdrawing. It was bitter-sweet news. The end of hostilities was welcomed by everyone, but the thought of another day and a half exposed to the elements without food was a killer.

The orders to withdraw to the extraction point came through during the night on 15 June, and we were instructed to be at the designated helicopter pick-up point by 1145 hours Zulu on the following day. It took an age to come, but we agreed to wait for the full light of morning before starting to move. The day dawned dull and overcast, although the visibility was good, and we took one last look at the Argentine positions. Nothing had changed.

The queue for the field kitchen still formed up, and the soldiers on duty still bailed out water from their trenches. The scope paused on the patrol at Sulivan House, conscious that we were within the effective range of their machine guns, which they continued to man from their dugouts. Even if they didn't know about the surrender, or felt unobliged to comply with it, and even if they didn't manage to cut us down with their machine guns when we unmasked ourselves, they could still call in the longer-range mortars and artillery located in the settlement.

We packed the scope away.

'What do you reckon, Ade?'

'Not sure, Splash. Perhaps if one of us stands up to, er, test the water, like.'

'You mean like a sort of sniff test? If one of us stands up and doesn't get shot, then we all stand up. If he gets shot, then we have only lost one man. Who you gonna dick to do that?'

'Um, good point. Fuck it, let's all stand up together.'

There was nothing for it but to reveal ourselves and hope that peace now prevailed on West Falkland. So we all stood up as one.

Our sudden movement was immediately detected at the enemy platoon position, as figures stood up in their dug-outs or moved about the position, gesticulating in our direction. The four of us stood motionless for a few seconds, unsure precisely what to do. So we waved. There seemed to be similar hesitation on the other side before they waved back.

With that, we turned and started to walk across the Bosoms. Laden with rifles and heavy packs, we moved slowly, as weak as kittens and nearly asleep on our feet after six days without sustenance and lying motionless in the cold for twice as long. As the patrol crested the top of the feature, silhouetted against the cold, grey skyline, none of us turned to look back before heading down the other side. The Argies held their fire. We were done, and our war was over.

# 40

Ten days later, we found ourselves standing at the back of a C-130 RAF Hercules with its engines running on the hardstanding at Stanley airport. We waited behind the aircraft's tailgate ramp, blasted by the prop wash and aviation fumes, as the Regiment's operations officer was in a heated discussion with a major from the Intelligence Corps about who was going to get on the first UK-bound aircraft out of Stanley.

Mountain Troop had taken no part in the rest of the Squadron's activities during the final push on Stanley. While 18 Troop had been stood by for operations on West Falkland, 16 and 17 Troops, beefed up by an SBS patrol, had made a forlorn diversionary raid in support of 2 PARA's final attack on Wireless Ridge, which was one of the last battles of the war. The Squadron's efforts to cross the upper reaches of Port William by rigid raiders were repulsed by heavy 20 mm Argie cannon fire. The boats got badly shot up, as did the fire support group on the home bank. Thankfully, the few casualties the Squadron took were surprisingly light, but Bilbo said it was pretty hairy.

Bilbo was the one surviving member of 19 Troop who took part in the operation, as it had been a toss-up between him and Roy as to who went on the OP patrol to Port Howard. Roy took the slot, as he had missed out on Pebble Island, due to not making the flight down to

367

Ascension at the start of it all. He didn't want to miss another opportunity for action and ended up getting a beltful of it.

As the Squadron licked its minor wounds from its foray near Stanley and the Argies capitulated, further to the west Roy was released from the wool press in Port Howard's shearing sheds. He had experienced no further hard-edged interrogation sessions following the incident with the pistol, and his captivity ended when news of the surrender reached the enemy troops based on West Falkland.

The Arg soldiers who pulled him from his hole in the ground seemed as happy about it as Roy was. They saluted him and presented him with an Argentine SF beret, out of respect for his bearing during his capture and the bravery he had shown in attempting to fight his way out of the OP. He was allowed to recover his kit, including his Gore-Tex jacket, which had been shot full of bullet holes during the firefight up on the ridge – remarkably none of them finding his flesh. He also found John's jacket, which was soaked with blood.

While the two Ruperts argued about the flight out of Stanley, I took in our surroundings. The small hard-strip airfield bore the scars of fighting. It was strewn with the debris of damaged and discarded Argentine equipment and aircraft. The one solitary hangar had been stripped to its metal framework by bomb blasts, and the tiny white terminal building was splintered with shellfire. It was also a scene of wanton abuse. The Arg troops had crapped anywhere that took their fancy, and the surface of the apron and taxiway was layered with human excrement. The terminal building was also full of it, as were the abandoned helmets that lay scattered across the ground. It spoke volumes about the way the unwanted occupiers had treated the islands and their people and the legacy they would be leaving.

Battle won, the thirty members of D Squadron trooped up the aircraft's ramp with our personal gear, leaving a disgruntled major and his people fuming on the filth-smeared tarmac behind us.

The light was fading as the C-130 began its final approach to Brize Norton almost three days later. The sun had slipped below the horizon, gilding the light clouds of a summer's evening with the last vestiges of a golden hue, to reveal a quintessential English landscape of patchwork fields, hedge lines and woods. Taking in the view from the port-hole window as the aircraft descended was like watching a giant banner announcing our homecoming being unfurled beneath us. I savoured the moment from my perch on the ramp, until the aircraft's wheels thumped down on to the runway.

It was the only welcome we received, other than the customs officer who was waiting for us as we shuffled off the aircraft and filed into a hangar. We had all been warned of the dire consequences of being caught with looted Argentine weapons. As a consequence, there had been a frenzied dumping of Argie pistols over the side of the landing ship in San Carlos before we headed to the airfield at Stanley.

We laid out our gear in a line on the hangar floor as a short, overweight bloke stubbed out a cigarette and came out of his office. He gave us a cursory glance and then asked where we had come from. Someone said the Falklands. He smiled, nodded and said, 'Well done, lads,' before turning and heading back to his office without a second look at the bergens and belt kit laid out on the floor.

The long flight had fatigued us, but it was the empty seats on the bus back to Hereford which made the enormity of it all hit home. Seven members of the Squadron had been evacuated as casualties, including James, Chris and Alex, who made it out of the Sea King when it ditched. All the injured would eventually make a full recovery and return to the unit. But those who went down with the helicopter would remain in its confines, which was later designated as a sea grave somewhere deep in the cold, unforgiving waters of the South Atlantic. The loss of people like Phil and Sid hit us all as we headed out into the darkening lanes of the Oxfordshire countryside, but it had far greater impact on the families they left behind in Herefordshire.

Lawrence Gallagher would never see his unborn daughter or watch his other two young girls grow up, and his wife Linda would never recover from the heartbreak of losing him. The losses were not all from D Squadron: Paddy O'Connor, whose training on the Stinger probably saved the lives of many of the blokes when the Pucara had them in its sights, would never know that his son followed in his footsteps into the Army and went on to join the Regiment he loved. John Hamilton was the only member of the Squadron to be buried in a known grave. The Argentine soldiers who killed him buried him with full military honours in a small, white-picket-fenced cemetery at Port

Howard, the settlers providing a Union Jack for the ceremony before he was laid to rest beneath the damp, peat-rich earth of West Falkland. John was awarded the Military Cross for his gallantry. Some, including the Argentine commander at Port Howard, said it should have been a VC for fighting it out against superior odds when there could only ever have been one outcome. It was little consolation for his grieving wife, and the child that they had been so desperately trying for would now never come.

Few people spoke during the journey back to Stirling Lines; most of us dozed or remained silent and alone with our thoughts as we drove through the night. We handed our weapons in to the armoury and dumped our kit when we got back to the camp. Then I went out of the back gate and made the short walk up to the married quarters patch. It was late. The lights were off as I went up the path and turned my key in the front door. Like the rest of the families, Liz had not been told of our imminent return. There was a startled shout from upstairs, as I let myself into the house, a voice from the darkness demanding to know who was there. 'Who the fuck do you think it is?' I replied, surprised by the edge in my own voice. And with that I was home.

Entering the house was the first brush with the normality of everyday things: the immediate warmth, the smell of cleanliness and a sense of ordered arrangement. I didn't find it difficult to adjust, although not having to carry a weapon or have my belt kit to hand was alien. For the first few days I savoured the appreciation of simple pleasures and sights: being with Liz, having dry feet, taking a bath, watching TV, or going for a drink and watching

371

people as they went about their everyday business without fear or danger.

There was no threat of air attack or sudden compromise, and all those things I had dreamed of when I was wet, tired, cold and hungry were suddenly a reality. But it didn't change me. I just got used to it again and cracked on. But as I spent time with Liz and tripped round the country and caught up with family, I found myself yearning for the company of the blokes and men who had been through it too. I didn't have long to wait.

Two weeks later, we were back on task and straight back into the black kit. D Squadron had assumed the roster responsibility for the Regiment's counterterrorist role. In truth, it was a relief to return to the fold.

When, in the middle of July, the rest of the Task Force returned, we watched the fanfare of it all on the TV in Stirling Lines as we sipped mugs of tea and waited quietly on standby, dressed in our CT rig. It stood in stark contrast with our own homecoming. There were no parades, flypasts, crowds or dignitaries to meet us as we slipped back to our base in the middle of the night. Some might have felt let down by the lack of attention, but that was not our way, and we didn't begrudge it of others.

In the preceding three months, D Squadron had travelled far and seen much. We prevailed because we were more professional, better trained and had greater motivation than our enemy. We also recovered from our setbacks, adjusted, adapted and overcame the environment we faced and the challenges it threw at us. But the return of the rust-stained ships, many of which had played a role in our story, like *Hermes, Antrim, Brilliant, Intrepid* and

*Canberra*, was testimony to the fact that we were only ever a very small part of a much larger military machine.

The people who walked down those gangways were the men who had fought hand-to-hand up the hills around Stanley with bayonets and grenades. They were the people who protected us as they defended their ships under heavy air attack and who flew us into combat and took additional risks when we were in trouble. Like us, they were servicemen doing their part and putting themselves into harm's way for a national cause. We had no call on some superior drive or some superhuman reserve to draw from; any mythical status we had was dubious. Our motivations were the same as theirs: to do the job well, to be tested in combat and not to let our mates down. Like them, we shared the same fortunes of war and its frictions of mistakes, faulty intelligence and the random chance of good and bad luck.

Success in the Falklands came from a willingness to take risks, determination, endurance and improvisation, but it was also the result of a collective endeavour by every individual and unit that took part. Some may have spoken about their experiences when they came back; many did not. D Squadron was no exception. As far as we were concerned at the time, what was done was done. Thomas Hardy could not have summed it up better when he wrote in *Far from the Madding Crowd*: 'They spoke very little of their mutual feelings; pretty phrases and warm attentions being probably unnecessary between such tried friends.'

# Epilogue

The islands are still a land where the weather dominates everything and makes for a bleak and unforgiving place. The wind never ceases as it blows incessantly across the empty expanses of the South Atlantic from the west. The oceanic surrounds also bring a preponderance of thick bands of cloud, rain and low temperatures, which struggle to lift much above 20 degrees centigrade, even in the height of summer. But when the sun shines from aching blue skies and the winds ease, kinder conditions reveal a raw, spectacular landscape of dramatic spine-topped features, nestled coastal settlements, white sandy beaches and rolling grass moorland.

These days, there is little evidence of the fighting that took place there all those years ago, and the ridgelines that were fought over are absent of the sounds of battle, although, if you know where to look, you will find the scattered remains of Argentine aircraft, the twisted wreckage of their fuselages burnished and rusted by the passing seasons and weather, lying forgotten on the hilltops and in the valleys where they were brought down.

There is little left of the carnage we wreaked that night on Pebble Island. The two upturned wings of the Skyvan we destroyed lie dragged to one side of the grass strip. If you look closely enough, the salt-encrusted remains of a Pucara's engines lie among the sea-washed rocks at the foot of a bluff on the west side of the airfield. The rest of our night's work has either been removed or claimed by the waves to leave a small, remote island of tranquil calm and peace inhabited by just two families.

If you climb up the rear slopes of Mount Kent, you will find our old positions up on the rocky saddle almost untouched by the passage of time. A pile of sun-mottled empty greenie mortar carriers lies under the sloping crag of quartzite, just where we discarded them. A few feet away, the round circular impression of the mortar we set up and fired is still imprinted indelibly in the peaty ground, along with the embedded slab of rock I used to stop the baseplate from digging itself in. Off to the right, in the lower ground, you can still make out the gun emplacements used by our artillery, along with the bunkers their crews fashioned from earth-filled metal ammunition boxes. But while little-altered signs of war can be found by the discerning, much on the Falklands has changed.

I never spoke to or saw a civilian the whole time that I was on the Falklands during the war, but I have met many since. Ask any of them if they think that the war was worth it, and the majority will reply with a resounding 'yes'. Given a say on their future and whether they wanted to remain part of the UK, in a referendum held in 2013, 98.8 per cent of the population turned out and 92 per cent voted in the affirmative.

If you ask any of us who came back after fighting down south whether it was worth it, most of us would reply in the affirmative too. Unlike more recent conflicts, the cause of the Falklands was clear-cut. But perhaps hardly any of that matters. We were professional soldiers who were just doing our job. Regardless of where we came from, we joined the Army voluntarily, we wanted to face the challenge of combat and we willingly answered the call, just as the British Army has done throughout its history and will continue to do. Those of us who served down south are now the older generation, of course, but when I look into the eyes of Paddy O'Connor's boy and note the crest of a sergeant major on his wrist, I know there is no difference.

I am often asked if I was affected by my experiences of battle. I think that question relates to suffering from some form of trauma. Being in combat is, of course, a traumatic and brutal business. That night on 19 May, thirty-plus years ago, was bloody dreadful, and there are other events that sometimes make me shudder when I think of them; a sight or smell, such as the whiff of aviation fuel, sometimes evokes a heightened sense of recall. But these sensations are part of the normal experiences of war, as much as they are part of life's experiences in general. However, there was, and is, no trauma.

I suspect some counsellor would claim that I am in denial, but they would be wrong. Clearly there were people who served in the Task Force who suffered from what is now called post-traumatic stress disorder. There has also been much subsequent comment that more veterans have taken their own lives than the 255 British servicemen killed in the conflict. Recent studies have disputed this, but it underlines the fact that PTSD is an extremely complex subject, not least as it is an invisible injury of the mind. When traumatic experiences remain trapped in the memory, unprocessed and undealt with, then recurring flashbacks, nightmares, aggression and dysfunctional behaviour can be the manifestations of PTSD.

I didn't see anyone who served in D Squadron suffer from any noticeable trauma, and I have seen no evidence of it, when I meet up with former comrades and hear how their lives have progressed since all those years ago when we climbed on that C-130 on a shit-strewn airfield. James continued to serve in the Regiment and became an officer like his father. Roy left the Regiment and returned to the Seychelles, where he set up and ran a successful security company and then became active in politics on the island. Bilbo also went on to the security circuit and now lives happily in the Balkans, but still manages to return to the UK for every England home international at Twickenham. Sadly, Alex has passed away as a result of illness, as has Binsy. The green turtle population on Ascension, once nearly extinct, has flourished, and I would like to think that he and I played a small part in that.

Cedric went on to command the Regiment and, like Mike Rose, become a senior general in the Army. Danny West continued to serve in the Regiment, before retiring as a more senior late-entry officer. The valiant Wessex Mk III helicopter called Humphrey survived the air attack on HMS *Antrim* in San Carlos Water and is now in the Fleet Air Arm Museum in Yeovilton, where it sits, still pock-marked by shrapnel, next to a bullet-ridden Mentor aircraft that was recovered and brought back from Pebble Island. Both rest adjacent to an Argentine 109 helicopter, which was pressed into service with the Regiment after the war. I have often seen it since and wondered whether it was the same one that was flown over our heads on West Falkland by the moustachioed pilot who thankfully never looked down.

My own service continued after the war. I spent four more years with 19 Troop and then parted company with them when I was posted as the Regiment's Special Forces instructor to NATO's long-range reconnaissance centre in the Bavarian Alps. Liz and I also parted company. The demands of the Regiment and being married to an SAS man eventually became too much for her, and, absent the domestic stability she craved, we ended up getting divorced. I stayed in the military and returned to the UK to take up a tied SAS post as a sergeant major at the Army's own recce training establishment on Salisbury Plain, undoubtedly becoming the bane of the students' lives as I stripped aspiring young recce commanders of their GPS and forced them to rely on a map and compass. However good they were as soldiers, at first most struggled without the instant gratification of digital technology, which confirmed that the Falklands conflict really was the Army's last analogue war.

I then re-established my love–hate relationship with regularly jumping out of aircraft when I became the regimental sergeant major of the RAF's parachute training school at Brize Norton. I spent the final years of my career as the RSM of the company commander's course in Wiltshire, before retiring from the Army at fifty-five. Although out of uniform, I continued my association with the military for another ten years, working as a civil servant in the Infantry Trials and Development Unit, testing and developing equipment for frontline units. During that time, I also returned to the Falklands.

On my last visit to the islands, one morning in February 2019, I watched the smoke drifting from the rooftops of Port Howard in a gentle, easing breeze as the sun rose above an idyllic, tranquil setting. The dogs barked and cocks crowed, much as they would have done when John and Roy watched down on Port Howard from their OP position up on the higher ground of the ridgeline lying behind me, although there were now no Argentine soldiers stationed in the buildings or dug in on the surrounding hills.

I looked back down at John's grave and the wreath that I had carried with me from England. Edged in blue rather than traditional red poppies, it contrasted with the grey quartzite of his headstone, which carried a simple inscription below the double cap badges of the Green Howards and the SAS: 'Captain G J Hamilton MC, 22nd Special Air Service Regiment, Age 29'. I stood in silence, feeling the wind on my face and the lump constricting my throat, as I thought of John and all the others who never made it home. It is the same sensation I feel rising in me as a sad stopper of emotion each time I visit the memorial to those that have no marked grave and are commemorated in the cemetery of St Martin's Church in Hereford, located a few hundred metres from where Stirling Lines used to be. Built from local red sandstone, the tall Gothic spire of the Victorian church stands sentinel to the low cemetery wall behind it, which is flanked by the white Portland headstones of the Regiment's more recent war dead. John's name is there, along with twenty other plaques, each tablet of marble commemorating a name of those who went down in the Sea King.

Perhaps they are the military men to ask whether it

was worth it, although they cannot answer. I think that they would also have said yes. As soldiers they stepped voluntarily into the arena of battle and wanted to be tested. Like all of us, they would have accepted that risk and loss are part of the business that we were in and they wouldn't have wanted to be anywhere else. The sadness of their loss will never leave me, but I feel fortunate that I was counted among their ranks, that I marched and fought with them. We stood together and enjoyed a comradeship forged in war, which triumphed over adversity, and we became better men for it, whether we survived it or not. Age may have wearied me and those who also came through it, as we were but warriors for the working day. But I regret nothing. If I were a younger man, I would do it all again, and I know that the others who did not make it home would too.

# Glossary

| | |
|---|---|
| CASEVAC | casualty evacuation |
| Conops | concept of operations |
| CT | counterterrorist |
| ETD | estimated time of departure |
| FN | Fabrique Nationale (a Belgian arms manufacturer; the automatic rifle they made, used by the Argentines, was referred to as an 'FN') |
| full screw | corporal |
| FUP | forming-up point |
| gat | rifle |
| GPMG | general-purpose machine gun |
| HE | high explosive |
| heli | helicopter |
| HLS | helicopter landing site |
| IED | improvised explosive mine |
| klick | kilometre |
| LAW | light anti-tank weapon |
| LCU | landing craft utility |
| LS | landing site |
| LSL | landing ship logistic |
| LUP | lying-up position |
| MFO | movements forwarding office (a form of plywood packing) |
| NVG | night vision goggles |

| | |
|---|---|
| OC | officer commanding |
| OP | observation post |
| ops | operations |
| ORBAT | order of battle |
| Pack-How | 105 mm howitzer |
| QRF | quick reaction force |
| RHIB | rigid-hull inflatable boat |
| RSM | regimental sergeant major |
| SBS | Special Boat Squadron (now Special Boat Service) |
| scaley-back | signaller |
| SHQ | squadron headquarters |
| SITREP | situation report |
| SLR | self-loading rifle |
| SOP | standard operating procedure |
| TEZ | Total Exclusion Zone |
| 2IC | second in command |
| 66 | see LAW |

# Index